For the Love of a Child

Also by Betty Mahmoody

Not Without My Daughter
with William Hoffer

For the Love of a Child

921/
m

BETTY MAHMOODY

with

ARNOLD D. DUNCHOCK

St. Martin's Press

New York

This is a true story.

The characters are authentic, the events real. But the names and identifying details of certain individuals have been disguised in order to protect them and their families against the possibility of arrest and execution by their governments. These are: Don and Miriam; Sarah; Nelson Bates; Beverly and Sabrina; Meg, Fereshteh, and Kayvan; and Marilyn and Feridun.

Library of Congress Cataloging-in-Publication Data

Mahmoody, Betty.
    For the love of a child / Betty Mahmoody with Arnold D. Dunchock.
      p.   cm.
    "A Thomas Dunne book."
    ISBN 0-312-08194-4 (hardcover)
    1. Mahmoody, Betty.   2. Mothers—United States—Biography.
   3. Mothers—Iran—Biography.   4. Kidnapping, Parental—Iran.
   5. Reverse culture shock—United States.   I. Dunchock, Arnold D.
   II. Title.
   HQ759.M317   1992
   305.4′092—dc20
   [B]   92-20974
                                                  CIP

First Edition: September 1992

10 9 8 7 6 5 4 3 2 1

I want to dedicate this book to all the children who have been abducted and taken to foreign countries and to those who live with fear.

Contents

Acknowledgments

I was fortunate in 1986 to have been put in contact with the William Morris Agency. Those I have worked with there have proven that they are more than just doing their job. They have had a profound effect on my life in that they have guided me through this career change, have helped build my self-esteem through their faith in me, and have become very close friends with whom I can even share my personal life.

Michael Carlisle has been more than a literary agent. He has become a true friend who has been there for me through both ups and downs. Whenever there has been concern for Mahtob's and my safety, Michael has always been available for support and guidance. On more than one occasion, he has calmed us and helped us cope. He has been my defender, business advisor, and general contractor in my new career.

Marcy Posner has been invaluable in providing a worldwide market. She has a daughter who is the same age as Mahtob, which has given us a special appreciation for each other.

Randy Chaplin has opened a door for me in the lecture arena. He believed in my abilities and promoted me on the lecture circuit, which has added great joy and satisfaction to my life, along with the opportunity to meet new and interesting people.

Antoine Audouard of Fixot Publishing (my French publisher) was actually the spiritual father of this book. Early on, he understood the importance of the issue of international parental child abduction and encouraged this project by suggesting I come to France, where I would not be distracted, to work. It was through Antoine that I was introduced to the Mothers of Algiers, who have been a true inspiration in my life. Antoine had invaluable input into the editing process of this book.

Anja Kleinlein of Gustav Lübbe Verlag in Germany has become more than an editor for my German translations. Mahtob and I love her so dearly that we have emotionally adopted her as a family member. Anja literally got into the trenches with her heart and soul when I suffered vociferous attacks in Germany after Moody's interview surfaced on German television.

Tom Dunne of St. Martin's Press has been a tremendous help in this project. He spent an enormous amount of time editing this book. His interest in the ideas that have grown from *Not Without My Daughter* is especially inspiring to me.

The talents of Jeff Coplon in his collaboration on this book have made it what I hoped it would be. He worked with me in writing these stories and brought to them his journalistic insights and understanding.

Mahtob and I have been fortunate in that, having lived the nightmare of *Not Without My Daughter,* we were received with open arms and given the opportunity to turn this horror into something that has affected other people's lives in a positive way. Through this process, we have made innumerable new friendships and met many people who have affected our lives in a way that will always be remembered.

Part One

1

Changed Lives

Wednesday, February 5, 1986

Mommy, look, the American flag!" Mahtob exclaimed as we approached the American Embassy in Ankara, Turkey. Her breath frosted the air; I could barely feel my feet. With each step, our sore muscles reminded us of our five-day trek on foot and horseback over the Iranian-Turkish mountains, the route taken by the smugglers who enabled our escape. I was a forty-year-old woman with a six-year-old daughter. We had both been pushed to the breaking point.

Trapped in Iran for eighteen months, our glimpses of the flag had been limited to photographs, where it was invariably desecrated by flames or rendered in crude, painted images on the cement floors of schools, for children to stamp or spit on before they entered their classrooms. To see it fly freely over our heads meant something special to me that day. The flag was a symbol of our deliverance.

There were many days in the past eighteen months when I feared I would never see such a sight again. In July 1984 Mahtob and I had accompanied Sayyed Bozorg Mahmoody, my Iranian-born husband, on what he promised would be a two-week visit to his native country. It was only after we arrived that Moody, as everyone knew him, declared that none of us were leaving—that we were in Iran to stay. My daughter and I were torn from my two teenage sons from my prior marriage. We were taken half a world away from my parents, from our friends, from all that we held dear and familiar.

Worst of all, I discovered that I had lost control of my fate. Under Iran's fundamentalist Islamic law, both Mahtob and I were considered Iranian citizens, and Moody was our absolute master. We could not leave the country without his written permission. Without it, we were bound there for life—even as Moody's behavior became increasingly erratic, and his beatings of Mahtob and me grew more frequent and severe.

I had not wanted to leave Iran this way, but all attempts to reason with Moody had failed. Three weeks earlier I had pleaded with him to reconsider his decision to force us to stay in Iran. "Please, Moody, tell me five years or ten years, but don't say never. If you say never, you don't give me anything to live for."

His reply: "The answer is *never*! I don't ever want to hear about America again." I knew he meant it.

Over the next few days I came to the most fateful decision of my life: we must break away from Moody, at any cost. I realized that neither Mahtob nor I were likely to survive a trip over the mountains in February, a time when even the smugglers normally deemed them impassable. The perils were many. We might freeze to death, or fall off a cliff. Our guides might rob and abandon us, or turn us in to Iranian authorities—the most chilling prospect of all, since I could be executed for taking a child from her father.

Yet I felt an eerie calm, an absolute peace with what we were about to do. I had come to know there were worse lots in life than death. The day we fled, Moody had cruelly told Mahtob that she would never see me again. He'd already booked me on a flight to the United States—alone—that would depart in two days. It was clear to me that we had no choice but to run. And after seeing her father's violence resurface, more crazily of late than ever, Mahtob had come to agree with me.

Eight days later, as I sat inside the embassy lobby, I had no reserves left. I looked up wearily at the U.S. consul, who told me, "You may need to go to the police station to resolve this issue with your passports."

"*Please* take care of it for me—I'm *afraid* to go to the police station," I begged. Our new U.S. passports, obtained through the

4

Swiss Embassy in Tehran, were unstamped; as far as Turkey was concerned, we were illegal aliens. If a warrant had been issued in Iran for my arrest, the police might jail me—a separation neither Mahtob nor I could endure. They might even extradite us back to Iran.

The American consul, already alerted to our plight by the State Department and obviously moved by our physical condition, said, "I can't make any guarantees, but I'll see what I can do."

As it would take some time to get our travel documents in order, he suggested that we sample Ankara's sights. *No, thank you!* We'd survived the air raids of the Iran-Iraq War in Tehran. We'd dodged rifle shots from snipers in the Kurdish civil conflict. We'd made it over those treacherous mountains, enduring with five days of little food or sleep. After all that, I was not about to give my husband a chance to grab us while we strolled down a Turkish street. For now I was just where I wanted to be, safe in the shadow of our flag.

I had another compelling reason to act at once. A few days before we'd left Iran, my sister had been able to reach me with the news that my father was about to undergo a life-threatening surgery for colon cancer. During the days of our escape, I had no way of knowing whether he was alive or dead. After phoning him the night before, I feared he might not last another day. "Hurry home," he had urged me, and I was determined to reach his side before it was too late.

I told the consul, "I want the first flight home!"

The Turkish police represented the latest in a long line of potential crises. According to Iranian law, Mahtob and I knew we could never leave Iran without written permission from Moody. From Tehran to the border our driver had been stopped many times by the *pasdar*, the Islamic vice squad, for routine checks. Each time a guard approached the vehicle, my heart raced. I shrank behind my *chador* for whatever camouflage it could give me, knowing this could be the end. For some reason they never asked for our papers.

After the smugglers left us inside Turkey, we boarded a bus

from the mountain city of Van to Ankara. Our luck held. I saw other buses pulled over, their passengers standing outside and presenting their documents for inspection. Our own bus was periodically stopped and boarded by khaki-uniformed men who spoke briefly to the driver, but each time they waved us on. No one demanded to see our papers until we arrived in Ankara in the middle of the night, and tried to register at a hotel across the street from the American Embassy.

There is no explanation for what happened; I believe we were saved by the grace of God.

We were invited to lunch while at the U.S. Embassy with the consul and vice consul. We were thrilled by the promised menu: cheeseburgers and french fries. When we reached the oversized wooden doors to the American compound, opened crisply by a brace of marines, we were stalled in a gridlock of mutual courtesy.

"After you," the consul said.

"No, after you," I echoed, without thinking.

"After you," the vice consul said.

"After *you*," I insisted. Our Marx Brothers routine ended only when I realized that I'd been habitually walking behind Moody and all other men in Iran. No one had to tell me to do so; I simply fell into step with the millions of other women there. It would be months before I could comfortably precede a man through a door.

As we waited in the embassy for news from the Turkish police station, Mahtob drew a picture of a boat on the Thunder Bay River, which flowed behind our house in Michigan. In the background she drew rows and rows of mountains and said, "I don't *ever* want to see another mountain."

Then the consul returned, obviously pleased with his success. "Everything's been taken care of. You can go home now."

Six hours later we were on a plane, the tickets paid for with my only credit card that hadn't yet expired. As we couldn't get a direct flight to New York, the airlines paid for our room and meals at the Munich Sheraton. Despite the temptations of a Western menu, the lingering tension—not to mention our shrunken stomachs—left us unable to eat. After I coaxed Mahtob into ordering some raspberries, she peeked over her bowl and said with a sly smile, "Mommy, you're teasing me. I know we're in Michigan because these are *real* raspberries."

Due to a flight delay into Kennedy Airport, we missed our last connection to Detroit. After clearing customs, we walked directly to the gate for the first flight out the next morning. Although we were so close to home, I still felt vulnerable and alone. The night would give Moody a chance to shorten the distance between us. I looked suspiciously at every passerby.

When we reached the Northwest Airlines gate area, the airport was nearly deserted. After making Mahtob as comfortable as possible in the plastic chairs, I began my vigil. Tired as I was, I dared not sleep and leave my daughter unwatched. Mahtob couldn't get much sleep either, but she never complained. As I gazed at her drowsy face, I was reminded of just how remarkable she was—how mature, and patient, and self-composed. Many parents would have done for their children what I did for mine. But there are few six-year-olds who *could* have done what Mahtob did. I was proud to be her mother—and grateful that I'd been able to keep my promise, never to leave Iran without her.

The next morning, as the plane's captain announced our descent to Detroit Metropolitan Airport, Mahtob awoke, hoping what she'd just heard was not still another dream. "Did they just say *Detroit?*"

We both bounded down the ramp. Michigan! Freedom! Family! Protection! We were greeted by a half dozen of my siblings and their spouses. When I'd called from Munich two nights before, they'd asked me what I'd missed most. All I could think of was . . . *Snickers.* I'd probably never eaten more than one or two Snickers in a given year, but now my family was pressing bags of the chocolate bars into my arms, enough for a lifetime of Halloweens.

They presented Mahtob with two dolls: a Cabbage Patch, and another one dressed in purple, my daughter's favorite color. While still in Iran, Mahtob had asked, "When we get out [she never said 'if'], before we go to Grandma and Grandpa's house,

7

can we go to McDonald's for three days?" Now that our return was a reality, she had no desire for McDonald's. She wanted only to see everyone at home.

I felt immediate disappointment that my sons Joe and John weren't at the airport. Neither of them had been told of our arrival until after we touched down in Detroit. With the family's nerves frayed to the breaking point, no one dared believe we had actually made it, and no one wanted to get the boys' hopes up if something fell through.

Our welcoming party had been waiting at Detroit Metro since the night before, our planned arrival time. When we didn't come off the plane as scheduled, one of my sisters started screaming. She was sure something terrible had happened—that we'd somehow been intercepted.

By the time we actually arrived that Friday morning, we were beyond exhaustion. Our excitement kept us going, and as we motored over the slippery highway, I saw the familiar landmarks with new eyes. Mounds of fresh snow lined the road. Though I'd long had a special place in my heart for my home state, Michigan had never looked so good.

We finally reached my parents' home, a ranch house in very rural Bannister. As we entered the winding dirt drive, I saw an indicator of how long we'd been gone. Years before I'd helped Dad plant dozens of pine trees around the house. When you see a tree every day, you don't notice its growth, but these pines had grown so much since I'd been there last. They were a jolting sign of what lay in store for me—of how much I had missed of my sons' lives and of my dad's tenacious struggle to share this day.

The house was built on three levels; we entered at the landing, then climbed half a dozen steps to reach the kitchen. Just as we got to the top, we received the most meaningful gift of all: a weak "Boo!" from inside the half-bath to our left. We peered past the door, left partially ajar, and there was Dad, leaning heavily on the sink. He'd greeted Mahtob with a "Boo!", invariably sending her into gales of giggles, ever since she was a baby. Dad was too sick to get up (he'd needed considerable help to get to the bathroom), but he insisted on preserving the ritual, to do something special for his granddaughter. He shouldn't really have done it—he *could* not have done it, if not for the strength of his love—but Mahtob will never forget it.

Mom greeted us in the kitchen; she'd baked blueberry and banana cream pies, as per Mahtob's request from Munich. The family hadn't yet been able to reach Joe, but there was my younger son, John. Two months from his sixteenth birthday, he had grown five inches since I'd seen him last, and now towered over me. John hugged and kissed me, and couldn't hold back his tears.

We moved to the long living room, where my father had returned to the hospital bed that confined him. Before becoming sick, Dad was a robust, stocky man, about five-foot-three and 175 pounds. He always had tremendous, almost inexhaustible energy. When I left for my "brief visit" to Iran, his colon cancer was already advanced, but mostly invisible. Dad had retired from his job at an automotive subassembly factory, but he was still up and about in his work clothes, tending his garden and mowing the lawn. He particularly enjoyed relaxing in a lawn chair and listening to radio broadcasts of his beloved Detroit Tigers' games.

At the time of my departure in 1984, the Tigers were in a pennant race. For the next year and a half, every time someone from Iran returned from the States, I would ask, "What happened to the Tigers? Who won the World Series?" No one seemed to comprehend what I was talking about. I never received John's letter announcing that Detroit had won.

The cancer had exacted a dreadful toll from Dad over the past year and a half. He had been reduced to an eighty-pound skeleton; he looked like a famine victim. Dad had lost most of his hair to chemotherapy, and what was left had blanched from salt-and-pepper to white. He lay there flat on his back in his loosely hanging pajamas, with barely enough energy to turn his head in our direction. He took in oxygen from a tube; he was still panting from the exertion of having gotten up to greet us. I would never see him dressed again.

Dad had fought so hard to stay alive to see this day. He had beaten all medical odds. He had been eaten up inch by inch by

9

the cancer, but never gave up. Throughout the ordeal, he'd been the only one in my family who truly believed I'd find a way to escape with Mahtob. He'd *expected* me to return—and in all our years together, I'd rarely disappointed him.

He looked up at me and smiled. "I knew you could do it," he whispered. "You've got stamina." I would receive many honors over the next six years, but his was the highest.

Everyone was eager to catch me up on what had happened over the past year and a half. While I appreciated their excitement, I was too exhausted to enjoy it. After all I'd been through, I had to put things in a new perspective. I'd lost my taste for small talk.

It was clear that no one in my family wished to hear what had happened to Mahtob and me in Iran, much less to resolve his or her own feelings about it. When I made some reference to my life in Tehran, they would gently brush me off, saying "That was a bad time. You're home now—why can't you just forget about it?"

With no place else to go, Mahtob and I moved in with my parents. The entire family assumed the role of our protectors. Being trusting, rural people, they had never locked their doors before, but now the bolts were drawn at all times. Dad's rifle was always loaded, and every adult was ready to use it if the need arose. Moody knew my parents' house well; it would be the first place he'd hunt for us. Given the lack of legal protection in such situations, there would be little to prevent him from taking Mahtob back to Iran.

During our first week home, I called the FBI and the U.S. Marshall's office about how they might help us with security. Both made the same reply: They were *reactive* agencies. "It may seem cold and cruel," the FBI agent told me, "but we can't do anything until *after* a crime has been committed."

Everyone's nerves were on edge. We listened for each and every strange sound. We watched the road for unfamiliar cars. If the phone rang and no one was on the other end, my family figured it meant trouble. Mahtob and I never answered because we had no way of knowing when it might be Moody.

While planning our escape from Iran, I had assumed that

10

upon our return Mahtob and I would go underground, with new and untraceable identities. I had a rude awakening within days after our return, when I consulted with Teresa Hobgood, my caseworker at the U.S. State Department, about changing Mahtob's name. Teresa explained that while I could call my daughter whatever I pleased, her name could not be changed legally, absent Moody's permission, before her eighteenth birthday. Also, she cautioned, an underground life would force me to relocate and cut all ties with my family or friends from the past. I wouldn't even be able to call my sons.

Why did I leave Iran in the first place? I could have survived the rationing of water and fuel, the two-hour lines for bread and eggs, the daily Iraqi air raids. But I could not tolerate being a prisoner. Nor could I let Mahtob be raised in a society where she would accept her imprisonment as a normal way of life.

Moody had jailed us in Iran. I would not allow him to become our warden in America.

There was a further consideration. In Iran I had met several women and children in situations similar to our own. I felt it was crucial to alert other people to the implications of intercultural relationships. I'd had no idea, for example, that marrying Moody, even in my own country, had automatically made me an Iranian citizen. I learned this only after I went to the Swiss Embassy in Tehran and discovered it could offer me no haven. I wanted others to ask questions before it was too late. I wanted to share my hard-learned lesson: that you can't pack your rights in a suitcase and take them wherever you go.

Whatever name I called myself, one thing was clear: I needed money. Not only had I escaped with nothing, but I found myself in a deep financial hole. A month after we had arrived in Tehran, Moody had wired all our savings out of Michigan. I'd never asked anyone for financial help in the past and I didn't want to start now. I cashed in my small retirement account to sustain our bare existence. The money would not last long, and it would not even begin to meet the $12,000 I needed to pay for the cost of our escape, let alone the capital gains tax owing from the sale of our house.

I had a negative net worth, no job (I'd quit my position as a personnel manager just before I married Moody) and no security. But I felt it important to keep a promise and repay Amahl, an Iranian businessman who engineered our escape from Iran. Against the advice of friends, I went to the National Bank of Detroit in Alpena, the last place we called home before leaving for Iran. I spoke briefly with Francis Flanders, the vice president, and said, "This man trusted me and he risked his life for us." I walked out with $12,000 cash in my hand and went directly to Western Union to wire it to an account "someplace in the world." Mr. Flanders's confidence in me at that desperate time in my life was something I'll never forget.

I had never doubted that I would write a book about Iran, from the first day I stepped into its buffeting heat, heard its chorus of high-pitched voices, and saw the obedient legions of women in their flowing, black *chadors*, many with but a single eye peeking through. Nothing in my twelve years with Moody—who had left his homeland in 1959, when it was still a westernized nation under the Shah—could have prepared me for this searing impression. I'd seen many photos of Iran before the revolution of 1979, complete with women—including Moody's relatives—in modern hairstyles and short skirts, and I was astounded by the country's transformation after the Ayatollah Khomeini came to power.

Though I lacked formal training as a writer, I resolved on the spot to describe this otherworldly society. I would write about how the country had changed after the Islamic revolution but also about what had endured: the customs, the cooking, the daily routines of ordinary people. As a guest of my husband's family, I would have an immeasurable advantage over those who saw the world from their five-star hotels. True, I would only be in Iran for two weeks. But I knew I could learn a lot if I put my mind to it.

After those two weeks multiplied into eighty, I had more of a story line than I'd bargained for. While I still planned to do a book, I put the project off indefinitely.

My life began to detour on my second night back in Michigan, when I took John and Mahtob to meet Karen McGinn and Doug Wenzel, our friends from Alpena, for a Saturday dinner out. Since we didn't have a car in Iran, it was my first experience behind the wheel in a year and a half, disorienting and wonderful at the same time. Our late-model, midnight-blue Ford LTD had barely been used before our departure, and I luxuriated in its sleek power and velvety interior—very different from the boxy, rattletrap Pakons that packed the streets of Tehran.

As I relaxed at dinner among friends, I had my very first opportunity to open up and talk about what had happened to Mahtob and me. It was too painful for my family to hear the details of our ordeal and escape, but our friends were transfixed. "You've got to write a book," Karen exclaimed when I finished.

"I'm going to," I said. "But first I have to get a job. I don't have a dime."

Karen wasn't about to let the thought slide. "I have a brother who works for a publishing company in Chicago. Shall I call him to see what you do to get started?"

"Sure," I said drowsily. I had barely slept the past two weeks, and in this relaxed setting, after a toast of champagne, my fatigue had begun to tumble in on me. The book idea still sounded abstract and far away.

Sunday I was thrilled to be with my elder son, Joe, for the celebration of his twentieth birthday. As I helped Mom prepare lunch, including birthday cake, Dad began to have trouble breathing. Dad's doctor, Roger Morris, was called to the house, and then an ambulance. "It doesn't look good," Roger said. "It's a miracle he made it this long."

I was devastated—I'd waited too long and come too far to lose Dad so soon. *It's not fair! Please, dear God, don't let him die yet!* Then I reproached myself for my selfishness. In Iran I had offered countless prayers for Dad to survive until we could get home. Those prayers had been answered—but the more God gave, the more I asked.

Monday, as Dad struggled in critical condition, I received a call from Steven Starr of the William Morris Agency in New York. Karen had worked fast. Steven's enthusiasm came over loud and clear: "You have an incredible story, and we'd like to talk to you about the possibility of a book."

Still exhausted, and knowing that I'd need to spend every spare minute with Dad, I said, "I'd be interested at some point in the future, but not right now."

"This could be worth a lot of money," Steven went on. Penniless, I turned him down.

Tuesday Steven called again and said, "We really want to talk to you. This is an *incredible* story." He added that he was sure he could get me a sizable advance—and then I realized that a book might enable me to stay home with Mahtob while I wrote, to protect her while I earned some money. It could be my job!

We made a date to meet in Detroit a few days later. While I shared my family's fears about our security, I finally agreed with Steven that the publicity from my book would provide the best possible protection. If I could bring my story to enough people, and enlist them to my cause, Moody might be too intimidated to make a move.

Wednesday, my sixth day back in the United States, Dad was prepared for his eleventh surgery in five years, to clear a bowel obstruction. We were offered little hope for his survival. After surgery, the doctor looked at Mom and said, "Someone better get her out of here for a while." My brother Jim drove her home. No sooner had they walked through the door than the phone rang. Mom answered to hear a familiar voice: "This is Barbara Walters calling for Betty Mahmoody." She wanted me to tell my story on "20/20"! When I heard about the call, I decided that Mom's heart must be stronger than the doctors gave it credit.

Friday, one week after my return, I went to see my younger son John play basketball. I had missed his football career while I was in Iran, and I relished the opportunity to cheer him on. I was thankful I'd gotten home in time to see John play for his high school team.

In preparation for the game, everyone stood for the national anthem. It was the first time I'd heard the anthem since my return, and suddenly the words had new meaning for me. Tears streamed down my face, and I was too choked to sing the words.

Amid this swirl of activity, I tried to readjust to the life I'd left behind. With Mahtob and I joining John, Dad's nurses, and our many visitors, my parents' house bulged at the seams. There was no time or space to catch our breath.

As busy as we were, we never lost sight of what mattered most: We were home. Early on we traveled to Alpena, a Lake Huron port city that was the only hometown Mahtob had remembered. The air there is tinged with the smells of a local paneling factory. When we got out of the car, Mahtob inhaled a deep breath and said, "*Ah*, this smells like home—and listen to the birds sing." When Mahtob was small, flocks of birds would gather at the feeders in our backyard. Among my daughter's first spoken words were "robin" and "bluejay," and to hear their song again was like revisiting old friends.

It wasn't long after the call from Barbara Walters that a producer came to Michigan to decide what to tape. Within a few days Mahtob, John, and I were scheduled to fly to New York to meet with Barbara. Joe, my elder son, declined; he didn't want anything to do with publicity.

As we flew into New York, the Statue of Liberty had never looked so beautiful. There she stood, proudly, and I had a new appreciation for what she symbolized.

We stayed at the Park Lane Hotel, overlooking Central Park. Our interview was at the Mayflower Hotel, just around the corner. When we walked into the room the cameraman tried to charm Mahtob, who was gripping onto my skirt for dear life. "Come here," the man beckoned. "Your mommy can stay there." He wanted Mahtob to look at me through the camera, but my daughter wasn't going to let anyone separate us again. She screamed and clung to me, tighter than ever. It wasn't an easy task for John and me to get her settled enough to begin taping.

We loved Barbara, who seemed genuinely interested in our story. By the end of the session Mahtob was sitting on her lap, exchanging hugs and kisses.

Barbara had given us prime tickets to see the Broadway musical *Cats*, seats so close to the stage that several actors ap-

15

proached and spoke to Mahtob during the performance. Barbara also suggested that we have dinner at Benihana of Tokyo, a Japanese restaurant that was a favorite of her daughter's.

Months later, when my children and I were looking for a home of our own, Mahtob said matter-of-factly, "Oh, we could move to New York. We've got friends there. Barbara Walters is our friend."

The segment was aired on June 20, 1986: Moody's birthday. Doug and Karen threw a party for us in Alpena, where many of our old friends watched the program with us. That same evening Dad had to be rushed by ambulance to the hospital again. The nurses turned "20/20" on as he was wheeled in, but he wasn't strong enough to watch.

My new eating habits reflected the changes in my life. During my first two months in Iran, as I battled depression and dysentery, I lost fifty-two pounds, until I was thinner than I'd been in high school. My face was a gaunt mask. My weight stabilized only after I made a conscious effort to survive for Mahtob's sake.

When I got back to the United States, I found myself surrounded by all the foods and drinks I had missed in Iran: Colby cheese, mustard, and an occasional glass of wine that was absolutely prohibited under Islamic law.

Most of all, I found myself drawn to desserts. I'd never been a big sweet-eater before. As a veteran of Weight Watchers I knew my metabolism wouldn't allow it. Now I had the opportunity to indulge myself after a long period of enforced self-denial, and my family encouraged me: "Oh, go ahead, it's okay—you couldn't have it over there." It didn't help when Dad, who would beat the odds again and survive his operation, developed a craving for frosted jelly rolls. He never wanted to eat alone. "Come on and have one with me," he'd say, and I'd oblige.

To make a grim story short, I put the weight back on—plus plenty more—as fast as I'd lost it, and have struggled with it ever since. "This is ridiculous," I told Mahtob last year. "I've gained all these pounds and I just don't seem to have the willpower to lose them. I think I'll go to a fat farm."

Mahtob's large brown eyes looked up at me as she said, so innocently, "But Mom, you've got enough. You don't need any *more!*"

My reaction to shedding my hated *chador*, the black fabric designed to cloak Iranian women from head to toe, was bizarre. On our bus to Ankara, Mahtob noticed that Turkey's dress code was more relaxed, and that some women were wearing neither *chadors* nor scarves. "Look," she said, "there are women uncovered. You can take your scarf off now." I declined because it had been many days since I'd washed or combed my hair. I'd had only one permanent wave in eighteen months. Brown and carefully coiffed when I'd left the United States, my hair was long, straight, and gray when I got back. John could barely bring himself to look at me. "Mom," he said after we'd finished our first hug, "you don't look like Mom."

On our second day home my sister Carolyn, a Mary Kay Cosmetics consultant, had brought a beautician to my parents' house. They gave me a cut, color, perm, and facial. My face was like a sponge, and the facial stripped away years; had they taken before-and-after pictures, Mary Kay could have used them in an ad campaign. My dad had always disapproved of makeup—he'd forbidden his daughters to wear it while they lived in his house—but this time he liked what he saw. "Well, that's more like it," he said.

But even after my hair was in shape, I felt strange going out bareheaded. It was as awkward for me to uncover in Michigan as it had been to cover in Iran. Donning my scarf and *chador* had become second nature, as required by a rigidly conformist social system. I remembered too well the days when a strand of loose hair would invite a twenty-minute harangue from the rifle-toting *pasdar*, the vice squad that roamed the streets of Tehran in white Nissan trucks and Pakons. When I spied an American policeman—or anyone in uniform, even a mailman—my arms would fly up as if to hide my head, and my heart would pound for minutes. It would be at least a year before the reflex passed.

Mahtob had her share of flashbacks as well. Most people

17

would not have noticed the plane that flew low over my parents' home a few weeks after we came back. For Mahtob, its harmless drone recalled the terror of Iraqi air raids in Iran when our stucco rowhouse would shake to its foundation and the air would smell of burning flesh. I found my daughter huddled in the corner of the living room, crying and trembling. She could not be coaxed out until many minutes after the plane had passed.

Dad fought on through the spring and into the summer. There were more surgeries and more pain than anyone should have to bear. Once his lungs filled with fluid. His breath came in gasping rattles, and we were sure he would suffocate. On another occasion he fell into a coma for three days. As my sister Carolyn and I stood by his hospital bed, Dad suddenly opened his eyes. He looked refreshed. His voice was stronger than it had been since I'd come home. Happy and at peace, he began to talk, and he didn't stop for an hour. He described what he'd seen: bright skies and sunshine, lush green valleys filled with flowers. He'd been with his twin brother, who had died six years earlier. He smiled as he told us all about it.

Seeing and hearing the tranquility that emanated from Dad's mind—his soul—made those last moments less difficult to accept. We were comforted with the hope that Dad would die in peace, and with our strengthened faith that he was nearing not an ending but a prelude of what was to be—forever.

When Dad was first diagnosed with colon cancer, he was given six months to three years to live. He'd prevailed for *five* years now, and his staunch will gave us precious time together. Each night I slept on a sofa by his bed, ready to fetch him a drink of water or tend to any other need. I wondered how many nights he'd slept by my crib in my infancy, when our roles had been reversed.

Dad was the only person in the family I could speak to freely, but he was too weak for long conversations, and I didn't want to burden him. For all that, he remained the head of his household until he drew his last breath. Everyone respected him, and his word was final. When Barbara Walters asked permission to send a film crew to my parents' home to tape part of the "20/20" show, most of the family stood opposed, arguing that publicity could only harm Mahtob and me. My mom said, "They're not coming to this house." Overhearing the discussion from his bed, so frail that he could hardly speak, Dad rasped, "They're *coming*." And they came.

On August 3, 1986, precisely two years after Mahtob and I had arrived in Tehran, nearly six months after we'd returned, Dad died at Carson City Hospital. He was sixty-six years old. When I told Mahtob she said, "Thank God we got to see him."

Dad had been a rare patient, the kind who worried about causing extra work for the hospital staff, about the other patients—about everyone except himself. For all his suffering, he never complained. Several nurses and doctors came to the funeral home to pay their respects. For years I would hear stories of how he had inspired the lives of others.

In the weeks of mourning that followed, I raged silently against Moody. He had stolen so much of my good time with Dad, and now he was absent when I most needed a spouse's support.

In time, there would be consolation from people like Dr. Jack Dilts, Dad's friend and surgeon. When I met him at a wedding, years after the funeral, Jack took me aside and said, "I don't know if I ever told you about your father's will to live. I operated on him at least five times when a normal person never would have made it through surgery."

A few days before Mahtob and I left Iran, when my sister had called to tell us that Dad was going to have another emergency surgery, the prognosis for his survival was bleak. Moody used this opportunity to talk to my father and tell him we would all come home. In reality, however, Moody had other ideas. He planned to hold Mahtob hostage while I returned alone to liquidate our assets—chiefly the furnishings from our home and two cars. He wanted the dollars before I returned. I was sure that once he got the money, he would not allow me to reenter Iran.

Something good came from Moody's deceit. It helped me

resolve that I had to take chances and do whatever was necessary to escape from him with Mahtob.

The other positive result, according to Dr. Jack Dilts, was that when Dad was rolled into the operating room, he was determined to live. He told everyone there, "They're coming home. I talked to Moody today and he said they're all coming home."

"He had this incredible desire to live to see you and Mahtob—he always talked about taking Mahtob fishing," Dr. Dilts told me. "I never experienced such a strong sense of love between parent and child as your dad had for you."

Jack's wife added that in church on Father's Day, when individuals were telling their father-child stories, Dr. Dilts stood up presumably to speak of his father but instead spoke of mine.

I was fortunate to grow up with Dad's love and to renew it before he was gone. Dad died—but not without his daughter at his side.

2

Bringing to Light

The William Morris Agency occupies three floors atop what was once the MGM building in midtown Manhattan. Its windows frame the power and glamour of New York, and of the publishing industry that was about to transform my life. It was March 1986, a month after my return from Iran.

The week before my "20/20" interview with Barbara Walters, I'd met the agency's president and Michael Carlisle, the gentleman who was assigned as my literary agent and who would become a very dear friend. I had been taken to lunch, and I was eager to get down to business. It was time to choose a collaborator for my book. I knew whom I wanted: Bill Hoffer, the co-author of *Midnight Express*, the dramatic account of an American drug smuggler's escape from a Turkish prison. While in Tehran, I'd heard about street demonstrations against *Midnight Express*, though the book and the movie based on it were banned there. I wanted to write with the person who'd had such a profound effect on ordinary people in Iran—the people who'd had such total control over my own life.

"You know," said my agent, "Bill Hoffer is a pretty big author. Maybe he'll say no."

But I persisted. If this writer could move the Iranian fundamentalists so strongly in absentia, I thought, he must be very effective. Perhaps he would say no, but I had to try. Those protestors in Iran would never know just how much they influenced my decision.

As it turned out, Bill was excited by my invitation, and even volunteered to catch a flight from Washington to meet me in New York that day—a gallant offer, as he detests flying. When we got together the following week to prepare an outline, we felt comfortable from the start. I found Bill soft-spoken, sensitive, and reassuring, a friend I hope to keep for life.

In June our book and movie contracts both came through. With my initial advance I paid off the $12,000 loan I'd obtained from the bank in Alpena and set aside another sum for Mahtob's college fund.

Bill drove up to Michigan, and we began working fervently. He had the knack of eliciting my feelings and Mahtob's without being intrusive. We trustingly opened up, and this helped us discover and express some of our most guarded emotions. Bill understood the vital role Mahtob played in our story and the dynamics of our relationship. My daughter came to accept Bill as a comfortable member of our little cocoon, the only male she trusted aside from my dad, Joe, and John.

In my new routine, Bill would arrive at 8 A.M. at the house I'd rented as an office, where we'd have breakfast and plunge into our work. We sat and talked all day long into a tape recorder as I attempted to re-create that strange, nightmarish chapter of my life. Bill's wife Marilyn did the word processing at the other end of the Federal Express route in Virginia. When Marilyn's transcriptions came back, we'd expand on each segment. Bill's questions would stimulate my recollections of sounds, smells, tastes, weather—everything I could possibly summon back from an event. Every couple of hours Bill would declare a break and slip out a deck of cards for a hand of pinochle. Refreshed, we would return to the tireless tape recorder again, until evening came and I took Mahtob to see Dad.

It was painstaking work, but well worth it. After *Not Without My Daughter* was published, I took pride when readers told me that they'd frozen with me in the mountains, or felt the layers of dirt we lived in, or smelled the sautéed onions in the air.

On the Fourth of July, Bill's wife and son joined us to

celebrate the holiday. Bill held Mahtob up to hang the American flag, ever so proudly, on the pole to the side of our house. Mahtob was one patriotic six-year-old who truly understood the meaning of freedom.

Bill and I worked for seven solid months. Our progress was steady, but we had to overcome two hurdles to make it to the end. The first was mostly a question of craft. I was having trouble describing an Iraqi air raid that had caught Mahtob and me waiting in line at a Tehran bread shop. On paper, the scene was good, but it wasn't great. Despite many rewritings, it didn't convey the terror I felt as I raced through the twisting alleys that led to our home, my daughter in my arms, dodging chunks of deadly debris from antiaircraft fire. The words just didn't sweep the reader along with me.

Then Bill made another set of changes . . . and something wondrous happened. Suddenly the scene was *there*, exactly as it had happened. Up to that point, I'd had doubts that my story would interest people who didn't know me. After Bill's magical revision, I doubted no longer.

The second hurdle was more serious, to the point where it jeopardized the completion of the book. It was in September, shortly after Dad's death, when I was most vulnerable. Bill and I were working even later into the night, sometimes until two or three in the morning. I was drained and exhausted, at my outer limit.

The process of writing had been emotional for me from the start, but I'd accepted that emotion as the core of my message. At one point I lost control. It came to a head when I unpacked some gifts that Moody had given me over the years. There were books with special inscriptions, and a music box that played Brahms' lullaby while rotating a specially chosen figurine: a mother who cradled a child.

The gifts triggered astonishing feelings that I'd repressed. I could deny them no longer: I missed Moody. More than that, a part of me still loved him. He'd been my closest friend from the time before we were married, my confidant. Now I was alone.

Once I acknowledged these emotions they set off waves of

guilt and self-doubt. How could I have *any* feelings toward Moody—aside from vengeful anger—after what he'd done to us? Whom could I talk to? Who would understand?

Like the rest of my family, I'd become an expert at avoiding conflicts of the heart. Now I was launched on an irreversible voyage of self-examination, and I found the ride excruciating. I wanted desperately to get off—to forget the book and the movie and all that went with them. There were weeks when I began each morning session with Bill by jumping up and running off for a cry.

To their everlasting credit, Bill and Marilyn never told me what to do but were always there to support me. As I sobbed away in my bathroom, Bill would patiently puff on his pipe and work by himself until I could return to the table. Had he been more aggressive, I might have given up the project for good. Had he not stood by me, I might have actually telephoned Moody— there were days when the urge to do so was almost irresistible— and forfeited everything.

I survived that month, and in surviving I turned the biggest corner of my life. I dealt with my conflict, I talked about it, I wrote about it, I relived it. My catharsis lifted a great burden from me. For the first time ever, I was a free person.

The idea for the movie version of *Not Without My Daughter* surfaced within days of my return from Iran. The William Morris Agency saw it as part of the package from the start, and the movie deal with Metro-Goldwyn-Mayer fell into place four months later, just after I signed my book contract.

As I originally understood it, I was to be a "consultant" to the MGM producers, Harry and Mary Jane Ufland. The Uflands were a classic Hollywood couple. Harry was a man in his late fifties, probably five-foot-seven at most, who radiated nervous energy. Mary Jane looked to be in her mid-thirties. Taller than Harry, she was very slim and had long, straight blond hair.

My first business meeting with the Uflands came a few days after our contract was signed. We met at a hotel restaurant at Detroit Metropolitan Airport and proceeded to wait three hours for a prominent, Detroit-based screenwriter to show up. Harry was being very nice to me, but I could tell he was furious—he doesn't wait for anybody.

The writer finally appeared and slid into our booth. Without so much as an apology, he looked at me and said, "Well, I'll tell you what I think about this. We've got to make it a love story between you and the man that got you out of Iran."

"But that's not what happened," I protested.

"That doesn't matter," he rolled on. "We need to make a movie that will appeal to an audience, and that's what they like."

Harry and Mary Jane eyed him in stony silence. I was appalled. If this was the movie business, I wanted out—even though I lacked control over the script, since I'd signed a release. "I really wouldn't like to see it done that way," I said.

"All right," the writer said, "if you don't want a love story, we have to get you rescued by the CIA—one or the other."

After he left, the Uflands tried to comfort me. To my relief, they assured me that they liked the story line as it was and that they saw no need to fabricate a plot.

The Uflands were eager to meet Mahtob. A few days after Dad's funeral, we got together at an elegant French restaurant in Washington, D.C. Realizing that the evening would be a long one for a six-year-old, Harry apologized: "We should have gone to some place for kids. She won't like anything on the menu."

"I never worry about Mahtob," I said. "She likes all kinds of food." After I directed my daughter to one of her favorites, white fish, Mahtob waffled. "Oh, I don't know, Mom," she said. "Do they have lobster? I'm really in the mood for lobster tonight."

When we first returned to Michigan, I didn't even consider sending Mahtob to school for the balance of her first-grade year. It was too much to throw at her all at once. While she'd learned to read and write Farsi in Iran, her English was behind her peers. She'd had so much to cope with: the loss of her father and all her young friends in Iran, the death of her grandfather, daily living in a new and frenetic household.

During our first months back Mahtob had a different kind of

education. Nelson Bates, a local detective, would come to our house in uniform to make her comfortable about approaching police officers. He schooled her on how to react to any would-be abductor, at home or on the street. I said, "Mahtob, I don't want you to be kidnapped. If it happens, you know what you have to do. We'll do everything we can, but it will be up to you."

In September of 1987, when Mahtob turned seven, I had no choice. I enrolled her in a private school, under an assumed name we chose the night before she started, one that she still uses. For the first few days she began her writing assignments by consulting a scrap of paper upon which I'd printed her alias. The teachers and principal were all informed—but sworn to secrecy—about her past.

Mahtob took her new identity seriously. One evening, after she'd invited one of her classmates to spend the night, her brother John came home and gave her his standard greeting: "Hi, Tobby, how ya doin'?" Mahtob rushed up to him, grabbed his hand, and dragged him into the laundry room. "Shhh," she said quickly. "Don't call me that in front of Katrina." As in Iran, a secret was absolutely safe with her.

Her first-grade teacher, Ruth Hatzung, understood what it meant for Mahtob to be apart from me. She drew my daughter out and lent her a sympathetic ear. Most important, she helped her refocus on our life in America and place the past in perspective. She did it so well that Mahtob didn't need any special counseling.

Our first Thanksgiving back held special meaning. Our Pakistani friends, Tariq and Farzana Ali and their two children, had come from upstate New York to join us for the holiday. I had met them years before, when Moody and I lived in Corpus Christi, Texas, a city with many expatriate professionals. We belonged to an informal Islamic social group, which also included families from India, Egypt, and Saudi Arabia. We'd all get together for a big Sunday meal, to which everyone would bring a native dish. I've always loved to cook—I won the Betty Crocker Homemaker of the Year Award in high school—and it was in Texas that I expanded my repertoire. To this day I cook more Middle Eastern dishes than standard American fare.

Moody and I became especially close to Tariq and Farzana, and stayed in touch after they moved away.

When they heard what had happened to Mahtob and me in Iran, the Alis traveled to Pakistan and hired someone to try freeing us from Tehran. Through Helen Balasanian, my contact at the Swiss Embassy, I got a local phone number for the man and had one of Mahtob's teachers call him. Unfortunately, he spoke no English and was too nervous to communicate through the teacher in Farsi. He hung up, and the plan was dead.

Don and Miriam were also special guests that Thanksgiving. While we were in Iran, my family had contacted the couple through a former business associate of mine who knew that Miriam was from Iran. Miriam immediately enlisted her sister Sarah, who lived in Tehran, to our aid. Again Helen played the intermediary and put me in touch with Sarah, who became my secret friend.

On the day we left Moody for good, it was Sarah who was waiting in her car at Mahtob's school bus stop to whisk us to a flight to Ziadon, near the Pakistani border. The plan fell through, as Moody became suspicious and accompanied us to school that day.

Given our guest list, the leading topic that Thanksgiving was our life in Iran. I could tell that Joe and John felt uncomfortable with the discussion, as they excused themselves early to visit their dad. Later that evening, after they'd returned, Joe kept repeating that he needed to go home to stoke his wood stove. "This house is already heated," I said. "Why don't you stay here for the winter?" He spent the night and stayed the next two years.

On January 2, 1987, at 2:47 A.M., I nudged a grumpy Mahtob awake to proclaim that Bill and I had finally finished *Not Without My Daughter*. My daughter had grown tired of the tape recorder and legal pads. She seized the moment to extract a sacred promise: "Mommy, *please* don't ever write another stupid book!"

Later that month Mahtob announced to me that she wanted to be baptized. A few days later, noting that I hadn't attended to her request, she firmly repeated, "I want to be baptized. If you aren't going to take care of it, I'll talk to Pastor Schaller myself." Purely by coincidence, the pastor chose January 29, 1987, the first anniversary of the day we began our trek to freedom, as the baptism date. Mahtob's entire first-grade class attended the moving ceremony as her witnesses. Bill and Marilyn Hoffer extended us the honor of becoming Mahtob's godparents.

Meanwhile, I was busy editing and proofreading the galleys. I'd worked on my story so long that it had become stale to me—I thought no one would ever want to read it.

On a bright winter day early in 1987 I laid aside the galleys and drove to Mahtob's school to pick her up. I watched her emerge through the school doors, surrounded by a bubbling circle of friends, trading good-byes all the way to the car. After she climbed in and gave me her usual kiss, I told her the news: "Honey, there was a plane crash today in Iran. Two hundred people died." With no hesitation, my gentle seven-year-old blurted, "Good, I hope my dad was on it!"

A pained silence hung between us. I'd heard Mahtob's anger before. "I hate Daddy for doing this to us," she'd told me in Turkey, when we were on our way home. Up to this moment I hadn't understood the depth of her bitterness and how much she'd repressed it. How could Mahtob grow up with a healthy attitude if she wished her father dead? I resolved on the spot to mount a systematic campaign to try to balance her feelings toward Moody.

At home that evening, I dragged out photo albums from happier family days. I reminded Mahtob of all the fun we'd had with Daddy in Michigan, of the weekends we'd spent at a nearby Sheraton for the swimming, sauna, and Sunday brunch. I told her I'd never felt ashamed that I married her daddy, that he'd been a devoted husband and father, and a dedicated doctor who truly cared about his patients. He'd been especially warm with my father, helping Dad to overcome depression after a colostomy and to fight to live. The problems we had in Iran, I said, didn't cancel the good times we had before.

Over the next several weeks we talked regularly on this

subject. "Mahtob, Daddy's birthday will be in a couple days," I said at one point. "I'll bet he is thinking about you right now, I'm sure he misses you. You know it's okay to miss him—if I had a daddy someplace in the world, I'd miss him too." I needed to give my daughter *permission* to care for the man who'd been so close to us both.

It was around this time that I unpacked Moody's office materials from storage. I found several dried-up felt pens and threw them away. A few days later I discovered the pens in Mahtob's dresser drawer. She had salvaged them secretly, and still keeps them, as if to hold on to her father.

About two months after the plane crash in Iran, Mahtob came home from school and said, "Mommy, tonight when I say my prayers, I want to ask God to take care of all the people in the world, even our enemies." From that night on she included Daddy by name. The wounds, I thought gratefully, were healing. Like myself, Mahtob was becoming a free person.

There remained, however, considerable scar tissue. Mahtob continued to fear her father even as she remembered loving him. Moody would always be linked in her mind to our time in Iran and to the abuse we suffered at his hands. As my daughter has told me more than once, "I don't want my eyes to ever see Tehran again."

Hostility can damage a child's sense of self. I've always wanted Mahtob to be proud that she's half-Iranian and to learn more about her heritage. In March of 1987, our second spring back in Michigan, we resumed our celebration of *No-ruz*, the Persian New Year. We dressed in our Easter finest and decorated the table with the *haft sin*, the seven symbolic foods whose names begin with the letter S.

Together we waited for the clock to tick to the second of the vernal equinox, when the sun reaches the sign of Aries, and the earth, according to Persian legend, shifts from one horn of the bull to the other. At the precise moment, we hugged and extended New Year's wishes to one another. I left the room and returned with a gleaming new purple bike.

After the two-week celebration it was time, I reminded Mahtob, "to gather all your bad memories and throw them away, as you throw the *sabzi* [fresh greens] into the river—to begin the new year without enemies and with good feelings toward everyone."

Whenever we travel to cities that may have Iranian restaurants, we check out the local telephone directories and do our best to try one. Mahtob is especially fond of *jujeh* (chicken) *kebab* with *zereshke pollo* (rice with barberries), a vegetable soup called *osh*, and *ghormeh sabzi*, in which finely chopped greens are sautéed with diced lamb, pinto beans, onions, and dried lime. When we visit Middle Eastern shops, Mahtob selects music tapes and storybooks in Farsi (my daughter was bilingual when we left Iran, but in Michigan she tried at first to forget her Farsi, saying "I don't want to hear Khomeini's language").

The publication date of my book was fast approaching. With each phone call from Michael there was more good news that brought us closer to the release of *Not Without My Daughter*. The book was given a full-page advertisement in the fall catalog of St. Martin's Press. *Ladies Home Journal* was the first magazine to do a serialization of the story. But the best day of all was when I received the first hardbound copy of *Not Without My Daughter*. It really was a book!

In September Mahtob and I kicked off the hardback release with a network television appearance on *Good Morning America*. Joan Lunden was on maternity leave and Barbara Walters happened to be filling in that day—a pleasant surprise for us. During a commercial break, when we were preparing for the interview, Barbara asked about Mahtob. I pointed to the side of the set and said, "She's fine—in fact, she's right over there."

To her producer's dismay Barbara immediately said, "Get her over here." Mahtob hadn't been to makeup, and there were only two chairs on the set. Barbara said, "She can sit right here on my lap and use my mike." Discarding her prepared questions, Barbara began the interview by referring to Mahtob and saying "This is my friend, my friend Mahtob—right? We've known each other now for over a year."

Bill Hoffer met us in New York and arranged to take Mahtob by train to his home in Virginia, where I would join them that weekend. She happily went off with Bill; he'd become part of the family.

I could no longer stay anonymous, and dropped my assumed name. To my relief, my new friends understood why I'd gone incognito and continued to stand by me. I set out on an eighteen-city, cross-country book promotion. As draining as writing my book had been, the tour was even more arduous. I would jet into a city at night, go directly to the hotel, check in, press my clothes, sleep for a few hours, and get up at dawn. Then I'd rush around town all day to do the local television, radio, and newspaper interviews, leaving just enough time to catch the flight to the next stop. Between appointments my mind would drift constantly to Mahtob, outside my protective presence.

In the fall of 1987, after arriving in Los Angeles on a flight from Miami, I went directly to the Beverly Hills Country Club, where I was to give my first on-the-road lecture. I shared the podium with authors Leonard Maltin, who compiles an annual TV movie and video guide, and Clifton Daniels, who put together *The Chronicle of the Twentieth Century*, a collection of front-page stories of historic events.

At the time, Maltin's review of my film seemed a long way off. As we talked, I realized that I knew nothing about the movies released during the time I'd been away. When I opened Clifton Daniels's book, I was fascinated by the world news headlines from August 1, 1984, through February 7, 1986. I realized then how isolated I had been, with all other Iranians, from what was really happening in the world. In Iran I had read or heard only what had been approved by the Islamic Guidance Ministry.

A few days and a few cities later I arrived in Tucson, Arizona, where I was one of four authors to speak at an annual lecture event. One of the other invitees was Dave Barry, the humorist for the *Miami Herald*, who would win the Pulitzer Prize three years later. By this time Dave was not a stranger, as we'd been meeting in green rooms (where talk-show guests gather before the show) around the country the past few weeks.

As at previous lectures, several people wanted to relate their experiences to me. A woman I'll call Beverly nervously expressed her fears: "I know my daughter Sabrina is going to be kidnapped to Iran. What can I do?" As she continued, it became clear that Beverly had already decided what she would do: avoid the issue and hope it would go away. "Although Majid is becoming abusive and we have so many problems, I won't divorce him until Sabrina is grown, because I know that will only make him angrier and he'll take our daughter," she said.

"Believe me, I understand," I said. "Had I not gone along to Iran, I am sure Moody would have taken Mahtob anyway. There just wasn't anything I could do to prevent it. Now we still don't have protection. We live with the fear that he will come back for her." I apologized for not having more to offer by way of encouragement and said, "If you need me in the future, you can reach me through St. Martin's Press."

I had been on tour for five weeks—a blur of airports and hotel rooms. I'd left Tucson at five o'clock Saturday morning, only to be stalled by a delay in Chicago. When I got home it was seven in the evening, and I couldn't wait to crawl into bed and sleep.

As I reached for the doorknob I heard sirens—a *lot* of sirens, from all directions. Minutes later Joe came through the door and said, "Gee, Mom, there's a real bad accident on the highway. They've got the road closed off—I had to go the long way around to get into town."

Joe took a shower and left. I was about to retire when Jan and Gale, my neighbors and old friends, came to the door. I knew something was up when Jan asked to talk to me in a room I used as my office. "John's been in an accident," she said. "He's in the hospital." I rushed to my friends' car and rode the longest five blocks of my life in the dark of the night.

The emergency room scene was worse than I could have imagined. As I stood before my son's broken body, I felt destroyed. John was encased in metal braces to protect his spinal cord in case his neck or back was broken. They hadn't yet taken x-rays, but it was obvious that he had several fractures, as I could see bone poking through skin.

32

John's face was a mass of cuts from flying glass. A friend stood next to him, holding a towel on his head. I soon found out why. His scalp had been sliced just above his hairline; without the towel it would have sagged from his skull.

I later learned that John's Plymouth had collided with a motor home. Pinned between his car's steering wheel and the door, my son had been extricated by firemen using the jaws of life. John's hip was crushed. His left leg was fractured in two places. Both arms were broken, his left shoulder cut to the bone. As bad as it was, John was truly lucky to survive that crash.

With no orthopedic surgeon on call locally, John had to be transferred to Carson City Hospital. It was the place I knew best and trusted most, where I'd met Moody when I was a patient and he was an intern there, and where they'd taken such good care of Dad.

The ambulance trip—the first of so many we'd take that year—was pure torture. I rode up front and kept urging the driver to go faster. Every little bump in the road brought a new round of groans from John. Roger Morris, our family doctor and long-time friend, met us at the emergency room. As he began stitching John's cuts, a train of specialists swept through: an internist, an orthopedic surgeon, a cardiologist. Despite their efforts, John's condition worsened. His face was gray, his breathing labored—both signs of heart failure. There was much concern about kidney damage and other internal injuries.

Within a few hours the doctors at Carson City decided to fly John to the University of Michigan Hospital in Ann Arbor, home to one of America's great trauma centers. As they moved my son from his bed onto a cart, to be carried to a nearby helicopter, he was screaming and moaning nonstop—piercing, curdling sounds. Gerald Brenton, the orthopedic surgeon, saw the alarm on my face. "Don't worry, he won't remember this," he told me. Then he put his hand on my shoulder and said, "I don't have any medical basis for saying this, but my gut feeling is that he's going to make it."

Jan drove me to Ann Arbor, a three-hour trip. I closed my eyes and prayed.

When I found John at the sprawling trauma center, he was

breathing more regularly—thanks to the 100 percent oxygen that he'd been given—and looked much better.

Later that day, after his condition stabilized somewhat, John underwent nine hours of surgery. Even at that, they could only work on his leg and hip; his left arm was left to heal on its own, and remains crooked to this day. The operation was a success, though John remained in critical condition for more than a week. After the rest of the family went home, I took a room at the medical center hotel for patients' families and canceled the balance of my book tour.

Mariette Hartley, then the hostess of the "CBS Morning Show," had shown a personal interest in my story, and I felt especially sorry to cancel my appearance on her show. She called the hospital several times to talk to me and check on John's condition. Even though I couldn't get to New York, she broadcast a special segment about the book and extended "a special hello" to John.

During our first few days in Ann Arbor, John was so overwhelmed by pain that he barely responded to the many family members and friends around him. I would go to his room, stand by his bed, and simply stare at him for hours at a time. One day I turned around to find Sherrie Bourgois, a newspaper reporter who'd recently written a story about me, standing there crying. Though we'd only met that one time, she stayed by me throughout John's long hospital stay, and another dear friendship developed.

I was grateful that this hadn't happened while I was still in Iran. Now I would be there when John most needed a mother, to support him and show how much I loved him.

As his shock subsided, John latched on to me as his lifeline. He was terrified to be alone. Every time I went to my room for a nap or a shower, he'd have the nurses call me back. Then he'd vent his anger at me, yelling incessant demands. The nurses explained that they saw this all the time, that victims of life-threatening accidents would lash out at the ones they loved most.

My son's facial scars were already healing—Roger Morris had done a great job suturing—but his emotional wounds still

34

festered. I tried to take his mood swings calmly, knowing that they too would pass.

Six weeks after the accident John came home, though he'd need round-the-clock nursing care for another four months. He was encased in a plaster body cast, torture for a teenager as active as he was. He had to be lifted hydraulically every time he needed to use the bedpan. The cumulative trauma of the last three years—my vanishing, his grandfather's death, and now this near-fatal accident—was almost more than he could bear. He would cry, "Why *me?*"

John made remarkable progress; like Dad, you couldn't keep him down. In January 1988, three months after the accident, he hopped to the kitchen in his body cast to make chocolate chip cookies. He worked with a homebound teacher and honor student classmates every day; his goal was to make it to his high school graduation that June.

Even after part of his cast was removed, John's arms weren't strong enough to support his weight on crutches. The doctors said he could take part in graduation exercises in a wheelchair, but that wasn't good enough for him. Each day he practiced on his crutches, until he was strong enough to file into the high school gymnasium with his fellow graduates, in step with everyone else.

When it was John's turn to receive his diploma, and he walked to the front—on crutches, but definitely under his own power—everyone cheered. They knew he shouldn't have been there that day and how hard he'd driven himself to make it. I was proud of John. He'd taken as tough a punch as life has to offer, and he'd refused to go down for the count.

When Mahtob and I made it back to the United States, I didn't realize that others shared my fear of losing their children to a parent in a foreign land. But after my book was published, I came to realize that cross-cultural abductions were more common than anyone suspected.

While on book tour, I enjoyed call-in shows the most. I particularly remember a local TV morning program in Cleveland. A woman called in and said, "You saved my life! My husband wanted to go to Jordan. I saw you on '20/20,' and I called the State Department, and then I decided not to go. My husband never came back. If I'd gone with him, I know I would have been in the same situation as you."

That woman set a pattern that held true around the country. Someone would call and say, "My children were taken to Saudi Arabia three years ago." Then someone else would report, "My children were taken to Spain five years ago." I kept in touch with these people and with many others who sent letters to me through my publisher. My mail kept getting heavier, and a number of the letters carried pleas for help.

Many left-behind parents had been told by the U.S. government they should "keep quiet, and maybe something can be done for you." Often they felt that no one else had ever experienced this situation and therefore it must be their fault—that they should have known better in the first place. I would tell one left-behind parent about another . . . and soon, out of nowhere, we had a little network. My correspondents no longer felt so isolated. They had each other—and they now dared hope they might have their children back some day as well.

It was the most serene of settings—a quiet café in Alexandria, Virginia—but I sensed that something was wrong. I looked curiously at my trustworthy dinner companion, Teresa Hobgood of the U.S. State Department's Foreign Consular Service Section. Normally cheerful and relaxed, she'd been on edge all afternoon.

It was February 1, 1988, five months after *Not Without My Daughter* had been published by St. Martin's Press in the United States. Since then my life had been consumed by book tours and lectures, like the one I'd made that morning to a Jewish congregation in Washington. I then proceeded to the State Department to discuss the issue of international parental child abduction.

Teresa had been our caseworker when Mahtob and I were hostages overseas. She'd kept my family informed through my contacts at the Swiss Embassy in Teheran, and had become my mother's trusted confidante. According to Mom, the family couldn't have withstood the unknown without Teresa's caring. Since our return Teresa had helped me monitor Moody's whereabouts. Over time we had developed a warm friendship. I learned that Teresa had been verging on burnout when they'd assigned her our case. Mahtob and I provided her with something all too rare in her business: a happy ending.

My afternoon at the State Department had passed quickly. I practiced my Farsi with Richard Queen, a U.S. Embassy hostage who'd been released from Iran several years before. I also discussed abduction statistics with Fabio Saturni, who headed the desk on international child custody cases. The desk, which had been established the year after my first national television appearance on "20/20," marked the State Department's first formal response to the issue, a tremendous milestone.

From the time I arrived, Teresa seemed uncharacteristically preoccupied. We chatted through dinner—about my book, other abduction cases, and John's convalescence. When my companion ordered cheesecake, I *knew* something was up. Teresa was slim and health conscious, and I'd never seen her eat dessert. She was putting something off.

Teresa reached across the table and placed her hand on mine. "You know, Betty," she said, "whatever happens in the future, we think you've done the right thing by telling your story. We get so many calls now from people asking questions before they marry a foreigner or travel to another country. They're learning from your experience that they cannot take the Constitution out of America with them. It's wonderful how many people you've helped from ending up in the same situation as you and Mahtob."

Teresa paused, her eyes holding mine. It was a look that foretold bad news, and suddenly I felt alarmed. She went on. "Today I had a call from Annette of the American Embassy in Berne, Switzerland." Teresa's grip tightened. "Dr. Mahmoody has left Iran."

My heart began sprinting. Blood rushed from my head, until I felt dizzy. I couldn't believe what I was hearing. Teresa sounded as if she were speaking from the far end of a tunnel. "We don't know where he is. All we know is that he has left." The news set off my worst fear, what I dread more than death itself—that Mahtob's father will someday leap out in revenge and steal her away again to Iran.

"But when?" I sputtered. "How did they find out?"

"Just today Annette received a message in the pouch from the U.S. Interest Section of the Swiss Embassy in Tehran," Teresa explained. "It stated that he'd left his job and his home, and they felt it was recent." She proceeded to read an excerpt from the cable: " 'He is in possession of a green card. It should not be ruled out that he has returned to America to recover his wife and daughter.' "

"They feel," she said heavily, "that your lives are in danger." Seeing my distress, Teresa did her best to calm me. "Please, *please* don't feel guilty about anything you've done. We all knew this would happen some time. We just didn't know when. It would have happened whether or not you went public with your story." She would try to get more specific information the following day.

My mind spun a million miles an hour. What should I do? I needed to call home to check that Mahtob had arrived safely from school . . . to get more security at our house . . . to make sure that no one could reach my eight-year-old daughter.

The minutes slipped by unnoticed, and we had barely enough time to get to National Airport for my flight to Michigan—the last one of the day. I *had* to make it; I had to get home, to touch Mahtob and hold her in my arms.

They called for final boarding as I approached the ticket counter—no time for the phone—but held the plane at the gate until I arrived. I felt dazed. I was unaware of my surroundings, or even that we'd taken off. I could only relive the past and fear for Mahtob's future.

When we reached Dayton, Ohio, where I needed to change planes, I learned that weather had delayed USAir's flight by one hour. I tried to compose myself, and phoned Mahtob. She was fine, watching television, without a care in the world. Then I spoke to my mom, who was staying over. I ached to warn her, to blurt out the news, but I didn't dare test Mom's heart condition.

Think, Betty, *think*: who could help us? Nelson Bates, the detective who'd been so helpful with Mahtob, had told me, "If you ever need any assistance, please don't hesitate to call." Now was the time. I dialed the officer at home and hurriedly conveyed Teresa's news. He immediately volunteered to maintain all-night surveillance around our house.

I hung up just in time for a public address bulletin that jolted me: "Flight 454 has been canceled due to ice on the runway." This couldn't be—I *had* to get home that night. Then a reprieve: there was space on another flight to Lansing. I could rent a car there, or get someone to pick me up; at least I'd be in Michigan. I rushed to the gate and made it just before they closed the door. About an hour later the captain's voice came over the public address system: "In ten minutes we'll be approaching Capital City Airport in Lansing. The temperature is twenty-six degrees, with snow falling."

I don't care if it's twenty-six degrees below zero—just get me home! As we approached our destination, the captain came on again. "We are now over Capital City Airport. The airport has been closed due to ice on the runway. We will now return to Dayton. Airline personnel will meet you at the gate with information on a hotel for tonight and will reschedule your flight. . . ."

It was near midnight before we touched back down, and every rental car had been taken. Close to tears, I resigned myself to staying the night and caught a bus to a nearby Sheraton. I could not begin to sleep. Repeatedly I played out various scenarios—all the ways that Moody might get to Mahtob. I doubted that he would fly directly into the U.S. His green card might get him through Immigration, but he'd be taking a chance, as his lengthy stay in Iran had made the card invalid. Given his notoriety from *Not Without My Daughter*, he'd likely be discouraged from applying for a visa. The State Department couldn't arrest him, because technically he'd broken no law.

Moody might have flown into Mexico, then crossed the

border with the assistance of relatives in Texas. In Iran he had told me that if the need arose he would hire someone to kill me. He could hire someone to kidnap Mahtob for him. . . .

Or perhaps I was panicking needlessly. Perhaps Moody had just become fed up with conditions in Iran and decided to move somewhere else.

What was I trying to tell myself? I always *knew* he would try to recover his daughter someday. I knew too that he wanted me dead—he told me more than once that he'd kill me if I ever managed to escape from Iran. I wasn't ready to die. As I remembered Iran, I felt stronger, more resolved.

Now I would do whatever I had to do to keep her here. Mahtob was *mine,* and no one could take her away from me. Moody didn't deserve to see her—much less seize her—after what he'd done to us.

As it turned out, Moody didn't show up that night. For the next two months, as his whereabouts remained unknown, I lived every moment as if he was lurking around the corner. Even after our contacts reported that he'd returned to Iran, I could not relax. I knew that he could leave again any day, or send an agent to get what he wanted: my death and my daughter.

Part Two

3

Crisis

Mahtob and I had always known that Moody might come after us. Until my meeting with Teresa, we'd begun to relax a bit. We'd lowered our guard as we became caught up in our daily activities.

No longer. Now I realized that we'd been kidding ourselves. Now I knew that Moody could be closing in on us—at any time, in any place. I heard that he'd had a falling out with his family, which might give him even more motivation to focus on Mahtob.

How could I protect us? I asked for advice from every direction—from security companies, private investigators, bodyguards. While some of our security measures should not be revealed, others can be told. I followed one recommendation within a few days of my return from Washington: I obtained a permit to purchase and carry a handgun.

I had our house wired with the best security system I could find. But I still didn't feel safe. I found myself riveted to the windows, suspecting any car that paused for an extra moment at the stop sign on our corner.

Guns and alarms were important, but they weren't enough. I knew I had to get a custody order for Mahtob, and quickly. Without one, as Teresa had warned me, it would be perfectly legal for Moody to take her away again. He was her father, after all. Even if he and Mahtob were to be found at the airport, on their way out of the country, she could not be rescued.

At the same time, I feared that filing for custody might jeopardize the security of our little haven. If Moody were alerted to our whereabouts by the legal documents it might even hasten his return to America, which I so desperately wanted to avoid. And I vividly remembered the legal system's response to my cry for help before I left for Iran. . . .

In the summer of 1984, as the time dwindled before our two-week family "vacation" to see Moody's relatives in Tehran, my misgivings had increased by the hour. I dreaded going but felt I had no choice. If I refused to go, I felt certain that Moody would try to take Mahtob to his homeland—for good. There was only one way I could conceivably avoid the trip: by getting a protective order to keep my husband away from my daughter.

At that time I'd never heard of an international parental abduction. But I couldn't ignore my intuition.

I had ample grounds to suspect Moody's intentions. His renewed devotion to Islamic rituals; the recent phone calls to his family in Iran, and Moody's refusal to tell me what was said; the surreptitious talks with his visiting nephew, Mammal—all were ominous signs.

After I unburdened myself to an attorney who was a friend to both Moody and me, the man responded with disbelief. "First of all, if you think he would do that, you need a psychiatrist. Besides, there isn't a judge in this country who would listen to you. Moody hasn't committed any crime. There's no way you can prevent him from having visitation rights."

I saw then that I had no choice. I *had* to accompany Moody to Iran, or else risk losing Mahtob forever.

Shortly after we escaped from Iran, in my effort to get a divorce and sole legal custody of Mahtob, I went to various attorneys with the hope of a different response.

There were two legal barriers. The first concerned "venue"—the place where papers would be filed and my divorce hearing held. According to state law, I would have to file with the court in my county of residence. If I tried filing elsewhere, I was told, I'd have to perjure myself, and Moody might well be able to set the divorce aside anyway. The second barrier was "due process," the requirement that I try, to the best of my ability, to give Moody advance written notice of the divorce and custody proceedings.

Taken together, these two legal necessities might serve as a lightning rod—an open invitation for Moody to return to Michigan and search us out, to make good on the threats he had made against me in Iran.

"There's no way to get a divorce unless you try to serve notice on Moody in Iran," the attorney insisted.

"I can't do that," I protested. "Moody will find us—he'll kidnap Mahtob again."

"But there's no way around it," the attorney said. "You have to give him an opportunity to defend himself in court."

After several other lawyers confirmed the bad news, I shelved my plans for the divorce.

Now, in 1988, I was faced with the same basic dilemma that I'd confronted before my trip to Iran. Would the legal system be any more responsive than before? I hoped for the best but feared the worst.

Ever helpful, Teresa, my State Department worker, told me that she had briefed a Friend of the Court, one of the appointed officials who advise judges on cases involving children. Yet from our first contact it was clear that the official and I were of different minds.

"I don't believe in restricting visitation from fathers," he began. "I think it's better for the children to have open visitation by both parents."

"But don't you know what my daughter and I went through to get back to America?" I asked.

He coolly replied, "I have little sympathy for adults who get themselves into awkward situations."

At that moment I grasped what we were up against. If someone like myself—with all the publicity, and with my case documented with the State Department—received this kind of response, what chance did other parents have?

I was caught in a Catch-22. I had to get a divorce and custody order to protect Mahtob from Moody. Yet the same process would make my daughter and me even *more* vulnerable than before. There seemed to be no way out.

In the spring of 1988 I looked forward to a European book tour with both excitement and apprehension.

Strangely enough, I felt more unprotected in my own country. Moody wouldn't suspect we were in Europe, and even if he got wind of our tour, we'd be gone by the time he found out. This trip would buy Mahtob and me a little more time. Out of caution I consulted with the State Department on travel to France, England, and Ireland, the countries on our itinerary. Officials confirmed that Moody was back in Iran, though we were never able to find out where he had traveled.

I could not even consider taking this trip without Mahtob. I had to have her by my side; I couldn't endure another panic like the one two months before, when I'd been stalled in Washington.

According to my family, I should have learned my lesson and never left the country again. But that would not be freedom. I wanted our lives to be as unrestricted as possible, given the circumstances. If Mahtob developed a fear of travel it could inhibit her for the rest of her life. While it was difficult for me to summon the courage to leave my home country again, I felt it was a necessary step in our healing process. Despite my pleas for understanding, my mother convinced herself that we would never return again. She became so upset that she made herself sick and was hospitalized.

We spent *No-ruz* (the Persian New Year) of 1988 flying over the Atlantic to Paris, where I met the people who would give me the greatest hope of a solution to this heinous problem of terrorism against children. Antoine Audouard, my French editor, told me, "A group of women here have asked to meet with you. I didn't make a commitment because I didn't know how you'd feel about it."

At that point, though I'd already been inundated by international parental abduction cases, most of them involved Americans. I was intent on exploring the problem further and welcomed the opportunity to expand my knowledge.

My first contact with the Mothers of Algiers—an advocacy group working on behalf of French women whose children had been abducted by the children's fathers to Algeria—was at a café along the Seine in Paris. I was astounded by the number of French cases and intrigued by what these women were doing. I wanted to get as much information as I could before I continued on to England. The problem of international parental child abduction, I realized, was by no means confined to the U.S. I couldn't stop thinking about the Mothers of Algiers, and I resolved to see them again.

The following month, at a lecture before a Michigan service organization, I voiced my frustrations about these divorce and custody issues. After the speech, during an informal talk with members of the audience, the topic came up again. One of the guests, a soft-spoken, bearded man in his mid-forties, was especially attentive. When I discovered that he was a lawyer with experience in family matters, I began asking *him* questions. Before we left he said, "I'm not an ambulance chaser, but I think I can help you." He gave me his business card and said, "If you're interested, give me a call."

Within forty-eight hours of my first visit to Arnold Dunchock's office, he had obtained a temporary custody order that denied Moody visitation with Mahtob. This was a great relief, though I still would be faced with the more stringent requirements for a permanent custody order as part of the judgment of divorce.

During that visit Arnie told me that he would like to help my cause. I didn't know it at the time, but Arnie would become my co-crusader—not only in protecting Mahtob, but in advancing the interests of children everywhere.

In addition to my book promotions and lectures, there were new developments with the film. Harry and Mary Jane asked me to go to California to meet Brian Gilbert, who was keenly interested in directing. "I love your story, but I want a new script," Brian told me. "The only way I'll direct this movie is if I can rewrite the script with you." Flattered by the proposal, and not guessing what lay in store for me, I agreed.

47

I liked Brian from the beginning. I found him jovial and unpretentious, and he seemed very caring about keeping the script as close to reality as possible. I made several trips to Los Angeles over the next two months to help Brian and the Uflands with the research that would help make the film real. Every day we went to Iranian restaurants and Persian cultural centers. When we went to cafés for afternoon tea, I'd eavesdrop on the surrounding tables. When I heard a phrase of Farsi, I clued Brian in. He observed how the people ate, drank, talked, and walked—and how the women often followed a few paces behind the men.

That summer, Brian came to Michigan to spend time with Mahtob and my family and to pore through my photo albums. Even after he returned home to London to begin writing, we kept the international phone lines and our fax machines busy. Brian really seemed to understand what I was trying to express.

But when his script finally came to me, the true feeling still was not there. I was getting desperate. Despite all our work, we were hardly closer to production than we'd been two years before. With nothing to lose, I thought it was time to try my hand. Rather than call the Uflands to commiserate, I got a baby-sitter for Mahtob, checked into a local motel, and rewrote Brian's opening scenes in longhand. I honed in on every seemingly trivial detail of my experience in Iran, the shadings known only by me. I was not a professional scriptwriter, but I was the only one (besides Mahtob) who had *lived* this story, and I struggled to translate the immediacy of my feelings to the page.

When I finished a scene, Lori, Arnie's secretary—the fastest word processor I've ever known—drove over to pick it up, then returned to her office and typed it into her computer. After working around the clock for four days, I sent a large block of the script to Harry and Mary Jane. They had no idea what I'd been up to, and I'll never forget the message Harry left on my answering machine the following day: "You blew us away! That's exactly what we want!"

In the midst of my work on the screenplay, the doorbell rang: United Parcel Service. I knew at once what was in the package. When I called Mahtob, she grumbled, "It's probably just another stupid script." It took considerable coaxing to convince her to open it. She bent down and struggled with the box. Finally she tore it open and reached inside. "Ah, my bunny!" Mahtob gasped. "It's my bunny!" A smile flitted across her face.

Mahtob embraced the green-and-white bunny, a replica of the beloved stuffed animal she had to leave behind in Iran. "It's so small," she said, as she held the three-foot-tall bunny in front of her, not realizing she had grown. She squeezed and kissed it. She twirled in a circle with "Tobby Bunny" in her arms. Then she reached down and hooked its elastic straps around her feet, and danced with Tobby Bunny just as she had so many times before.

Mahtob hadn't been so happy in such a long time. She sat on the sofa with Tobby Bunny next to her. Then her smile faded. I could sense her mind drifting back to Iran. She looked so sad, and tears began to trickle down her face. I could tell that Tobby Bunny was evoking memories of her father, the man who once provided Mahtob with so much warmth and security.

After reading about the left-behind bunny in *Not Without My Daughter*, several people had written to ask if we'd been able to replace it. In fact we had searched extensively, but to no avail. Then Mary, the daughter of Mahtob's first-grade teacher, volunteered to make a new one if we provided her with the bunny's dimensions and a photo. Later, when we hung it on the knob of Mahtob's white chest of drawers, the bunny fit just like the original. Despite Mahtob's powerfully mixed emotions, Tobby Bunny holds a place of prominence in her room.

My life in Iran was dedicated to one purpose: getting back home with Mahtob. Hearing her sob at night often prevented me from escaping into sleep. I wanted desperately for someone to help us get out. It was during this time I made a sacred promise to myself that I would never turn my back on others who needed help.

Since returning from Iran, another force has joined my constant worrying about Mahtob. Now my insomnia is spurred not by Mahtob's sobbing, but by the cries of the thousands of children who still suffer the repression my daughter encountered. Now I want to help them, as others helped me, to find a way out.

In October 1990 I returned an urgent phone call at the request of St. Martin's Press. A panic-stricken voice answered, "I don't know if you remember me. My name is Beverly. I contacted you three years ago when you were in Tucson. I told you that I was afraid my daughter would be taken to Iran. He *did* it! She's gone!"

Beverly's husband had taken Sabrina to Tehran and barred her from even talking to her mother. Beverly's first instinct was to join her daughter in Iran, but her husband rejected the idea. He wanted a divorce—and knew he could get more favorable treatment under Islamic law in Iran than in an American court. As Beverly tearfully noted, "I can't even get *into* his country without his written permission."

Beverly was distraught about her daughter's plight: "Sabrina can't speak the language. She doesn't know those people, and the culture will be so difficult for her to understand alone. Her teddy bear is still here; she can't sleep without it. My poor baby! What can I do to help her?"

I advised Beverly not to cut her ties with Majid—to maintain a line of communication, no matter how difficult.

Several months later, after much pleading, Beverly's husband agreed to allow her to go to Iran. She left her family in America behind, knowing she might never see them again—and that Sabrina almost surely will never be allowed to leave Iran. They remain there to this day.

At the other extreme are those parents who go to desperate lengths to avoid losing their children, who attempt to foil a parental abductor by hiding. But as Kristine Uhlman can testify, going underground is no guarantee of a child's security. I was put in touch with Kristine through my growing network in 1987. She had met Mustafa Ukayli years before, while they were both graduate students. They were married at the Ohio State University Lutheran Student Center in 1975 and had two children—a daughter, Maisoon, born in 1977, and a son, Hani, born in 1978.

After Mustafa became physically abusive, Kristine managed to free herself and her children from him. "I changed my name and went into hiding, knowing that he would make every effort to recover the children." She told me she communicated with her parents only through a third party and that they didn't even know what state she was living in. Ultimately she won temporary custody of both children from a Denver court.

As is often the case, Kristine's parents had trouble understanding why she would want to leave her handsome, smart, generous husband. While Kristine was in hiding, Mustafa stayed with her parents, sobbing his heart out, convincing them that his values were similar to theirs. During this time, he would sneak out of the house to close the couple's joint bank accounts and organize the paperwork he needed to "steal" the children.

On September 11, 1981, Maisoon and Hani were kidnapped violently from in front of their home. "Within three days," Kristine told me, "Mustafa had divorced me in the Islamic court in Saudi Arabia and was given custody of the children and all our assets."

With no possible recourse from her country, Kristine asked the Saudi government for help. But she quickly found that it would recognize neither her American custody order nor the two counts of felony kidnapping against Mustafa. The Saudi ambassador promised to help her gain access to her children—but only if she refused to speak to the press. Kristine complied. At the time I was being contacted by several other left-behind parents, who said they'd been told the same thing: "Keep quiet, and maybe we can do something for you."

Desperate to make contact with her children and willing to try almost anything, Kristine followed the advice of the U.S. State Department and the Saudi Embassy. Her plan was to establish residency in Saudi Arabia and then bring her case before the Islamic court. It took nearly two years for the Saudi government to grant her a special residency permit to live and work there as a civil engineer.

A week after entering the kingdom, Kristine was arrested and put in a women's prison, where nearly half the population consisted of toddlers and small children. "Islam protects the mother-child bond to the point that if a mother is imprisoned, her child remains with her in her cell," said Kristine. "The first night I was attacked by a lesbian. There was no one in the prison who spoke English. There were no mattresses or sheets, and we weren't fed regularly because food had to be donated by family or friends." While she was there, a representative of the Saudi Embassy called her parents in California and told them that Kristine could be helped—but only if they avoided the press. After five long days Kristine was released. She has yet to find out why she was arrested.

Still cut off from her children, Kristine went daily to the Saudi Foreign Ministry for the next three months. She sought permission to go before the Islamic court, because Islamic law explicitly grants a mother custody of her children until they reach the age of seven. As Kristine was a legal resident of the country, she hoped she'd be afforded equal treatment under its laws.

On August 2, 1983, almost two years after their abduction, Kristine saw her children. Hani, by then four years old, could describe every detail of the kidnapping, down to the toys his father gave him to stop crying. "He told me that a man dressed like Santa Claus helped their daddy 'steal' them from their mommy," Kristine said.

The following week, she finally convinced the court to consider her case—making Kristine the first non-Arab woman ever to be heard in the Shariah (Islamic) Court of Saudi Arabia. On her second day in court, her Saudi lawyer told her "there is no money in divorce cases" and abandoned her without a translator in an all-Arabic proceeding. On the third day, a piece of devastating evidence was introduced against her—a picture of her leaving a church with her children. The judge declared that Kristine could not have custody of the children because it would "affect their religiousness." She was denied regular visitation. During the next year, while she continued to live and work in the kingdom, she was allowed to see her children only five times.

Finding the situation intolerable, Kristine left Saudi Arabia. Since then she has had to beg her ex-husband for visits with her children. In 1986 he allowed her to see them, but only in the company of his new wife. All contact with the children was monitored. "I had to sleep in the same bed with his current wife," Kristine said. "My children argued about who they would sleep next to—neither of them wanted to sleep next to me. My daughter told me, 'America is a bad place. America has no mosques; America gives passports to Jews.' My son told me, 'My eyes are not blue, my eyes are brown. I am an Arab.'"

Kristine's mother's last request, to see her grandchildren one more time, was not granted. Once again I realized how lucky Mahtob and I were to get back from Iran in time to see my father before he died. At least he knew we were home.

After Iraq's invasion of Kuwait in 1990, Mustafa took the children to Holland, where Kristine had a most unpleasant visit with them. Maisoon and Hani were now total strangers to her. It was difficult to understand their broken English. They had become deeply religious Muslims. Worst of all, they'd been convinced that Kristine didn't love them and denounced her as their mother. Kristine's father was to join them for the visit, but on the day he arrived Mustafa changed his mind and left a note in his hotel mailbox: "When you read this, we will be back in the Kingdom of Saudi Arabia."

Kristine told me, "I just want to sleep, to dream of them. I wake up comforted, submerged. I dream I can smell them and feel my daughter's curls and skin." Unfortunately, dreams are all she has had to hold on to since 1981. She can only hope that Maisoon and Hani might choose to return to the U.S. for college and that the three of them might pick up their lives together. But given the children's current beliefs about their mother and her country, that too may be only a dream.

After spending countless hours on the phone, Kristine and I met in January 1988, when we appeared together on "The Phil Donahue Show." The show's guests, including an American university professor who had converted to Islam, all stayed at the Drake Hotel in New York, and we waited together for the limo to pick us up to go to the studio. As we walked toward the car, I encountered the professor's Palestinian husband. The man held the Koran at the entrance of the limo for us to kiss as we passed under. Though I declined, I immediately felt intimidated by this man. Not about to demote himself by sitting in back with the women, he took the seat next to the driver. As the car merged into traffic for our short trip, he and his wife began chanting from the Koran. When the professor stopped briefly to join us in conversation, she was sharply reproached by her husband for behaving improperly. "I have to pray," she said, and resumed chanting. Once we arrived at the studio her husband demanded that she change into a different dress, and she did.

While we waited in the green room, Phil Donahue passed through and graciously greeted each of us with a handshake and small talk. As Phil reached his hand toward the professor, her husband said loudly, "Don't touch my wife!" Phil withdrew immediately and cut short his visit.

I felt nauseated; it was as if I were back in Iran. For a moment I was unsure whether I could do the show, but decided I wasn't going to let this man control me.

Kristine's strongest advice to me that day was to never hide: "I went through the whole thing, the name and the identity change, and living where nobody knew me, and they still found me. It was a waste of time and money." When her children were abducted, it took too much time for Kristine to convince people around her what really had happened and who she really was.

Kristine has suffered more pain in the last ten years than most of us can imagine. She holds no bitterness, only remorse that she has been robbed of her children. Recently she told me, "There's nothing I can do, but at least I can talk to others." And she has. Kristine has given many hours of her time, at her own expense, to console and advise other parents in similar situations.

When I first expressed my concerns about safety to my literary agent, Michael Carlisle, he confirmed advice I'd previously received, noting that "the publicity could *become* your security." Now, more than ever, I am sure that was correct. If the people around me know my situation, they are better able to warn me of any suspicious actions. A mom of one of Mahtob's classmates told me after the book was published, "I am so glad we know your story. Now every day when I pick up my children, I watch Mahtob to see who she leaves with." Yes, I did make the right decision in not letting Moody make us captives in our own country. After all, that is why we left Iran—to be with our family, and to be free.

Unfortunately, there are probably more women trapped in male-dominated countries than we can imagine. There are no statistics because most are not trying to get out. They become broken women, sacrificed to their own despair.

A midwestern American woman named Meg demonstrated just how much a mother will sacrifice to protect her children. In 1982 Meg filed for a divorce, spurring her husband Hossain to kidnap their son Kayvan and their daughter Fereshteh to Iran. Desperate, Meg followed to be with her children. For the next eight years she lived with her husband's large family in a two-room house in Tehran. She might as well have been caged. During all that time, she had not a single opportunity to communicate freely with anyone from the West. She wasn't even permitted to stand in line to buy food without supervision.

In 1990 Hossain gave Meg permission to take their third child, then a baby, to see her aging parents. The State Department called me, sketched some details of the case, and asked, "Would you please talk to her? We feel so helpless—there isn't really anything we can do for her. Maybe just talking to someone like you may comfort her."

I spoke with her often, wanting desperately to help her, but like the State Department I lacked solutions. She said, "I just read your book, and if my life in Iran were half as good as yours was, I would have it made." Her description of her family's way of life in Tehran was horrifying, but certainly realistic to me. I remember that southern section of the city, with its two-room houses holding fifteen inhabitants, with no air conditioning and no modern facilities.

As much as Meg dreaded returning to her imprisonment in Iran, she could not desert her two older children. On the day she was scheduled to leave a heavy snowstorm closed the airport, canceling her flight. That same day she received a letter that Fereshteh had smuggled out. Across the top of the letter her fourteen-year-old daughter had written:

Mommy, please read this two times!! Mom, don't come back. How stupid you are, Mom, if you come back. Mom, I will nag him, like that time that he stole us. Me and Kayvan screamed a lot. I will do it again. I'm bigger now. I can do it better.

Mom, believe me, we have a good life. We have meat, eggs and fruit too. So don't worry for us. Mom, I got your letter today and the pictures. I love everybody just like they are. I saw your picture. I could read your face. I could see how lonely you are, but . . . if you come back you will be miserable. I wrote all of this, but I don't know if you will listen or not. But Mom, think about what you are doing. OK? Mom, say hello to everyone. I pray this letter gets to you fast.

Meg was deeply torn. I hoped the storm would be a reprieve and that she would reconsider going back. My heart ached for her two young teenagers who were trying so hard to find a way out of Iran. I could feel the desperation, Fereshteh grasping at straws, just as I had in Iran. It didn't seem fair that children should have to carry this heavy burden. Like Mahtob, these two children had to grow up in a hurry.

Meg's sense of guilt and responsibility overpowered her. She couldn't forget how, during the Iraqi missile attacks on Tehran, Kayvan had run outside their post-office shelter to get bread, the family's only food—risking his life to save theirs. She could not bear the thought of leaving him and his sister in Tehran, not knowing what their fate would be.

On the day Meg was to return to Iran, she told me that Kayvan had carried on so much after he was taken that they put him in the basement. After she arrived in Tehran, he boasted of his success: "Mommy, you got to live with us because I was bad." Meg went on to say "I memorized your book. It gives me hope. I'm going. I don't have any choice. Maybe someday?"

After Meg left, I received a letter that expressed her feelings further: "I can't explain, but I'm scared to separate the kids. Someone will get hurt or left behind. Family and old friends can never understand—only someone who has been there. Fereshteh is trying to be the adult woman in the family. She's trying to live my dream. When did the child become the adult and the adult the child, I don't know. But I'm going to try to keep the kids together and give them some sort of dream." I have not heard from Meg since.

Through my involvement in these frustrating cases, I've learned that one possibility never can be ruled out: a reconciliation, which often results from a woman's dependence upon her abuser. Pressure to reunite the family may come from many sources—not least from the two parents' families. Frequently the hope for reconciliation is the frayed thread connecting an abandoned parent to a child, and it compels the parent to maintain contact with the abductor.

Although reconciliation is almost always a desirable approach, it is often unsuccessful. After all, the relationship broke in the first place for a reason. But if a reconciliation actually resolves the parents' differences, it can be a true solution.

In 1988 I was contacted by the sister of Marilyn, a Detroit-area woman who married an Iranian named Feridun. By this time I was beginning to recognize a pattern of the factors of an imminent abduction. Marilyn had been virtually held hostage in her own home by her husband. He taped her phone conversations and barred her from seeing relatives. According to Marilyn, he had put gasoline in the house and alternately threatened to burn her and their four children alive, or to drive off a bridge with the family in the car. He told Marilyn, "If you go to the authorities, I will kill your family."

Fearful for their lives and frustrated by the court system's demonstrated lack of understanding, I consulted government officials and a battered women's shelter. Arrangements were made for Marilyn and her children to escape from her home, and she and her children were networked through shelters to a faraway state. She established a new identity and attended a university, which built her self-esteem and prepared her for an independent life with her children.

57

A year and a half later, when her husband demanded visitation, she told me she would rather go to jail than reveal her children's whereabouts. She was so concerned about their security that she would park her car in Ohio before proceeding in another car to a court appearance in Michigan.

Marilyn's situation had all the signs of a disaster in the making. Feridun had few ties and no family members in the United States, and had recently traveled to Iran. It was a typical scenario for an international parental kidnapping.

Finally the date came for the family's custody hearing. Marilyn had been ordered to produce her children—or to go to jail for contempt of court. After several interviews, the official known as the Friend of the Court recommended against visitation for Feridun—a major step forward. I was scheduled as an expert witness in her trial, and felt confident that this case would turn out different from most.

At last the stage was set for the showdown. I waited in the corridor, along with Marilyn's mother, sisters, and attorney, for Marilyn and the children to arrive. Feridun was also waiting, his arms filled with belated Christmas gifts for the children. The elevator opened, and Marilyn and the children stepped out, walked past all of us, and went to her estranged husband. They asked for a private room to talk, and it became apparent that a reconciliation was likely. Several months later I'd heard that she and her husband were still seeing one another and that Marilyn had cut off all ties to her family.

This case reflects an especially disheartening aspect of the battered women's syndrome: the more violent, the more outrageous, the more bizarre and life-threatening the man's attack, the greater the likelihood that the parties will reconcile. Typically, the abused person rejects any helpers when returning to the abuser.

After this pathetic courtroom drama, the attorney turned to me and said, "What will you do when the next one asks you for help?" Feeling hurt and betrayed, my response was "I won't help." Not only had I spent considerable time with Marilyn, but I'd invited her to stay at my home when she'd come to Michigan for court appearances. I had jeopardized my security, and Mahtob's as well, by trusting and trying to help her. Still, for the sake of all the other children, I knew I had to go on.

In June 1990 Arnie and I met in Brussels with Patsy, a Belgian. Her English, which she'd learned in Israel, was very good. As she cradled her nine-day-old daughter in her arms, she said sadly, "Though we've been separated for eight years, my husband is refusing a divorce. I have been living with someone and we decided to have a baby and start a new life. But I'm not forgetting my first life."

Patsy met Ben, a nonpracticing Jew, in Israel, a place she loved to visit. They were married in a civil ceremony in Brussels, where he asked a priest to be his witness. "As long as we were living in Belgium, he acted in a European manner," Patsy told me. After they returned to Israel with their son and two daughters, however, his behavior changed drastically (this is a common thread among abduction cases).

"He was beating me, locking me in the apartment, and not giving food to the children, so I took the children and left him," Patsy explained. "I never tried to tell the children that their father was bad and that I was good. I didn't have to tell the two older ones, who remembered all too well the times he beat me in front of them."

Nine months after the move to Israel, Ben tried to kidnap the children. The smallest one could not yet walk and was the easiest to take. Ben put her in the car, and when Patsy rushed to retrieve her Ben tried to slam the car door on Patsy's back. The other children screamed and attracted attention, forcing him to withdraw.

Patsy obtained a court order awarding her custody from the Belgian court. But her trust in the system was limited, and so she went into hiding. The children had to change schools in the middle of the year and had a hard time understanding what was happening. Her older daughter seemed especially upset, but refused to discuss it. After the girl started wetting herself during the day, Patsy explained that Ben was trying to take them away.

59

In November 1985 Ben showed up at the children's school with a bodyguard and two cars. Remembering the first incident, the older daughter said, "I don't want to go with him to France." Once again the abduction attempt failed.

The next year passed without incident, despite sporadic police reports that Ben was in Belgium. But in December 1986, when the children were seven, five, and four years old, Ben's latest attempt was successful. Through intensive efforts Patsy traced him from Brussels to Amsterdam, London, and finally to New York in February 1987. Patsy went to the United States ten times in eight months trying to locate her children. She worked with the National Center for Missing and Exploited Children and did a segment on the television show "America's Most Wanted."

In January 1989 Patsy's husband was arrested in New York and jailed on a kidnapping charge. He said he had taken the children because he didn't want them raised as Christians, and Patsy was Catholic. Ben would not reveal the children's whereabouts (she later learned that they had been secreted in a Hasidic Jewish community somewhere in the U.S.). Seven months later Patsy won her fight to have Ben extradited back to Brussels—the first extradition for a parental abduction in Belgian history.

Under Belgian law, parental child abduction is a crime punishable by eight days to one year in prison. If the abductor refuses to cooperate, the maximum sentence may be extended indefinitely—as it has been for Ben, now in his third year in a Belgian jail. In talking to Patsy, I realized that she was not seeking revenge against her ex-husband. She sought to keep him in jail because he was the only person who could lead her to her children.

Back in the United States, Patsy and her father doggedly followed the children's trail. They found two Hasidic groups among whom the children had been living; on one occasion they were within six weeks of catching up to them. But apparently their progress was leaked to Ben's co-abductors, and the children were moved to yet another community. For all Patsy knows they could be in Paris, Amsterdam, Mexico City, or any place in the world.

Patsy joined forces with Anne-Marie Lizin, a Belgian government official, to form a nonprofit group called Missing Children International, whose operations began in September 1989. The organization counsels parents before and after their children are abducted and strives to educate judicial officials about the seriousness of this crime. In Belgium, as in the rest of the world, potential problem cases rest in the hands of judges.

Kit Bell was swept off her feet by a handsome Libyan named Sabri Hashim while they were studying for their master's degrees at Portland State College in Oregon. After their son Ahmed was born, Sabri convinced Kit to make a trip to Libya. Again, as in so many other cases, once there he refused to allow Kit or Ahmed to leave his country. Their daughter Camella was born in Libya.

After three years of unhappiness and confinement in this strange land, Kit coaxed Sabri to allow her and their children to vacation in the United States. Like Kristine Uhlman, she immediately filed for divorce and went into hiding. Sabri followed them to the States to contest the divorce.

The judge held the children's Libyan and American passports and ordered supervised visitation. When Kit resisted, pleading that she feared for her children's security and for her own life, the judge threatened to jail her for contempt of court. Realizing that the children would be at greater risk if she were in jail, Kit reluctantly came out of hiding. On his second visitation Sabri charmed the court-appointed supervisor into letting him take the children to a toy store unsupervised. He and the children vanished without a trace. Three weeks later Sabri sent a cable to his American lawyer, disclosing that he and the children were back in Libya.

When Kit begged her husband to let her come to Libya to visit them, he rebuffed her: "You don't exist for us any more." Three years after the abduction, the United States bombed Qaddhafi's headquarters in Tripoli, one mile from the home of Sabri's family. To prove to Kit that the children survived, Sabri later sent photos of Ahmed, who by then was six years old, and Camella, who was four. Though she yearned to know what they looked like growing up, the pictures "tore my heart out," Kit said.

Despite the pain of her separation, Kit said she knew her children would be loved as long as her mother-in-law is alive. At the same time, she added, "they'll be raised in a society that I really can't believe in. They'll be raised with values that are hard for me to handle, and the educational system there is very different from the one we have here."

Kit has learned a lot about cultural differences and now understands the role of a father according to Islam. She remains torn by a terrible dilemma. "I bore these children so they are mine. He loves them, and in his society they are his."

Kit acknowledges that she is more fortunate than many left-behind parents. "I know where my children are, and perhaps one day . . ." she said, her voice fading. When asked if she would ever consider a counterabduction, she replied, "I would only take them now if there was a peaceful agreement. It would be devastating for them; they don't speak English and they have been there so long." Because of her love for her children, Kit would not want to add further trauma to their lives.

Kit continues to write to Ahmed and Camella and sends them gifts, not knowing if they actually receive them. She continues to call, but has never been allowed to speak to the children. After ten years of incredible suffering Kit somehow goes on, inspired by hope that some day, after the children are grown, she might again come to know them.

In this case the judge followed a common misconception: that his court could protect the children by securing their passports (some judges rely on an even more naive tactic: they threaten to hold parental abductors in contempt if there is any breach of the court's orders—an empty threat for someone planning to leave the country). The court didn't consider an obvious loophole in the international passport network: the ability of any foreign national to get children across borders on his or her own country's passport.

Teresa Hobgood, the State Department caseworker who handled both my case and Kit's, noted that a custodial parent "can provide us with a certified copy of their custody order, and we will prevent the issuance of a U.S. passport to the children. Of course, the other parent can go to their own embassy or foreign consulate here and get a foreign passport, so it's not fail-safe."

In 1986 I proposed that the State Department implement a passport control check for all children up to sixteen years of age who are leaving the country. My suggestion was to file in a central computer the names of potential abduction victims, who could then be identified through *any* passport.

The State Department responded that my idea was not feasible because it would infringe upon the rights of American travelers. I countered that the cross-check would take no longer than getting an airplane seat assignment and that travelers would accept the minor inconvenience—just as they had come to accept airport security screening as a result of the obvious need for it. Don't the rights of our young citizens also need to be protected?

4

Pakistani Justice

*I*n April 1989 fifty people packed a tiny mid-Michigan town library to hear me speak. During the question period, I called upon a petite young woman in her twenties who was seated up front and seemed especially absorbed by my remarks. She stood and said in a shaky voice, "I came here from a shelter for battered women about a hundred miles away. My two-year-old son and I are hiding from my husband. He's threatened to kidnap our son and take him to his country, Lebanon. What can I do? Who can help me?"

When she finished, she was in tears. The rest of the audience, a rural crowd unaccustomed to such public emotion, fell silent. Then an attractive, well-dressed woman with a professional demeanor rose and introduced herself as Chris Korest. "I'm here today on behalf of U.S. Senator Donald Riegle," she began. "I feel very moved by what I've heard here, and I'd like to explore how we can help."

Chris was an answer to a prayer: totally committed to our cause, with enormous energy and a commanding intelligence. She conveyed her enthusiasm to her entire office, including her boss. Before long Senator Riegle had joined forces with Senator Alan Dixon of Illinois, an early congressional leader on this issue. Previously I would often discuss cases with the State Department and with Sara Pang, an aide to Senator Dixon in his Chicago office. It had taken time for other cases to surface in

Michigan, where as late as 1988 the problem seemed abstract. As my book received more attention I began to hear from Michigan residents as well, and with Chris Korest on our "team," I had a caring referral source.

When I was on tour or needed to leave the country, Chris was able to keep the ball rolling and stay in touch with the parents we were trying to help. She relieved the extreme pressure I'd felt ever since my book was published and provided me with an inexhaustible source of moral support.

One family took Chris's heart hostage: Christy Khan and her three sons. The trail traveled by Christy Khan was filled with many unexpected twists; it was filled with intrigue, danger, and finally resolution in a land very distant in many ways.

Christy was in an aunt's house, playing with her children, when a small throng of her husband's friends and relatives burst through the door. Their faces were taut, their voices besieging. She could make out only snatches of the talk—after nineteen months in Pakistan her Urdu was still limited—but she gathered that some police agency had just called from Michigan and that something was terribly wrong.

"Riaz is in jail," one brother-in-law exclaimed to her in English. "You must find out what happened!"

Christy's heart skipped a beat. Here was her worst nightmare, the news she'd been dreading ever since Riaz Khan, her Pakistani husband, had left her and their two young sons two weeks before to go to the U.S. *Please, God, let him be all right*, Christy prayed as the family's panic washed over her. *Please let him come back to us.*

It was August 6, 1990, nineteen months after Riaz had abducted Johnathan and Adam from their home near Detroit to his native city of Peshawar, then trapped Christy there after she'd followed. Since then Riaz had turned dangerously erratic—impossible to live with, even for his own extended family. Christy knew that Riaz represented her best hope, perhaps her *only* hope, of getting her children home again. He'd left strict instructions: Christy and the boys were not allowed to leave the house, much less the country, without supervision.

65

With Riaz gone she would have to deal with six men—his father and five brothers—rather than one. Unlike Riaz, none of those six had any ties to the U.S. In accordance with social custom they would want to keep Christy and her sons, *especially* her sons, with them forever. For all his gaping faults, Riaz was her lifeline to freedom.

Christy's return call to the police in Berrien County, in the far southwest portion of Michigan, took an eternity to connect. Her in-laws hovered over her chair in a positive frenzy, yelling five questions at once. As Christy strained to hear through the receiver, her thoughts raced. She had considered more than once all the disasters that might befall her husband on this trip. What if he were to drive after drinking and get hurt in an accident (although Islam forbade alcoholic beverages, Riaz was never an observant Muslim)? What if he looked up his former mistress and ran away with her, leaving Christy and the children to fend for themselves? Or what if Riaz's mysterious business dealings caught up with him and got him arrested?

"Police Department." The woman's voice crackled loud and clear over nine thousand miles.

"Hello, I'm calling about my husband, his name is Riaz Khan." Christy spelled the name. "We heard he's just been arrested." *Please, please, let everything be all right.*

"I don't believe he's been arrested," the woman said. As she paused, Christy exhaled—*it was all a mistake, something lost in translation.* Then came the real news, delivered so nonchalantly, beyond Christy's darkest imagining: "I believe that a body has been identified, and I think that's who you're calling about."

Christy dully repeated the message out loud—and her in-laws erupted in confusion and the first spasms of grief. Christy felt far away, as if she were dreaming about someone else. She could think only of what Riaz had told her shortly before his departure, in one of his typically cryptic threats that now rang metallically in her ears.

"You better hope nothing happens to me while I'm gone. Because if anything happens, you will never leave this country."

In June of 1985, after completing her junior year at Eastern

Michigan University, Christy had craved a change of scene. She traveled to Tulsa, Oklahoma, to visit a high school classmate then at Oral Roberts University, the school founded by the famous born-again evangelist. A devout Presbyterian herself, Christy liked the campus atmosphere at ORU. She also liked Riaz Khan, a tall, well-built student from Pakistan with thick black hair and a strong cleft chin.

From their first meeting, on a double date arranged by friends, Riaz was obviously drawn to the vivacious, fresh-faced, warm-humored Christy. At twenty-five he was four years her senior, a refreshing change of pace from the narrow-minded business majors Christy had dated in Michigan. He explained that he'd been trained as an advocate (the Pakistani equivalent of a lawyer), that he'd traveled throughout Europe, and that he hoped to pursue a law degree in the U.S. "He appeared," Christy told me years later, "to be a very honest, knowledge-seeking person."

Riaz had more romantic virtues as well. He was gallant, even chivalrous. He insisted on holding every door. He brought flowers on every date. He praised Christy constantly, "made me feel very feminine."

Though he'd been raised in a vastly different culture, Riaz was a fervent booster of the United States. He said he loved the people here and found life far freer than in Pakistan, where martial law had been imposed shortly before he'd left in 1982. Riaz spoke little about his home country and dodged questions about his family. They were "not much interested" in what he was doing, he said, and he rarely wrote to them.

He was similarly vague about his religion. Though Pakistan was 97 percent Muslim, Riaz affirmed that he was a serious, nondenominational Christian. He was trying to learn more about his faith at school.

Riaz called Christy soon after she returned to Michigan, and by autumn they were trading weekend visits. In December Riaz met her parents. He was already proposing marriage—avidly, relentlessly. "I can't live without you—I will die without you," he would declare. "You're the nicest person I've ever met."

In retrospect, Christy said, "I was extremely naive. I was the perfect victim to go along with whatever he was going to do."

In January 1986 Riaz told Christy that his student visa had expired. He would take a semester off, reapply in Pakistan, and come back as soon as possible. Despite the nagging feeling that she was moving too fast, Christy finally accepted his proposal, and they agreed to marry after he returned that fall.

Christy couldn't wait that long to see him again—she missed him too much. On romantic impulse, she left to join her fiancé without graduating. It was the boldest adventure of her life, but Christy set off without a qualm. Here, after all, was the perfect combination: an exotic setting with a man she could trust.

Peshawar was located in northwestern Pakistan, about fifty miles from Afghanistan and the Khyber Pass, part of the old land route between India and Russia. Though the mountains of the area were considered mere foothills to the Himalayas, Christy had never seen anything like them, or the spectacular vistas they afforded. The roads were narrow and twisting, with no guardrails; anyone who fell would drop a long way. The most dangerous stretches were marked on the mountain walls by painted skulls and crossbones.

Less splendid was the city itself. A noted tourist spot in the 1970's, with an especially famous bazaar, Peshawar had swollen with tens of thousands of Afghan refugees who fled there after the Soviet invasion in 1979. The newcomers lived in the poorest shanties and stretched the community's limited resources—especially its water and sewers—well beyond capacity. Isolated to begin with, Peshawar was now dirty, densely populated, disease-ridden, and shrouded by a brown haze of pollution. The Pathan tribe, which dominated the city and environs, was notorious throughout Pakistan for its hard, uncompromising manner.

Although Riaz and Christy stayed with an aunt in the city, most of the family lived in an agricultural village in a flat, marshy area fifteen miles west. To be more accurate, the family *owned* the village, along with the surrounding sea of sugarcane, mangoes, and cotton. The village residents, thousands of people living in simple huts, all labored in these fields plantation-style; there was no other source of employment.

68

By Pakistani standards the Khans, a huge extended family headed by Riaz's father and uncle, were super-rich. According to Riaz the family's wholesale fruit business was badly mismanaged and in decline. Their houses were large but ill maintained, even decrepit.

The second oldest of eight children, Riaz held a place of honor in the village. He'd always been the most ambitious of the Khans, the most adventurous, the one who'd cracked the narrow bounds of Peshawar to explore the world. Adored by his mother and deferred to by his father (a weak and emaciated man plagued by stomach ulcers), Riaz "was like a king to them," Christy recalled. "Even his older brother looked up to him. He'd been everywhere, so people assumed he knew everything." Riaz, she noticed, did nothing to discourage the assumption.

Christy fell in love with the Khans—with their warmth and hospitality, with their willingness to embrace a stranger who would soon be joining their family. Of the men, she was especially taken by Fiaz, the third-oldest brother, so gentle that he would stay behind to talk to Christy while the others went off to shoot their rifles, semiautomatics, and machine guns—for fun.

The family did all it could to make her comfortable. When Christy asked if she could deviate from standard Peshawar practice and wear her *chador* off her head to better cope with the heat, the women supported her. Riaz rolled his eyes at her unorthodoxy but went along with it—and Christy would gratefully fling the *chador* over her shoulder like a Mexican serape.

For their part, the family was flattered by Christy's willingness to learn about their traditions and daily life. "We heard that Americans are really awful to foreigners," one cousin confided.

"But America is made up of foreigners, people from different countries—that's all we are," Christy replied, to wide approval. She also upset their preconceptions of American women, "that we were loud-mouthed, aggressive, and treated our husbands badly." After observing Christy serve tea to Riaz's friends, the father repeatedly praised her "obedience."

So far, so good. But other incidents gave Christy pause, made her wonder what she might be getting into. One day a younger female cousin came to visit and asked, "Aren't you afraid of his temper?"

"No, what temper?" Christy said.

"Oh, Riaz has a terrible temper," the cousin said, "and everyone here is afraid of him."

Perplexed, Christy later approached Riaz and said, "Oh, so you have a temper." No, no, Riaz assured her: "These people just don't understand my way of talking."

A few days later another cousin asked Christy straight out if Riaz ever struck her. She was shocked. "No, of course not! If he hit me, boy, I'd be out of here so fast!"

Looking back, she said, "It concerned me that they would even ask, but Riaz had always been so wonderful with me. I thought maybe they just misunderstood him. I knew that people frequently didn't get along with their families, but they can still have a happy marriage."

Marriage was what Riaz was pushing for with all his might. He wanted to tie the knot in Pakistan, the sooner the better. Christy held back. She had assumed they would date awhile longer, then have a church wedding in her hometown. She was disturbed to find out that Riaz was actually a Muslim—less by the fact than by the falsehood she'd swallowed all this time. Christy noted, "As long as he had religious values, it wouldn't make any difference."

To persuade her, Riaz promised a second wedding after they returned to the U.S. He later went back on his word, claiming that Islam prohibited his participation in a Christian ceremony. Then he dropped a bombshell: the authorities had refused to extend his student visa. Christy later found out that Riaz had lost his place at Oral Roberts because he had cut too many classes. He had no way of getting back to the States—unless he married an American. "If you love me and you're going to marry me in America," he pressed, "why can't you marry me here? Then we can be together."

The very next morning Riaz woke Christy up to deliver an ultimatum. "You have to make up your mind," he said. "You're going to marry me now, or return without me." The *imam* (an

Islamic holy man) had already arrived at the house. There was no time to delay—nor even for Christy to wash her face.

Bewildered by Riaz's pressure tactics, Christy pushed aside a premonition that something was wrong. Riaz might have his contradictions, but she couldn't face the thought of life without him. On their way to the *imam* she steered him into a side room and said, "I will marry you, but you must understand that I cannot live here. Our kids cannot grow up here." She had seen too many cases of children with malaria and typhoid in Peshawar, even among well-to-do families.

"Of course," Riaz said. "That's why I ask you for this marriage—so that I can return to America and we can build our life there."

While Christy was agreeable to a Muslim ceremony, she made it clear to the family that she would remain a committed Christian. "But if you're marrying our brother, you're Muslim in our eyes," one sister said. "Will you take an Islamic name?"

As Christy recounted, "I had learned a lot more about Islam while I was there, and everything I learned was so nice—it is a very peaceful religion. I told them I would not convert, I made that very clear. I said I would accept an Islamic name, because it made it easier for them to accept me." Her marriage certificate would record her as *Miryam*.

The wedding itself was anticlimactic. Riaz and Christy exchanged their Islamic vows before two witnesses and a third man who stood in for Christy's father. The *imam* didn't speak English, Riaz told her, "so whatever he asks you, just say '*gi*,' " the Urdu word for yes. "Just nod and smile, and don't ask any questions."

After the ceremony, Riaz informed her that he would celebrate by dining out with his brothers. By tradition, he added, no women would be present—including Christy. He would bring her back a piece of chicken.

Christy spent her wedding night in her room alone, hurt but accepting. "I wasn't so naive as to think that you could mix cultures completely," she said. "I knew there was going to have to be concessions on both sides. I made the concession that night because it wasn't earth-shattering."

The days to come only compounded her confusion. Before the wedding Christy had always joined Riaz when his male friends came to visit. Now she began to be excluded. "You don't understand the language, and they're uncomfortable with you," Riaz told her, none too kindly. "They're not used to having a woman in the room."

It was, Christy related, "like the horror stories you hear, when the groom changes on the day of the wedding. I was frustrated and angry, but I knew my trip was winding down and I didn't want to leave on a sour note. It was the kind of situation where you just press your lips together—what can you do?"

As she left Riaz in August—his new visa would take several months to process—Christy held her husband close. She remembered the good things they'd shared and felt sure that all would return to normal back home. After all, they loved each other, didn't they? They would make it work.

Four months later, on December 24, 1986, Riaz flew into Detroit. It was their first Christmas eve together—and the first time Riaz had seen their infant son, Johnathan. The reunion was tender and exciting; Christy felt as if they were courting again. Looking back, she said, it may have been the high point of their marriage.

They rented a house in Livonia, not far from her parents, and Riaz took a graveyard shift at a Mobil station. He never missed a night, but Christy could tell he felt humiliated by his work's low status. It was only temporary, Riaz told her, until he could get his Oriental carpet business off the ground.

Riaz was a caring and attentive father, and those early months passed happily, though not without points of disagreement. It bothered Christy when Riaz told people he was five years older than he really was, or when he lied to his family that he *owned* the gas station. If he admitted the truth, he said, they would no longer respect him.

"Do *you* respect me?" he kept asking Christy.

"Of course I do," she said. "As long as you're working hard, who cares what you're doing?" Riaz never seemed satisfied.

Before long the marriage took a slide. Despite infusions of capital from his father (at one point a check arrived from Peshawar for $10,000), Riaz's carpet venture never materialized. No one would lease him space, he grumbled; they were prejudiced against foreigners. He worried constantly about money, and pushed Christy to go back to work as a legal secretary before she felt ready, when John was but a few months old. He lost interest in the baby, stopped helping with the housework.

"He told me it was degrading, and he didn't have to do it," Christy said. "Everything we had agreed on, every understanding between us, he went in the complete opposite direction. There was no consideration anymore—it all came to a screeching halt."

Christy was an accommodating person by nature—"*too* accommodating," she says in retrospect—but she began to bristle at the unfairness in their relationship. Despite Riaz's perpetual worries about money, he managed to buy his clothes from the top department store; to dine without her at nice restaurants; to wheel around town in large late-model rental cars, which he claimed were loaned to him by friends; and periodically to come home with a new gold ring on his finger, supposedly a gift from his family.

Christy had no idea where all the money came from, but she knew that she and John weren't getting their share. Riaz kept a separate bank account, out of which he paid for groceries and gasoline. Christy struggled to pay the rent and everything else, and the press of job and baby wore her down. She began to voice her dissatisfaction—usually over the phone, given their work shifts—and Riaz didn't like it. She was showing him "disrespect." One night he fumed, "When I come home from work, I'll fix you up!" Christy wasn't sure what he meant, and an hour later Riaz called back to apologize: "I'm tired, and it's the money stress."

That spring Christy had a miscarriage. Distraught, she called a friend for sympathy and said if she had more help around the house and didn't have to work so many hours outside, she might have kept the baby. Riaz overheard her and flew into a rage. How *dare* Christy insult him to another woman?

By July Christy was pregnant again. She called her mother, who urged her to cut back her office schedule. "I just can't, we can't afford it," Christy said. The next day Riaz was furious:

"Why did you tell your mother that we can't afford it? Now she'll think I'm a no-good bum!" As he railed on, Christy shelved a suspicion that she'd later confirm: *My husband is taping my phone calls.*

They had argued more and more frequently recently, but Riaz had never touched her in anger, and she'd almost forgotten his cousin's unsettling inquiry in Pakistan. So she was shocked that night when her husband grabbed her by the throat and squeezed, ignoring her gasps of protest. He released her only after she lost consciousness.

"The first time it happens you can't believe it," Christy recalled. "You can't believe in a million years that this person, no matter how mad he was getting, would do anything like that."

That night Riaz apologized abjectly: "I'm sorry, sweetheart, I'm sorry. This is not your fault, this is my bad temper." He literally kissed his wife's feet. After he left for work, Christy stayed awake the whole night, thinking that she would get in her car in the morning "and take John and never come back." Morning came and she didn't leave. She was pregnant and filled with the optimism of new life. She was not inclined to consider a future with two babies and no husband.

The pattern was set. Riaz would attack Christy after some trivial or imagined slight, then beg for her forgiveness in a spirit of total self-loathing, then resent her, as if *she* had humiliated *him*, and turn surly once more. It happened two weeks later, when he slapped her and fattened her lip, and again the next month, when he choked her—Riaz's favorite method of abuse, one that left no marks. As Christy later recalled, "It was like when you show a dog you're afraid of him. The more fear I had, the angrier he got."

When Christy confided in her obstetrician, the doctor warned that Riaz was jeopardizing the health of the fetus, and gave her the numbers for several safe houses. Christy still thought the marriage might work: "When I commit to a person, I stay committed to them a long way." She couldn't help pitying her husband, so tormented by stress that patches of his beard were falling out.

As if to answer her faith, Riaz calmed down. In September

74

they moved from their house to an apartment, easing the financial squeeze. With Christy's encouragement her husband began seeing a psychiatrist, who suspected a chemical imbalance and put Riaz on medication. The mood swings smoothed out. The household seemed normal for weeks at a stretch.

Then, in late November 1987, the equilibrium was smashed yet again by a phone call. "Is Riaz there?" asked the pleasant-sounding woman. When Christy asked if she could take a message, the woman said, "Who are you?"

"This is his wife, Christy."

"Well, this is his girlfriend, Nicole."

At first Christy thought it was a joke. Riaz was always at work when she called the station at night, and he checked in with her every afternoon. Where did he find the time for an affair? "He must have had amazing energy," she concluded ruefully. Nicole's subsequent outrage at Riaz's double life made Christy a believer. Riaz had told Nicole he was living with a rich uncle, whom she'd thought she was calling; she'd found the phone number on some luggage Riaz had left at her house. He'd promised that he was neither married nor a father—the deepest cut of all for Christy. How could a man deny his own little boy? Their entire married life, it suddenly occurred to her, was stitched with treachery. She would not stand for it any more.

When she confronted Riaz, he took the offensive. Nicole kept a cleaner house, he told Christy. He was tired of Christy's morning sickness. Besides, he said, he only slept with Nicole because Christy was having her own affair at work—a charge she found ridiculous, given that the lawyers at her firm were all on the gray side of sixty.

After some high-decibel exchanges, Riaz admitted his suspicions were groundless and said sheepishly, "Well, we have to get a divorce then, don't we?" Christy, six months pregnant, took a different tack. She would work with him to save their marriage, she said, but only if he pledged to end the affair and to refrain from hitting her ever again. Sobbing, Riaz agreed to her terms.

Christy wasn't quite through. If they ever did get a divorce, she said, she would be strict about visitation, "because I've heard about fathers who take their kids out of the country."

Riaz was scandalized. He dropped to his knees and said, "As Allah is my God, I would never take these kids away from you. I didn't go through the agony of childbirth. You carry the children in your body, you nurture them, you take care of them. You're the best mother in the world. I could have many women, but no woman could be a better mother."

Christy felt reassured by this vow, however melodramatic. Even Riaz would not violate an oath to his God lightly. She chose to forget, for that moment, that she was married to someone who held very little sacred.

In early 1988 Riaz began talking incessantly of his family and of Pakistan, a conspicuous switch for a man who'd long denigrated his homeland. He booked a flight—for himself alone—for March, a month before his wife's due date. As they prepared to leave for the airport, Christy felt another surge of anxiety. Perhaps, she said, it would be better to leave John home with her parents.

Riaz looked hurt. "What do you think I'm going to do, grab him out of your arms in the airport and run away? Christy, I would never do that in a million years. The child belongs to the mother—I could never do for him what you do."

While Christy didn't miss the tension that shadowed Riaz everywhere, she hoped he might come back for the birth. Riaz refused to cut his trip short; he had no desire to be near her during labor. "I've hurt you so much that I can't stand to see you in that kind of pain," he said.

Adam was born on April 6, 1988. Riaz returned a month later. He looked suspiciously at the newborn and declared, "This is not my son. I have brown eyes, you have brown eyes. How could we have a son with blue eyes?" Christy pointed out that Riaz's brother and grandfather had blue eyes, but Riaz was adamant. Adam must have some other father. He was cold toward the baby from that point on.

Riaz no longer resorted to physical violence, but Christy knew something was missing. Her husband stopped taking his medication and seemed more and more depressed. He'd long found comfort in whiskey, and began to drink heavily. When

Christy became pregnant again, just two months after Adam's birth, her husband recoiled at the idea of another mouth to feed. "I can't take this any more," he complained.

By contrast, Riaz seemed happy and vital when he spoke with his relatives, who called with greater regularity and lobbied for another visit. "I need to go back again," he said. Christy proposed that they make it a family trip the following spring, after the baby came in April. Her pregnancy had been difficult, with acute cramping, and she was in no condition to travel. "I don't know," Riaz said. "I just need to clear my head." He wanted to leave the following March, as he had the year before.

In September, when their lease was up, the apartment manager called Christy at work and asked her to stop by and sign a new agreement. Riaz had asked for a month-to-month arrangement, the manager said, and had indicated that their family would be moving in December. Puzzled, Christy called Riaz, who said the manager had misunderstood—he had simply wanted to change the lease to a December starting date.

Later that fall, after Christy disclosed to her co-workers that she was planning a trip to Pakistan, several women expressed concern. They'd recently read *Not Without My Daughter* and found the story alarming. "He'd never take the kids without you, would he?" one of them asked.

After a year of relative peace at home, Christy had laid to rest her qualms on this subject. She tried to picture Riaz—so indifferent lately toward their sons—as a child abductor, and the image eluded her. How could a man kidnap his children when he couldn't change a dirty diaper? "No," she assured her associates, "he'd never do anything like that."

Wednesday, December 28, 1988, a bitterly cold Michigan day, Riaz checked in with Christy at her office about noon. She wasn't feeling well, she told him. She'd been fighting a bad cold and was thinking about quitting early.

Riaz took an unusually sympathetic tone but advised her to stay put: "Why don't you just stick out the day, and when you get home everything will be nice. You won't have to do anything, you can just rest."

When Christy finally came home about 6 P.M., hacking and exhausted, she found the apartment empty and a note by the front door. "Dear sweetheart," the note read. "We are going to Holly [a town about fifty miles away]. Right now it's 3 P.M. We will be back before 6:30. We are going to see [a] friend, Dr. S———. Don't worry, back at that exact time I mentioned. I love you."

Christy felt cross and frustrated at this break in the children's routine. Riaz had been terribly absentminded lately; he was perfectly capable of picking up one of their sons and forgetting the other. She called the day-care center, which confirmed that Riaz had collected John and Adam earlier in the day. Christy lay down on the sofa and waited.

By 9 P.M. she was nervous. What if Riaz had left the boys with people they didn't know while he went out drinking? What if some stranger grabbed the children while Riaz wasn't watching? John was barely two years old, Adam only eight months. They were so vulnerable and so cute, and Christy knew that babies were kidnapped all the time.

By midnight she was frantic. Her thinking had narrowed to two most likely scenarios: Riaz had been in a car accident, or he'd simply gotten drunk and spent the night in Holly. Maybe, her mother suggested, he was just too embarrassed to call. Christy tried the police, but there was nothing they could do until twenty-four hours after the kids turned up missing.

Early the next morning Christy and her father went to the local police station. A desk sergeant crudely speculated that Riaz had snatched the boys to his home in Pakistan: "Where the hell else would a man go with an eight-month-old baby?" Of all the possibilities, this one scared Christy most, though the physical evidence was against it. Not a single item—not one toy nor a change of clothes—had been missing from the apartment.

In full panic, Christy and her father drove every route they could think of between her apartment and Holly, looking for wrecked or deserted vehicles. Christy was beside herself, dreading to find what she was looking for and terrified of the alternatives.

That evening, having exhausted the local roadways, she

called the FBI, which informed her that Riaz was essentially free to do as he pleased. "As long as you're still married, he has the same rights to the children as you—we can't stop him from taking them anywhere," the agent said. "If we met him at the airport, all we could do is request that he call home. We cannot detain him."

The agent referred Christy to a federal hotline in Chicago, which confirmed that U.S. passports had been issued for both boys and forwarded to Riaz at a post-office box. Adam's passport had been delivered just the month before, but Riaz had filed for John's in July 1987—the month when their marriage was at its lowest point, when Riaz had first choked her.

The abduction was still theoretical, as Detroit airport officials refused to release their flight list to Pakistan. It remained that way till 9 P.M.—when Riaz called her from Karachi, Pakistan's largest city, en route with the children to the train to Peshawar. After this ultimate act of abuse, he tendered his most abject apology.

"I-I'm sorry, I'm sorry," Riaz stammered, over Christy's bitter weeping. "But wait, wait, I didn't take the children away from you. I left a ticket for you, sweetheart. It's in the cedar chest in the dining room. Believe me, things will be better for all of us here."

"How can they be better?" Christy cried.

"Here I have money, and you won't have to work," Riaz said. Then he put John on the phone.

The toddler sounded disoriented; he wasn't used to spending so much time with his father. "I want you, Mommy," John said. "When are you coming?"

"I'll be coming really fast," Christy said, straining to keep the panic out of her voice. "Take care of your baby brother till I get there."

Now that she knew the truth, Christy was stunned. Riaz had covered his tracks remarkably well. Through all his frenzied rages he had never threatened to abduct the children—the act he knew would hurt her most. His cold calculation made the deed even more shocking.

Christy dialed her husband's family in Peshawar and reached Tariq, Riaz's older brother, who said Riaz had asked to be picked up at the train station. "But he didn't tell me he had the kids," Tariq said. "Where are you? Why didn't you come with him?"

"I'm sick and I'm pregnant," Christy said, her voice quavering, "and I don't think this pregnancy is going well."

"Stupid Riaz, stupid man," Tariq muttered. "Don't worry, Christy, don't worry."

Christy knew she wouldn't stop worrying until her arms were around her babies. She took a leave of absence from work, booked the next available flight to Karachi, then checked herself into a hospital overnight. Sleepless and weakened, she was well on her way to bronchitis, with pneumonia in the offing. After her original flight was canceled due to bad weather, Christy had to wait several days for another seat; the flights were booked solid with returning holiday travelers. Meanwhile, she found that Riaz had taken the $2,000 she had saved and had overdrawn their checking account by $10,000. She later discovered that he'd applied for more than a dozen major credit cards in her name, from American Express to Sears, and left all of them with hefty charges.

She finally boarded on January 6, 1989. The flight took twenty-six hours, with layovers in Frankfurt and Istanbul, and Christy coughed almost every minute of the way. When she arrived in damp and chilly Islamabad, the Pakistani capital, at one in the morning, she felt thoroughly pathetic. When she made it through customs, the weakness passed. There, defensive and angry, stood Riaz; he'd always resented her illnesses and the inconvenience they caused him. There, unmistakably, were her sleeping children. Riaz's sister, Ambreen, placed Adam in Christy's arms. A female cousin held John. Christy relaxed for the first time in ten days.

Upon checking into a local hotel, where they would stay before driving to Peshawar the next morning, Christy inspected her sons more closely and was dismayed. In the space of less than two weeks, they'd come to show all the earmarks of neglect.

Adam's cloth diaper was soaking wet. When Christy laid him down on her bed to change him, she was shocked to find huge, raw blisters on his bottom. When she rubbed in a bit of ointment, the baby cried in pain.

As Christy rocked Adam back to sleep in a chair, John lay next to her on the bed, thin and sickly looking. She nudged him, and he slowly opened his large brown eyes. Ten days ago those eyes had been shining and alive; now they were as dull as old pennies.

Recognizing his mother, he stared at her as if she were an apparition. "Mommy, I told you to come to me, and you didn't come," he said softly. He closed his eyes again but awoke a few minutes later, climbed out of bed, and laid his head in Christy's lap.

It was then that Christy noticed the tiny needle marks on John's hands and feet, the telltale bruises of intravenous hydration. "They wouldn't let him drink the water there, because he wasn't used to it," she recounted. "And he wouldn't drink their milk—it's buffalo milk, really rich and thick, and it tastes a lot different than our milk. Nobody thought to give him juice, and he'd become badly dehydrated. My husband didn't know what to do, so he took him to the hospital and they put an intravenous drip in his hands and feet."

Christy pulled out two of John's favorite toys, a rubber crocodile and a stuffed bear. He'd had nothing to play with since Riaz had taken him, and he clutched his small possessions close as he drifted back to sleep.

Christy wasn't surprised to find Riaz at a loss in caring for the boys, or that his family had played pass-the-baby, with no one in charge. She was appalled at her husband's disinterest in their children's suffering. It made her angrier than she'd ever been, lent her a pure white fury that she made no effort to filter, despite the consequences. During her first days in Peshawar, she quarreled with Riaz unremittingly. "Don't you know this is Pakistan?" her husband said with a scowl, much affronted. "You can't fight with me here!"

Christy fought on, even after Riaz dashed her hopes that she and the boys might soon return to the U.S. Her husband controlled their exit visas, and none of them could leave Pakistan without his written and notarized permission. He claimed this power under his nation's version of Islamic law. As Christy soon found out, there was little that she—or the U.S. State Department—could do about it.

Riaz had used the time before Christy's arrival to build support within his family. "He had pretty well convinced them that we would be better off there," Christy said. "He told them horrible lies about our life in America—that I was miserable, that the children were never cared for, that my family hated him."

Moreover, Riaz had claimed that Christy was bent on a divorce and planned to steal the children from *him*. As evidence, he played his family a tape of a recent phone conversation. Upset that Riaz planned to leave her again before their baby was born, Christy had called her mother in tears: "How am I going to have a baby and take care of these two kids by myself?"

"If you need a place to stay," her mother soothed her, "you're welcome to come and stay with us. You know the door is always open."

The word "divorce" was never mentioned, but Riaz had insisted that Christy's mother was telling her to leave him. As the person in his family who knew the most English, he was able to "interpret" the tape to serve his purpose.

As Christy learned more about the Pakistani social structure, she better understood why Riaz had stolen children he scarcely seemed to care about. Had he come home to live without them he would have lost face—within his family and his Pathan tribe, even among prospective business associates. He would have been less than a man.

Despite the mores of their society, many family members openly sympathized with Christy's plight, most notably the women. Twenty-three-year-old Ambreen, in particular, was "the sweetest person on the face of this earth." While no one would buck Riaz directly, his brothers were becoming disenchanted with his arrogant, demanding ways and how he bossed them around the family business they'd worked in for years.

To keep the family peace Riaz was almost exiled from the village, with Christy and the boys in tow, to Peshawar proper, where his aunt deeded her house to him. Even though they now lived at a distance, Riaz and his brothers kept feuding. The principle bone of contention was land, the source of the Khans' wealth. While Riaz was in the U.S., the family had annexed a new tract and divided it among the brothers. The two most valuable parcels, those fronting the main road, were claimed by Tariq and Fiaz. To Riaz this was an unforgivable breach of protocol; as the second-oldest brother he should have received one of the front lots. The argument escalated until Riaz grabbed his gun and chased Fiaz out of the house, waving the firearm madly.

"He's your *brother*," Christy said, trying to cool Riaz down.

"It doesn't matter," her husband rejoined. "This is about money, and people kill for money."

Riaz was not a selective bully. At one time or another Christy saw him physically abuse nearly every member of his family, including his mother and aunt. One day he went so far as to choke his eighty-year-old grandmother.

"It's better if I don't say anything," Christy's father-in-law, the victim's son, said with a whimper as the beating ensued. "It will just upset him."

"What do you mean?" Christy yelled, incredulous. "Who *cares* if you upset him?" The cousin she'd met three years before had told the truth: everyone feared Riaz's temper.

Between her husband's eruptions Christy focused on the more mundane details of life in Pakistan. No longer considered a visitor, she was expected to conform to the rules that governed all other women in conservative Peshawar. Her *chador* was to cover her face during the family's five daily calls to prayer, whenever she left the house, or when company dropped in.

Christy's foremost challenge was cooking. At his father's urging, Riaz had tried to please her by installing some Western appliances at his aunt's house. The microwave didn't work; the electric stove burned out because Peshawar's current was erratic; and the gas stove exploded. Christy found herself back at a small gas burner set on the kitchen's concrete floor. Too often she had little to work with. For a time Riaz forced her to eat highly spiced native dishes—"This is my country, and you'll eat spicy food"—which gave the pregnant Christy stabbing stomach pains. On occasion her father-in-law would drop off loads of carrots or melons, on which John feasted. Aside from some hauls of black-market baby food, most often spoiled, Riaz wasn't much of a shopper, and Christy wasn't allowed to go out on her own. On many days she and the boys had nothing but pita bread and eggs. On other days they had only bread.

When the boys developed sores in their mouths, the family told Christy that she was brushing their teeth too much and that toothbrushes were dirty things. Christy suspected a vitamin C deficiency, but Riaz locked her chewable vitamins in a cupboard. If the children took them, he claimed, they would lose their appetite.

The hardships were all the more onerous as Christy felt a sense of imprisonment. The aunt's house was surrounded by a high stone wall, with a metal gate that was always locked. Christy was not allowed to walk around the block or even to approach the gate. When Riaz left on one of his frequent and unspecified "business trips," he left rigid orders for the servants to monitor Christy's phone calls and confine her movements. They obeyed without deviation, and so did the aunt, a warm-hearted woman who gave what moral support she could. Whenever Christy seemed sad she'd say, "Go home to America!"

On their sporadic family outings to the city's bazaar for ice cream, Riaz would make Christy wait in the car. She would have no opportunity to escape. Christy loved ice cream, but she began to dread these brief expeditions. To encounter something so familiar only reminded her how far she was from home.

As the weeks passed, and Riaz remained unyielding, Christy resigned herself to bearing their third child in Peshawar. She feared, from experience, that the fetus was not developing normally, and she worried that the delivery might be complicated. Prenatal strain was aggravated by her daily chores, especially by the laundry, which required her to lift heavy buckets of hot water from the bathtub to an agitating machine outside. On March 15, a five-bucket day, Christy went into labor three weeks before her due date.

The hospital was very different from what she'd been accustomed to in the States. Hygienic standards were low. The delivery room featured a bare wooden table, something out of a Norman Rockwell illustration, which was simply wiped off between patients.

The doctor who ran the hospital relegated Christy to two young and inexperienced midwives. First they gave Christy drugs to quell the contractions and delay the premature labor. When they realized that was hopeless, they gave her more drugs to intensify the contractions. "It felt like my body was being torn in three different directions," Christy recalled. "It was pure hell." Although the baby had yet to enter the birth canal, the midwives proceeded with an episiotomy. When Christy cried out they offered little sympathy: "Every woman in the world has pain!"

At that, Christy had gotten off gently. When Ambreen underwent a difficult delivery several months later, the nurses slapped her face every time she screamed, warning that she would upset the other patients. Ambreen's baby girl was sickly from birth and died of pneumonia two weeks later.

Riaz was out of town at the time on another business trip, but his brother Fiaz had stopped by the hospital. When Ambreen told him she could hear Christy crying, he almost shoved the doctor into the room to attend to her. Christy didn't know whether to feel relieved or alarmed when the doctor berated her assistants, saying "I'm very dissatisfied with your work—this baby needs help!"

After eight hours of labor, Eric was born with a forceps delivery. The doctor pronounced him a picture of health, but Christy could tell that her new son was weaker than the first two. His movements were feeble, his cries muted. Three weeks later, with Eric still struggling to get back to his birth weight of six pounds, Christy took him to Riaz's cousin Shabina, then an intern. She suspected a problem and referred Christy to her medical professor, who diagnosed Eric within five minutes.

85

There was a major heart defect, the professor told Christy. Whereas normal people had two separate valves, Eric had only one. Quick surgery was essential, and the only place for it was in the United States, where technology was most advanced.

To Christy's added anguish, the professor said he believed that Eric also had a mild case of Down's Syndrome. "Don't tell the family about the Down's," he cautioned Christy, "or they won't let you take him home. If they believe he's retarded, they'll say it's God's will that he die."

Riaz returned to Peshawar the next day and met with the professor. As Christy had anticipated, her husband resisted the proposed trip to Michigan: "I can't believe there's no other place in the world that can take care of him."

The doctor, who'd been prepped by Shabina, took Riaz to task. "What kind of man are you?" he said sharply. "Do you care for your child or not?" Faced with someone of higher status, Riaz grudgingly backed down. Christy's parents purchased plane tickets for the entire family. Her anxiety for Eric aside, Christy was heartened. At last Riaz had come to his senses—he could see that she and the children belonged back home. Once there, of course, his power over them would diminish.

On the day before their flight, as Christy packed the family's bags, Riaz announced that he had changed his mind. He was staying in Pakistan—and so were John and Adam. Christy stormed back to the room where a family meeting was in progress. Her in-laws' heads were bowed; they would not meet her eyes. *They've caved in to him again*, Christy thought. Finally her father-in-law looked up and said, "We do not interfere in matters between a husband and a wife."

Christy began weeping hysterically, until she hyperventilated and fainted. When she came to, her younger sister-in-law, Mahreen, was leaning over her. "Christy, you have to understand, there's nothing we can do," Mahreen said softly. "Our hearts are breaking for you and your children. When we say something to Riaz, he only gets angry."

For the first time, Christy blew up in front of the family. "You're afraid *he's* going to get angry? My kids are at stake—to hell with him if he gets angry!" She picked up some apples from a basket and hurled them in Riaz's general direction, but not so close as to risk hitting him—for she too was still afraid. Riaz sat on the floor, laughing, goading her on. "You're afraid of *my* temper?" he asked the family. "Now you see what *I* have to live with."

There was no reasoning with the man. Christy knew she had to go; Eric was so weak that he had to be fed with an eyedropper. Still, her certainty made it no easier to break the news to two-year-old John, who seemingly screamed for hours, or to leave Adam four days after his first birthday. As Christy entered a car for the Karachi airport, Adam reached back for his mother from the aunt's arms, calling out for her, bewildered.

Riaz, meanwhile, was his old bizarre self. Noting that Christy was booked first class (all coach seats had been taken), he said, "Boy, I should be going. I'd enjoy going first class." A day or two later, after the professor's diagnosis of Eric was confirmed by doctors in Michigan, Christy called Peshawar to brief Riaz on their son's condition. Her husband brushed aside the medical report; he was interested in something else. "What was it like flying first class?" he asked her.

His question reminded Christy of how much he missed America's amenities. It was puzzling. Riaz was simply too selfish to put up with Pakistan's spartan life-style for the sake of holding on to his children, or even to preserve their shell of a marriage. There must be something else that kept him there, that made him afraid to go back to America. What?

Four months later, in August of 1989, Eric underwent heart surgery at the children's hospital at the University of Michigan. The procedure was successful, but additional operations would be required down the road. Given that Eric also would need special help for his Down's Syndrome, his return to Pakistan was out of the question.

Shortly after the surgery, Christy and her father flew to Peshawar for a one-week visit. The separation's toll on her sons was all too evident. John was both subdued and nervous, so thin that his ribs stuck out in the back. In his grief for his mother, he was refusing to eat. Adam's hair was down to his shoulders. At sixteen months of age, he was wildly undisciplined and lacking in speech. He had no adult to talk to him; he and John were left all day under a servant's halfhearted care. With no toys in the house, the children's sole source of entertainment was an empty diaper box.

"And so I knew then," Christy said, "that I had to go back."

With Eric safe in her parents' care, Christy returned to Pakistan in October 1989 and stayed there—save for a brief Christmas trip home to treat a case of dysentery—for the next ten months. Leaving Eric, who'd been so close to death for so long, was even harder than leaving her older boys. "I was pining away for him—I just couldn't let go and forget him," Christy said. Shuttling between her needy children, never feeling settled or intact, was enough to drive a mother mad.

In Peshawar Christy tried a new tack with Riaz. Rather than pick fights with her husband, she gingerly pleaded her case for the family's return to the U.S., where they could all be together. Christy banked less on Riaz's paternal instincts—he referred to Eric as "a punishment from God"—than on his growing impatience with Pakistan and his nostalgia for the high life he'd enjoyed in the West. She insinuated that they might renew their love in America. Riaz seemed tempted but wary of leaving. "If I were you, I would divorce me," he'd say. He gradually lost interest in going.

By winter he had reverted to his dark side. The more conciliatory his wife acted, the angrier it made him. One especially emotional day, when Christy couldn't stop crying for Eric, she asked Riaz, "Won't you ever even consider going back?"

"You can never talk to me about going back," Riaz said coolly, sadistically. "You must understand that you and the children will live and die in Pakistan."

At such times, Christy related, "I called on my religion. I would reach really deep within myself and ask God to help me rise above him. . . . I was deadly calm at that point. There's something inside you that just clicks and says, 'I either have to defeat this thing or be defeated by it.' "

There were times when she feared her prayers might not suffice. Drinking heavily, Riaz had taken to slapping and choking her again. "Do you know," he would say, measuring his words for effect, "that it would be easier for me to kill you and just get rid of you?"

One memorable evening the threat became hideously real. Set off by Christy's insistence that John was too young to go off to preschool, Riaz went into a tirade. Christy told him she was taking the children out of their bedroom until he settled down. Riaz sprang up to lock the door and said, "If you go out that door, I'll kill you." As Christy sat paralyzed, with the petrified Adam burying his face in her shoulder, Riaz grabbed his revolver and held it to her head.

"You know I can shoot you at any time," he said. "If I kill you right now, no one will know. I'll just tell them you were having an affair with a man from Karachi." Christy stared straight ahead, praying for deliverance. Then, out of her peripheral vision, came an image to rend her heart: John, who she thought had been asleep, was standing five feet away, stock-still, speechless with horror. "Oh, forget it," Riaz said disgustedly. "I'll do it at my own time, my own way."

The boys were deteriorating. John seemed more high-strung by the day. Adam, once the most cheerful of roly-poly babies, coped by withdrawing. "He basically turned into a blob—he took no interest in anything," Christy said. "I don't have one picture of him in our last two years in Pakistan where he's smiling."

Christy's harsh daily regimen—the cooking, cleaning, laundry, and sole responsibility for two bored children—wore her down. She lost twenty pounds. There were times when she believed that Riaz was right, that she would never leave that land, just as I had felt in Iran. It is hard to convey this sense of utter depression and helplessness. When you are as isolated as Christy or I was, it can be very difficult to sustain any hope that things will get better.

Then in July, Christy sensed a possible breakthrough. Eric needed another hospital procedure. The Michigan social workers were moving to make him a ward of the state unless guardianship formally passed to Christy's parents—or unless Christy or Riaz came to vouch for their parenthood and reinstate Eric's state-subsidized medical insurance. Although Riaz had always deemed Eric's condition an embarrassment, his pride was punctured; he would not allow a son to be claimed by another. Besides, he said, he had business overseas to attend to—"a way to make a lot of money." He would go to Michigan.

As his departure date approached, Riaz became unhinged. He refused to take late-night phone calls. He no longer allowed a servant to walk John down the street to buy candy. He fretted constantly about "people" or "those men" who might kidnap his children. "Christy, leave me alone," he'd say. "I have problems that have nothing to do with you."

At other times he was vaguely combative. "You'd better hope nothing happens to me over there," he kept telling her, "or you'll never get out of this country." Christy might have passed this off as a paranoid delusion, until Fiaz made the threat more explicit: "If anything happens to my brother, it will be your fault."

Most chilling of all was Riaz's brooding farewell on the day he left. "I'm sorry for everything I've done to you, and I'm sorry for what I'm going to do," he said. He sounded like a man who didn't plan to come back. Christy was terrified—her worst fear was to fall under the thumb of Riaz's unpredictable male relatives, as provided by Islamic law in the event of a husband's death or disappearance. She begged to go to Michigan in Riaz's place, but he would hear none of it. He was ready to meet his fate—even if he wasn't ready to let her know what that meant.

Riaz's itinerary began with stops in Germany, to see a gem dealer, and in Britain, where he met an acquaintance from Peshawar. He reached New York in the first week of August and a few days later flew on to Detroit, where Christy's father picked him up. They reached her parents' house at about 8 P.M. When Riaz called Peshawar, Christy was almost relieved to hear the old sneering cockiness in his voice. "What's wrong with Eric?" he demanded. "Why didn't you teach him to walk?"

"I've been in Pakistan for the last ten months," Christy pointed out, which made Riaz laugh. *He must have been drinking again,* she thought.

It was the last time she ever heard his voice.

Riaz stayed at the house for two hours. He turned down an offer to remain overnight; he'd already made plans, he said, to stay with friends from India who lived nearby. At 10 P.M. a car stopped by the house and honked. Riaz declined any help with his bags, mouthed some hurried good-byes, and hurried out the door.

Six hours later his corpse was found in a park near the Indiana line.

After she hung up with the police receptionist, Christy was inundated with questions she couldn't answer. "How was Riaz killed?" her in-laws demanded. "When did it happen? Who is suspected?" She called her father and received his grim corroboration. Detectives had traced her parents' house from one of Riaz's credit card applications and asked Christy's father for photographs to help identify the body. He gave them several pictures—and then was staggered by a massive, stress-induced chest pain. While Riaz had made Christy and the boys hostages in the first place, he was also the only link her parents had to them. He was the one who held their exit visas, who might yet have been persuaded to release them. If he was gone, they faced the unknown.

Christy called the police back, and this time got through to a detective on the case. He told her that Riaz had been "traumatized."

"What does that mean?" Christy asked, as half a dozen in-laws tried to interrupt her.

"Well, he was struck," the detective said.

"Who shot him? Who shot him?" the relatives cried out. "Did the police shoot him?" Christy tried to correct them, to pass on what she'd been told, but they would not listen. Riaz had been shot, they were sure of it. As the news sunk in, the family began to mourn their prodigal son. Most of them walked about with a blank look on their faces, staring at the walls, every now and then striking themselves to vent their grief.

"He had a very pure heart," his mother wailed. "He had the heart of a king—he wanted to give everything to everybody."

The mourning intensified over the next week, as the family

waited for Riaz's body—a delay caused in part by the dead man's use of a British passport, one of many odd details in the case. While Christy found Riaz's distant relatives to be loving and supportive through this period, the immediate family members seemed locked into their private tragedies, impervious to one another.

The family's attentions to the widow were more curious than comforting. Within hours after learning of the murder, the sisters asked Christy to return the gold bracelet and necklaces Riaz had given her, claiming they were family heirlooms from their grandmother. Whenever Christy began to cry they reproached her: "No, you have to be strong, you must help us hold together."

Fiaz took a different tack. "Oh, my dear sweet sister, don't worry," he said unctuously. "I will take care of everything. You are mine now, and these are my sons." Christy thought he was speaking figuratively, until she remembered the custom directing brothers to marry and support widowed sisters-in-law. When Fiaz began making unacceptable advances—brushing up against her, stroking her cheek—she set him straight. "You do understand," she said bluntly, "that I'm going back to Eric when the funeral is over." Once rejected, Fiaz's manner turned ugly. She had made an enemy for life.

It was around this time that John, then three and a half, ran up to Christy yelping "Mommy, somebody's gonna shoot me, somebody's gonna shoot me!" He had misconstrued a heated family discussion about Riaz's death. Christy settled him, took a deep breath, and explained what had happened. "Daddy isn't coming home," she said. "God decided it was time for him to live in heaven now, and he is really happy and really free."

John looked confused and said, "Okay." He started to walk away, then came back and said, "But, Mommy, Daddy's not happy. He's an *angry* man!" If John appeared to take the news in stride, Adam barely reacted at all. Neither boy showed emotion, even when their uncles grabbed them and shouted, "Riaz Khan, Riaz Khan!" a spooky invocation of a father who'd been reluctant at best in the role.

On August 16 Riaz's body reached the village in the silk-lined casket paid for by Christy's father. The first ominous reaction came from Christy's father-in-law. He had nothing to say about his son but seemed obsessed with John and Adam. "I will never see these children again," he kept repeating mournfully. Christy wished he would stop. With Riaz dead, the family would have neither the interest nor the power to hold her there much longer. The status of her boys, who were dual nationals under Pakistani law, was more problematic. If the family chose to contest custody within the local courts, Christy knew she would have a fight on her hands.

To that point Christy had been treated as a fellow mourner. The family's demeanor changed drastically after it read the death certificate that accompanied the body—and found that Riaz *had* been shot after all (the police had withheld specifics to safeguard their investigation; as it turned out, Riaz had indeed been "struck"—by a single bullet to the back of the head). The revelation placed Christy in an awkward position. "You lied to us!" the brothers shrieked.

The dam broke when the family performed the Muslim ritual for the dead, in which the body is stripped, bathed, and finally shrouded in white cotton in preparation for the funeral. After a harrowing phone conversation with the Michigan funeral home—"When they do an autopsy," the mortician had warned, "the medical examiners aren't real neat about putting people back together"—Christy urged that the ritual be suspended. The family ignored her. When they saw the condition of the body, they were pushed over the brink. At Fiaz's house, the gathering point, an uncle ran into the sitting room, grasped Christy roughly, and shouted, "You bloody, murdering American!" (once considered a close ally, the United States had fallen out of favor in Pakistan). Men she had never seen before milled about, fixing her with glares of hardened hatred.

By the end of the funeral later that day Christy was officially an outsider, a *suspect*, someone not to be trusted. Why had Riaz been so nervous before he left Pakistan? It must be, they concluded, that he feared Christy's family. They told her, "After talking to the detectives, they have narrowed it down to two people. We have conducted our own investigation, and your father is guilty. It's just a matter of days before they arrest him."

Prohibited from calling either home or the Michigan police, Christy was helpless to counter the wild charge—or to defend herself against the rushing flood of threats. "We have our way of dealing with this," the once-gentle Fiaz declared. "Did you know that when our grandfather was killed, we killed twelve people to satisfy his death?"

"Do you really believe my father could do something like this?" Christy asked her in-laws.

"It doesn't matter what we believe," said Mahreen, Riaz's nineteen-year-old sister, who had taken the death especially hard. "If you hadn't married my brother, he'd still be alive." She glared at Christy and added, with utter calm: "I would just like to drink of your family's blood."

"Are you trying to scare me?" Christy said.

"Yes," said Mahreen, "we are."

They were succeeding—especially after they targeted Christy's children. Their contention, as far as Christy could follow it, was that Eric had been "brought to this world by Satan" and that it was the infant's fault that Riaz had died. As Eric had made them suffer, they would make John and Adam suffer—by preventing them from going back to the States with their mother.

Here was the agenda that Christy had feared most, no longer hidden. She was horrified and enraged: "You're going to make John or Adam suffer because you're mad at Eric? You're going to hold an eighteen-month-old baby responsible for his father's neglect?"

At that, one of the brothers slapped her face, shouting "He was a great father—don't you talk like that!" Riaz had entered the blameless world of the dead.

When Riaz was alive the family had assured Christy that they would never allow him to send her away from her children. Within ten days of his death the same people proceeded to do exactly that. "This is their father's country," said Fiaz, who pushed hardest for Christy to leave Pakistan by herself.

"But their father's gone," Christy shot back, "and the United States is their mother's country."

"We've been very tolerant of having you in our family," Fiaz said darkly. "Don't push us."

Christy dug in; she would not go without her boys. Her sons became the central topic of interest in the village, their names invoked with passion on every corner. John, who understood more Urdu than his mother, ran up to her and blurted, "You'll never leave me, will you?"

Christy, trying to console her son using words she'd soon regret, said, "Don't worry, darling, we'll never be apart again."

By August 26, with Christy still in limbo at Fiaz's house, the air was thick with animosity. People seemed to be moving in slow motion. An unspoken threat hung over her head, like a summer storm about to break. Then it happened: at 5 P.M. twenty male relatives invaded Fiaz's long back porch, surrounded Christy, and tried to pry her children from her arms. They yanked Adam away and handed him to a servant. As the servant retreated, the two-year-old looked back at his mother forlornly and then threw up.

John would not submit so easily. As Fiaz howled obscenities, the child screeched his protests and clung to Christy with remarkable strength. In a frenzy the men yanked at John's arms, even beat him on the back to loosen his grip. Christy pushed them off, shielding her son as best as she could.

"Don't fight with the men!" a brother shouted.

"I'm not giving up my kids!" she shouted back.

Christy was shocked to find Riaz's Uncle Hyatt among the aggressors. Hyatt had always been the dearest man in the family to Christy, her friend and protector, but he too had been swept up. Without stopping to think, Christy punched Hyatt in the neck with all her strength. "I'm not proud of doing it," she'd say later, "but they *needed* to be punched. They were out of control." Hyatt fell back with a groan. His cohorts lost steam at this unexpected female resistance and finally left the room grumbling. Adam was returned to Christy minutes later.

At this juncture the family seemed to divide by gender. Hyatt's wife stood up and declared that the men were completely wrong—an act of considerable courage in her male-controlled culture. Ambreen was moved to yell at her husband, which was unheard of in Peshawar.

Christy's strongest remaining ally was a male cousin named Shohob. "Whatever you do," he cautioned her, "don't let anyone in your room tonight." That evening Christy locked the door to her bedroom, though she knew it was considered taboo. Around midnight, as the boys slept, she saw the inside door handle jiggle; someone was trying to get in. She tiptoed over and peeked through a window slit that ran along the door's edge. The sight stole her breath: a man who looked like Fiaz, plus three others she'd never seen before, were clustered outside holding a heavy rope and a burlap bag. The handles of their ever-present knives protruded from their tunics.

Terrified, Christy sat on the floor and rapped as hard as she could on the inside wall with a penknife. A few minutes later she could hear Shohob's angry voice in debate with the others. "You can't do this to an American," Shohob declared. "The U.S. Consulate knows where she is, and the family will be held responsible." Warming to his task, he added dramatically, "You know, the American government sends in armies to get its people out." With a last round of curses, Fiaz and the rest finally left.

Shohob later told Christy that the men hadn't intended to kill her, but to keep her under wraps until the family could win legal custody of John and Adam.

The next morning Fiaz served Christy with a court injunction that barred her from leaving Pakistan with her sons. "If she succeeds in taking away the children," the family's petition noted, "[their] future will be ruined."

Christy's first instinct was to stay and fight. "I'm not leaving without my kids," she insisted. A friendly female cousin named Ronnie advised against it. "This is an evil thing that is happening," she said, "but you have a better chance if you go away and fight for your children from America." The implication was clear: the events of the previous evening were not a fluke or bluff. The men would be back for her.

Christy made her decision. She would be no good to her

sons if she was locked up, or worse. She called the U.S. Consulate and told them to expect her at the embassy in Islamabad the following day.

On her last night in Peshawar, Christy watched her sons slumber. She dwelled on the terrible choice she'd been forced to make, dredged her brains for an alternative that she knew did not exist. "There are no words for that night," she said. She left early the next morning without waking John and Adam; she couldn't bear another long good-bye.

Christy had often chafed against the limits of diplomacy over the past two years. U.S. Consulate officials had made it clear they could not offer haven for her children nor guarantee safe egress to the airport if Christy were to spirit the boys away. On this day her impatience was forgotten. She was grateful when an embassy official named Mike Gayle ushered her into the sweeping modern complex and when he told the in-laws who'd escorted her that the embassy would find her lodging that night. She was even more grateful when he provided an embassy vehicle—complete with darkened windows—to take her to the airport the next day, and when he stayed with her until she boarded her plane.

Before she left she made two important calls. The first was to the detectives in Berrien County, who assured her that her father had never been a suspect in Riaz's murder; the family had simply concocted the story. The second was to a cousin in Peshawar, who told her that John had stopped eating. "He is crying and begging for you all the time," the cousin said, as Christy died inside.

"I'll be back," Christy said, "as soon as I absolutely can." That was the truth as far as it went, she thought glumly. In this endless ordeal, there was no way of telling how soon that would be.

Of all the separations between Christy and her children, the one that spanned the next six months was the most frustrating. In the past she'd been able to call John and Adam regularly from Michigan. Now that Riaz's family perceived her as an adversary they cut off telephone access, until the consulate finally intervened in November 1990, three months after Christy had left.

When John came on the phone she didn't recognize his voice—at first she thought it was another child, that the family was playing a trick. John's Pakistani accent, negligible when she left, was now pronounced, and his tone was abnormally high-pitched. "Mommy, I'm happy, I'm no weeping," John said.

Then came a woman's voice in the background, one of Riaz's aunts: "Tell Mommy you go to school."

"Mommy, I'm no weeping, I go to school," John said.

Christy could hear the deep hurt in her child's voice. "No matter what anybody tells you," she told him, "you have a Mommy who loves you very much."

John burst into tears, his voice now poignantly familiar. "Mommy, I want you, I want you!" he cried. "Come get me!"

The aunt broke in and said, "You can't talk to these children, you're upsetting them." The phone went dead; Adam never had a chance to say hello.

I truly felt for Christy in this period. A forced separation is the most wrenching experience any parent can have. I went to Iran in the first place only because I feared that Moody would kidnap Mahtob if I didn't. When he actually seized our daughter from my arms in Tehran and separated us for two weeks, I felt buried in a chasm of helplessness and dislocation—for two weeks I lost my identity. It was the threat of a more permanent separation that convinced us to attempt our risky escape.

Even as Christy felt a raw urgency to get her children home, her Pakistani attorney, an earnest young man named Nasir Ul-Mulk, warned that a full-blown custody battle could take two years or more. In the end, Nasir said, Christy was sure to win. The teachings of the prophet Muhammad were clear—children under the age of seven needed the nurturing of their mother, regardless of the woman's religion. The fact that Christy was technically a Muslim, by virtue of her Islamic wedding name, would further bolster her position.

Christy had little faith in Pakistan's judicial system. She was attempting to do something with no known precedent—to retrieve children from a Muslim family by going through an Islamic court. Recently I have heard of a similar case, where an American mother was granted custody in Egypt—but with the strict provision that she remain in that country.

Christy was also less than confident that her lawyer would be able, or willing, to buck the Khans' influence in Peshawar and get the court to rule in time. In two years John would be going on seven, when a Muslim boy's upbringing automatically reverts to his father—or, in this case, to his father's family. In fact, John's Pakistani citizenship papers made him ten months older than he really was—another of Riaz's clever stratagems. If her in-laws succeeded in dragging the case out, they might yet win the day.

There was an alternative: to hire a mercenary to snatch the boys and run. Christy knew that Peshawar was a center for the Afghan resistance movement, with no shortage of armed men who had nothing to lose. She also knew it would be next to impossible to enter the family's village without being noticed and that the terrain to the nearest borders was forbiddingly mountainous. If an attempt failed, all contact with the children would be lost. She finally decided to persevere through the courts.

To reinforce her status as a Muslim, Christy took her Islamic vows with a holy man who lived in the Detroit area. "I believe there is one God," she intoned in English, then Arabic. "I believe that Muhammad was a messenger of God." Christy felt no deceit during this ceremony. She believed in God, and the more she read of Muhammad's teachings—and in particular of his high regard for women and children—the more she was impressed by them. Had Muhammad been alive today, the holy man agreed, he would have been appalled by her in-laws' actions.

Here again I could empathize with Christy's decision. I had studied Islam while I lived in Tehran. In my case it was a calculated move to gain the trust of Moody and his family. Once they were convinced that I'd accepted my life in Iran, I thought, they would give me more freedom of movement, the key ingredient to any plan for escape. After Moody took Mahtob away I felt compelled to pray to God, to Jesus, to Allah—to any potential source of help and sustenance, wherever it might lie. I was in no position to be exclusive.

The better I knew Christy, the more I liked her. In some cases brought to my attention, I couldn't be sure that the left-behind parent was the better caregiver for the abducted child. Parental abduction is a hurtful act and must be deterred as a matter of principle, but there were instances when I had to wonder whether the alternative was much better. In Christy's case, however, I harbored no such doubts.

I was immediately taken by her case. For one thing, Christy was an extraordinarily sympathetic person—warm, sincere, and motherly by nature. For another, the death of Christy's husband illustrated a dire pitfall for left-behind parents and their children. It reminded me of how I once prayed for Moody's death in Iran, how I even fantasized about shoving him under the wheels of a car in Tehran's heavy traffic. Like others in my situation, I'd assumed that Mahtob and I would have been able to go home—that Moody's death would end our imprisonment.

I was wrong. To my horror, I discovered that both my daughter and I would become the property of Moody's family after his death! His family might have allowed me to leave or, worse yet, insisted that I do so, but I was sure they would never have let Mahtob leave the country. They would keep her out of pride or out of spite—or because they were convinced that their way of life was superior to any in a hated America.

I was constantly impressed by Christy's commitment to her children and her depth of feeling. On a more secular front, she urged everyone she knew to write to the Pakistani Embassy in Washington. Before she was through, the embassy was bombarded with hundreds of letters and petitions. Although officials there told her they could not move her custody case out of Peshawar, they agreed to tell the judge that they'd review his decision—a scrutiny of no small significance.

Less than three weeks after the beginning of Operation Desert Storm, Christy's attorney informed her that her case was on the docket and would start any day. Her presence was not required, Nasir said, but it would likely influence the judge. The time was right. Christy was determined to go to Pakistan—and to show good faith, she would go there alone.

Her decision set off a frantic round-robin of phone calls between Christy's home, Senator Riegle's office, the State Department, and my office. Sally Light, the child custody chief for the State Department's Overseas Citizens Services, was genuinely concerned for Christy's safety, given the rash of anti-American demonstrations occurring in Pakistan. Sally believed Christy had no real chance to get her kids home, that she'd be taking a huge risk for no gain.

I told Sally I agreed with her—and that I also was concerned about Chris Korest, who had gone beyond her professional role and become emotionally involved in Christy's case. Chris believed that Christy would bring her children home. I worried that Chris wouldn't be able to handle the setback that seemed sure to come and that she might be so discouraged that her good work would suffer.

Even Chris was ambivalent about the trip to Pakistan. At one point she called Christy and said, crying, "I'm afraid that you're going to be killed."

On February 9, 1991, an hour before Christy was set to leave for the airport, Sally Light tried one last time to stop her. "Don't go," she pleaded. "I don't think you've thought this through. You need to understand that you and your children will be considered nonessential business by our people over there. We're at *war* now!"

"I don't care," Christy said. "I'm going." She hung up the phone and burst into tears. Then she was driven off to catch her plane.

It was her fifth trip to Pakistan in a little over two years, but this one was different: Christy was free. She relished the simple act of checking into a Peshawar hotel, of coming and going when she pleased, not that her movements went unnoticed. It soon became apparent that Christy was being followed by two men—undercover Pakistani agents who'd been designated as her bodyguards, on Senator Riegle's request to the Pakistani ambassador.

Even an interview at the U.S. Consulate couldn't douse her

optimism. "Oh, so *you're* Christy Khan—you've generated more mail than anyone I can remember," one officer said. "But I still don't think this is the right time to get your kids. I suggest you go home."

The preliminary court appearances had gone well, according to Nasir. Her in-laws had finally accepted that Christy's father was blameless in Riaz's death and were hinting that they would settle.

"I don't want an out-of-court settlement," Christy said. "I want my children free and clear."

A few days later Christy made her first appearance in Peshawar's civil court. The courtroom was the size of a two-car garage, with a cement floor and high ceiling. The judge sat up front behind a rough-hewn bench, the principals and their lawyers facing him around two small tables. The rest of the room was packed with dozens of hangers-on and refugees who stood and gossiped.

The proceedings were most informal; a hearing would begin whenever both sides happened to show up. As Christy and Nasir waited for her in-laws, the attorney gave her some tactical advice: "No matter what happens, don't cry. This is a sign of weakness. Don't look the judge in the eye—that would be too challenging. He's already going to be intimidated because you're an American, and he doesn't want you to think you're going to get away with anything." Christy decided to behave the same way that had kept Riaz's family off balance—to be respectful but not submissive.

With the eighty-degree temperature and crush of bodies around her, Christy felt drenched beneath her obligatory sweater and *chador*. She kept craning her neck for some sign of John and Adam, and was devastated when her in-laws entered without them. As she didn't dare reenter the village, this was her only chance to see them. The judge adjourned the case for another week and directed the family to bring the boys next time.

Fiaz was furious. "Don't think that you have any great power," he hissed to Christy outside the courtroom. "I could make it look like you just disappeared."

Back at the hotel Christy called her mother. "I'm so *scared*," she said. Her spirits were propped up only by a growing faith in her attorney, whom she'd selected at random from a list provided by the U.S. Consulate. "Time and time again," she recounted, "he showed himself to be an extremely honest and straightforward man, a man of tremendous integrity. I just think I was blessed—that God sent a whole regiment of angels, because I seemed to have one stroke of luck after another."

It was at her second court appearance, ten days after she'd landed back in Pakistan, that Christy saw her sons. As they entered the room with the family's attorney, she was delighted to see how well they looked, astounded at how large they'd grown. She ached to hold them. She strained to keep control, but a loud sigh passed her lips, and the buzzing courtroom spontaneously hushed. Christy struggled to hide her gushing tears behind her *chador*. She wasn't supposed to cry, she told herself, and then she glanced at the judge and caught his look of genuine understanding.

At Nasir's request the judge recessed the hearing to allow Christy and the boys to meet in his chambers. Christy's father-in-law went with them, doing his best to make a good impression. "I want to join with you—you are my daughter," he said. Christy paid no attention to him. Her whole focus was on the two small boys she hadn't seen for five months. John came right to her arms, but Adam held back. *He's not going to come to me,* Christy fretted. *He's not going to want me.* Christy sat John down with a small toy she'd brought and held out another toy to Adam, praying he'd respond. "I looked at Adam and he looked at the toy," Christy recounted, "and then he just reached for me. I tried to hand him the toy, but he just pushed it away. And from that time on he would not leave my lap." When it was time to go, Adam had to be peeled away by the father-in-law.

All seemed to be going smoothly—and then came another crisis. Early in March Adam contracted viral meningitis, an infectious disease with a high fatality rate in Pakistan. He'd always been the sturdiest of her three sons, but now he seemed so vulnerable: covered with spots, vomiting convulsively, his compact body stiff as wood.

Christy had to push for every step of treatment: first to get Adam admitted to the hospital on a Friday evening, a traditional day off for doctors there; then to get him into a private room, away from the typhoid and tuberculosis of the general ward; then to find the diluted penicillin that was critical to his treatment. Shabina, the cousin who had helped her with Eric and was now a pediatrician, doubted that Adam would pull through.

"He'll live," Christy said with an intuitive sureness. She was heartened that Adam was willing to take fluids, which were essential to ridding the infection from his system. There was something else—her conviction that she'd come too far and too long to lose her child now. It was a time of immense stress for Christy, when all the forces of parenthood kicked in. As she told me, "When things are that extreme, you become so hard and so focused on what you're doing that you're not emotional, you're not tired, you don't feel anything. You just do what you need to do."

Adam turned the corner two days later, and Christy spent her last two weeks in Pakistan at his bedside, leaving her legal affairs to Nasir. He reported that the family was buckling, that they now proposed that Christy take John but leave Adam, who'd always been more docile with them. Then Nasir came with his best news yet: the judge had put his foot down. He would allow the family no more adjournments. "This is no good for the kids," the judge had said, "no good for the mother, no good for anyone."

At that point Fiaz had lost all control. "What do you mean, this is no good for the mother?" he snarled. "The mother doesn't matter!"

The judge peered at him gravely. "If the mother doesn't matter, what is this sheet of arguments I have in front of me?" Fiaz had committed a colossal blunder; his family's basic contention was that Christy's sons should remain in Pakistan for their own good and that of their paternal grandmother, who needed consolation after losing *her* son. A flimsy argument to begin with, it now lay exposed in all its hypocrisy.

Seeing that they were beaten and that the judge seemed

determined to give Christy the boys, the family scrambled for the best possible terms of surrender. The attorneys worked out a court-approved settlement with several stipulations—including one that barred Christy from remarrying, under penalty of losing custody. The fight was over.

Christy and her boys piled into the backseat of Fiaz's car for the ride to Peshawar's airport. As the grumbling brother-in-law started the engine, a familiar face poked through the open rear window. "Christy, you were always one of my favorite nieces!" Uncle Hyatt shouted as the car pulled away. "I am glad everything worked out for you!"

Five years earlier Mahtob and I had bounded down the same ramp at Detroit Metropolitan Airport—the ramp to freedom! On March 26, 1991, Christy, Johnathan, and Adam alighted from the plane where John saw Eric for the first time in two years. He felt the need for a proper introduction: "Hi, I'm Johnny, I'm your big brother," he said with a four-year-old's solemnity. "I'll take care of you now." At last, Christy thought, they all could take care of each other.

Lacking income or savings, she had moved in with her parents in their working-class Detroit suburb, into the same modest, three-bedroom house she'd grown up in. Despite the tight quarters, the family is sustained by love and mutual gratitude, their ties all the stronger for the crisis they've shared.

Four months after their return John and Adam were still fragile, but they had made great strides. John no longer awoke at night gasping, soaked with sweat, begging Christy not to leave him and crying about men with guns. Adam stopped demanding a bottle and wetting his bed. Both were able to go to bed without clutching their toys, without fearing that their possessions—and their new, happier reality—might be gone the next morning.

Because he'd been older at the time of his dislocation, John's nature—sensitive, quick-witted, and profound—was already in place in Peshawar. Adam became a different child in his changed environment, "a hysterical new personality," in Christy's words. After the physical and emotional chaos of his splintered family

105

life in Pakistan, "he can't stand a mess. If his hands are dirty he has to run and wash them. If he sees Eric take a hairbrush out of the bathroom, he chases him around the house until he gets it back in the cupboard where it belongs. And he sits in the bathroom and looks around and says, 'Clean, clean, clean!' "

Almost every night, just as he drifted off to sleep, Adam dreamily asked his mother, "You no leave me?"

"No, of course not," Christy would answer.

"Yeh," Adam said, in his Pakistani accent, "togedder!"

With three boys under the age of five, Christy accepted the inevitable small conflicts. John and Adam could be especially intense in their sibling rivalry—a carryover, Christy believed, from the days when Riaz and his family pitted one against the other. Adam's emerging jealousy of Eric—it was this baby, after all, who kept taking Mother away from him—could get physical at times. Parenting for Christy was more than a full-time job. To promote harmony and structure, she was zealous about keeping the household routines: "Regular bedtime, regular wake-up time, regular bath time. We have rules in this house. My husband was extremely spoiled, and I don't want my kids to think they can go around and do whatever they please."

As it turned out, her load was lightened by the son who might be expected to demand the most. "Down's kids are like a gift of love, and Eric *reeks* love," Christy said. "He has a simple goodness that I just can't describe. He's the most well adjusted of the three of them—there's been absolutely no jealousy on his part."

One of Eric's reconstructed heart valves was leaking, and the doctors predicted that he'd need another operation within a year or two. Meanwhile, he took two diuretics and heart medication; if he missed a single dose he felt weak and fatigued. But there were no restrictions on his activity, and he loved the rough and tumble play with his brothers.

Eric was also the least upset when Christy went out alone on an errand—something she didn't even attempt until mid-June, two months after their return. For John and Adam, each of her absences, however brief, would summon high anxiety. Yet over time the boys were healing in this regard, too. When a sister-in-law baby-sat to allow Christy to attend an evening wedding reception in July, the children handled it well.

In truth, the separations may have been hardest on Christy. Protective by nature, she had to worry that Riaz's family would renege on its grudging agreement and try to take her boys away. "It seems kind of sad, because I adore my kids and I'm enjoying their childhood—they're such a riot," she said. "But I will be so relieved when they become teenagers. That's when I'll relax and enjoy them the most, when they'll be able to look out for themselves. They're so helpless now. I know the kids feel what I'm feeling, as much as I try to keep it from them. Sometimes I'll just be looking out the window, mulling things over in my mind, not even thinking it shows on my face, and John will say, 'What's wrong, Mommy?' "

Months after her legal battle, Christy was still trying to make her peace with her late husband's culture. She still felt uneasy in the comfortable Pakistani blouses and pants she brought back from Peshawar. She acknowledged the need to teach the boys about their paternal heritage, especially as they grew older, but confessed that it wouldn't be easy for her.

For the moment, at least, the boys were not crying out to learn. John, who'd become fluent in Urdu, refused to speak a word of the language. He blocked out any recollection of the cartoon version of *Charlotte's Web*, the only videotape available to him in Pakistan for two years—a strange lapse for a child who inherited Riaz's photographic memory.

Neither John nor Adam displayed much curiosity about their father. The subject rarely came up unless they went out somewhere and John saw a couple walking together. Then he knew he was missing something. "Don't worry, Mommy," he said. "God will give us a new daddy."

Christy was still preoccupied with their old daddy—and in particular, with how and why he met his end. The detectives doubted that she was in any danger. "Just rest easy," they told her. Whoever was looking for Riaz apparently found what he was after.

The murder case had yet to be solved. Christy knew the police were purposely withholding information for her protection. She felt frustrated that Riaz was as elusive to her in death as he was in life—that she knew so little about the man she lived with for the better part of five years.

The detectives *were* willing to disclose that Riaz owed money to "everyone and his brother" and that he was shot in a park that lies midway between Chicago and Detroit, a notorious meeting ground for drug smugglers and other criminals.

Christy was startled to hear that Riaz's blood contained no alcohol—an unlikely state for a man who was a borderline alcoholic and who especially liked to overindulge on plane rides. "When someone is going to do a deal," one detective remarked, "they frequently stay sober." Had Riaz been involved with drugs? Christy knew that Peshawar was a distribution center for opium from Afghanistan, and she'd heard it rumored that the Drug Enforcement Agency had entered the case. No one stepped forward to substantiate this theory.

What irked Christy most was her conviction that Riaz's relatives knew the real story and that they were covering up to protect their reputation. Despite repeated requests by stateside police, they refused to release Riaz's phone records for the weeks leading up to his last journey. Christy felt sure that those records could shed light on the crime. Though she'd understood only snatches of Riaz's high-strung phone conversations during that period, she did hear him make repeated references to the Afghan resistance underground. Was there a link there?

She kept playing back Riaz's words just before he left Pakistan: *Christy, leave me alone. I have problems that have nothing to do with you.* Riaz had enemies on every side, any one of whom would have been pleased to end his life.

By the fall of 1991 Christy was moving forward—taking courses toward becoming a certified court recorder, pointing toward a job within three years, when all three of her boys would be in school. She wasn't ready to blot out the past, nor did she want to. She'd had no time or emotional reserve to mourn Riaz in Pakistan—not at his funeral, or at his grave. According to

Riaz's tombstone, he was thirty-five when he died—or five years older than the truth, just as the deceased would have wanted it. Several months after the murder, Christy attended a memorial service for Riaz in Michigan. It was time at last for her grieving to begin.

"My friends say 'You shouldn't feel sorry—he's right where he belongs,' " Christy noted. "But he was still my husband. I loved him once, and we had children together. And he wasn't a monster, he was still a human being. That is not the way you want something to end.

"I felt bad for him, but in a way my faith saved me. I realized in Pakistan that there was a tremendous aspect of my husband's personality that I couldn't come close to understanding. But I think that God knows us better, and I believe with my whole heart that God is merciful. I just hope Riaz has found peace, because he had absolutely no peace of mind whatsoever in his life."

Christy was at home now, but not at peace. Just as I could be thrown upside-down by a report on Moody's latest movements, so would Christy wonder when her in-laws might try to win on the streets what they'd lost in court: her sons.

For all her worries, Christy is one of the lucky ones. The great majority of left-behind parents who go through foreign courts are thwarted at every turn. They become haunted by their loss, despairing of their future. They are people like Ramez Shteih, a Lebanese-born New Jersey man who lost his three daughters to South Africa in 1986. And they live out my worst nightmare every day.

5

Disjointed Systems

*R*amez Shteih became a naturalized U.S. citizen in 1980, fourteen years after he'd moved from Beirut to New York, to take an accounting job for Pan American Airlines. Among his benefits was the ideal perk for a man touched by wanderlust: free airfare to go almost anywhere in the world. On one such vacation in 1977, Ramez stopped for lunch at a roadside restaurant in the blooming hills of southern Scotland. A waitress caught his eye, and the romance of his life took wing. Muriel Dunlop was a day shy of her nineteenth birthday and Ramez was thirty-eight, but the two hit it off from the start. They exchanged addresses and commenced a heartfelt correspondence. When Ramez returned to visit six months later, they courted like old flames.

"The way I look at it, you don't judge a person by the age," Ramez said. "We felt very close, like we understood each other without really talking—like we read each other's minds. We didn't have to explain anything. Whatever we did worked out."

They enjoyed simple pleasures: picnics in the country or at the shore, evening excursions for ice cream, visits to Muriel's friends. Ramez met Muriel's parents, and he was well received. David Dunlop was a tool maker, his wife Isobell a hotel receptionist. They seemed like perfectly reasonable people, unconcerned about the age, nationality, or religious differences between Muriel and her fiancé. Ramez attended a Greek Catholic church, while Muriel was a nonpracticing Presbyterian. The

Dunlops too were adventurous travelers. The family had spent most of Muriel's childhood and adolescence in Rhodesia, where her parents had sought more lucrative employment, before the war for independence there drove them back to Scotland in 1975.

Ramez and Muriel married in a small Scottish church in February 1978. After Muriel's green card came through they settled in a Brooklyn apartment, then moved to suburban New Jersey—the proper spot, they thought, to start a family. Barely out of her teens, the adjustment was rough for the new bride. Impatient to get pregnant, she declined to look for work. She felt lonely, isolated, and out of place. Muriel did not often complain—she was the type, Ramez said, who "keeps it inside and suddenly explodes like a volcano." He hoped her discontent would pass.

In February 1979 Muriel flew to Scotland in anticipation of the birth of their first child. Victoria was born there in April, and Muriel stayed on for another three months, with Ramez flying in on weekends.

Six months after the birth of Maya, the couple's second child, Isobell came to New Jersey from Zimbabwe to visit. The Dunlops had resettled in Africa to be near their two younger sons, who had moved there seeking work.

On her second day in town Isobell asked Ramez where he kept his daughters' passports, and appeared dismayed to learn that they were stored in a bank vault.

The next day Isobell summoned Ramez to her room for a private talk. She got straight to the point: "I want my daughter and grandchildren to come back with me and visit the family in Zimbabwe."

Surprised and angered by Isobell's presumption, he answered, "I must discuss this with my wife."

"Oh, your wife has a mind of her own," Isobell replied calmly, as if the matter had already been settled. She never raised her voice; she knew it wasn't necessary.

Ramez sharply insisted that he must consult Muriel—and then found, to his distress, that his wife refused to talk to him about *anything*. When Ramez entered a room, Muriel and her mother would walk out. At night in bed she would turn her back to him, as silent as a stone. Only four days earlier Muriel had been calling Ramez three times a day at work, freely expressing her love for him, openly yearning to have another baby. Now their communication was limited to such issues as who should go to the supermarket.

"What is the problem?" Ramez kept imploring.

"If you don't know, why should I tell you?" Muriel countered. Her silent treatment lasted for the balance of her mother's visit.

"She was always totally loyal to me, and I to her," Ramez said. "There was no fight, nothing at all. But the moment she gets with her mother, her personality totally changes. She totally loses control."

Ramez went on to say "My father-in-law is just a wimp—a microphone for his wife. He has no say whatsoever. The same way my mother-in-law controls her husband, she wants to control her daughter and our family. If she can't control it, then she tries to break it." Ramez described Muriel as if she had been possessed; she ordinarily added fresh milk to her coffee, but now changed to powdered milk, like Isobell; she always smoked Merit filters, but now switched to her mother's brand, Marlboro; and worst of all was the change in Muriel's face. Normally open and relaxed, her eyes turned tense, her mouth sneering and contemptuous. 'I never experienced such hate from a person," Ramez said. He knew his life was spiraling out of control when he found a card from a divorce lawyer in the pocket of Muriel's bathrobe.

If the days passed in misery, the nights could alarm him. He'd often find Isobell pacing through the house, gulping coffee and chain-smoking. Isobell kept pressing, ever more bluntly, for Muriel's trip to Africa. "Your wife doesn't love you," she told Ramez. "I'm going to take her and the children to Zimbabwe, and if she decides she loves you she'll come back."

Ramez refused to release the passports, and two months after her arrival in October Isobell finally retreated and left their home. "It was," the beleaguered son-in-law said, "just like you switch a light on and off." Muriel snapped back to her old self, as if waking from a dream.

Seven months later, in June of 1982, there was an aftershock. Unknown to Ramez, Isobell had pummeled Muriel with a battery of high-pressure letters—including a $500 check for a lawyer. One Saturday, out of the blue, Muriel told her husband, "You are going to get what's coming to you."

"What do you mean?" Ramez asked.

"I want to divorce you," Muriel said icily. She would not name her reasons, and Ramez endured another two months of killing silence.

The breakthrough came one night with a phone call to Muriel from a friend. After Ramez reported that his wife was asleep, the friend decided to tell him the score. "Lots of things are going on behind your back," she said. "Your mother-in-law is inciting your wife against you."

None of this came as a total surprise to Ramez, but it reinforced his conviction that Muriel was a helpless victim of a personality far stronger than her own. The next morning Ramez didn't mention the phone call. He simply conveyed to his wife that he understood what was going on—that some people could be happy only through the misery of others.

"It was as if I said the magic word," Ramez recounted. "My wife hugged me and kissed me, and she told me, 'I love you.' She called me three or four times in the office, and when I came back in the evening, she said, 'I missed you. I won't allow my mother to control me anymore.' "

For four placid years, Muriel was true to her word. Isobell continued to write—Ramez found it galling that she excluded his name from her salutation to Muriel and the girls—but Muriel took the letters in stride. She ignored her mother's entreaties to come to Zimbabwe and cut Isobell short on the phone: "I won't listen to you break up my marriage." In a letter to her husband from this period she wrote, "Believe me there is no one I love more than you. Even my parents take second place now."

In December 1983 their third daughter, Monica, was born.

Although peace now reigned in their household, Muriel had never adapted to the States. Each year she and the girls would make extended visits, two and three months at a time, to Ramez's family in Lebanon. In September 1984 they went for a whole year, with Vicky attending a British school in Lebanon. Ramez could join them only for short stays and found the separations hard, but he knew that Isobell could be kept at bay only if Muriel was content.

"I don't know what it is," she wrote her husband from Beirut, "but I find a certain peace here. I'm always happy and laughing. If I feel low at all I go to Leila's [Ramez's sister] or Nohad's [a doctor's wife and neighbor], and what seemed big at the time is soon forgotten." She kept urging Ramez to move there permanently—to take a job with Middle East Airlines, or move into the import-export field. Ramez protested that he couldn't make enough money in Lebanon and that the interminable war—which ultimately would kill 150,000 people, or nearly 3 percent of the population—made life too unstable there. His own family had been lucky enough to avoid injury, but the danger was ever apparent.

In 1986 Muriel proposed a trip to visit her family. She would take their three daughters for two weeks, then Ramez would join them for one week, and they would all return together. Ramez was uneasy with the idea but could think of no good reason to resist the trip. His wife hadn't seen her family for five years, and she missed them.

Muriel seemed committed to their future together. She'd circled September 3 on their kitchen calendar with the notation "school starts." Vicky would be entering second grade, Maya kindergarten, Monica nursery school. Desperately wanting a son, she'd recently visited her doctor to find out why she hadn't gotten pregnant since Monica's birth. Just before leaving she told a neighbor, "Look after my husband while I'm gone."

On August 12 Muriel and the girls arrived in the barren hills of Natal Province, about fifty miles inland from the coastal city of Durban, South Africa, where her parents had moved from Zimbabwe and rented part of an old farmhouse from a man who harvested tropical flowers for export. It was a cheaply made, isolated place, with no other buildings in sight save one for the farm's thirty black laborers, who lived up the hill. Muriel professed to have found paradise. "Ramez, you are going to love it when you come," she wrote five days later, with her typical warmth. "It's so like Beirut and the mountains."

For Ramez, the letter was most exhilarating at its close: "The girls miss you and so do I. They always ask when you are coming. I love you!"

Toward the end of August, Ramez boarded a seven-hour South African Airline flight to a desert island west of Morocco, sat through a three-hour layover, flew another eight hours to Johannesburg, and finally caught a one-hour shuttle flight to Durban, where Muriel's brother Gordon picked him up. Ramez reached the Dunlops' home well after midnight and quietly slipped onto the large bed shared by Muriel and the girls. Too excited to sleep himself, he lay still there for hours, watching his daughters' soft breathing.

"As they woke up one by one," Ramez would write in his journal, three years later, "they too laid still, wondering if I was a dream or a reality, staring at me quietly with loving, sweet, and longing eyes. As soon as they realized I wasn't a dream, they all jumped with exceeding joy over me: happy, very happy. We were a bundle of joy and laughter."

For the first day or so Isobell was friendly, and all seemed well. Then Muriel began to act strangely. At the family's night-time get-togethers she began to edge away from Ramez, often moving to the next room. "She was walking in a coma—she was like a zombie," Ramez said.

On September 3, the day before their scheduled departure, Ramez couldn't shake the feeling that he was about to receive some very bad news. He saw it on the faces of some family friends that afternoon—a look of sympathy and disappointment. He heard it when the ever-observant Victoria said offhandedly, "Oh, Mommy's going to get a car and a job." Surely, Ramez thought, she was referring to some office job in New Jersey. He didn't dare let his mind wander elsewhere.

That night Muriel's parents excused themselves to their bedroom at 8 P.M.—suspicious in itself, since they usually stayed up talking till midnight.

"I don't see anything packed," Ramez told Muriel, after the girls had been put to bed.

She joined him on the living room couch and appraised him with a stranger's gaze. "I don't want to go back," she said. "I've lost my love for you."

Ramez felt as if he'd been punched. "What about the children?" he demanded. "Think of how you're going to hurt them—and hurt me."

"That's your problem," Muriel said mechanically, as if reciting a message she'd rehearsed. "They're staying with me."

Ramez was stunned. Even as his wife confirmed his worst suspicions, he tried to deny the dark reality closing in on him. Muriel couldn't be serious. "We must work this out in our home, in the U.S.," he insisted.

Muriel was impervious to argument—as were her parents, who readily answered Ramez's call to join the fray. Isobell could barely contain her gloating. "Your wife doesn't love you any more," she said. "Why should she stay with you?"

"She can divorce me in New Jersey if she doesn't want me, but she can't keep my children away from me," Ramez insisted.

Isobell was undeterred, as if she and Muriel spoke with one voice: "Why should she go back to New Jersey and fight you on her own in the courts? Here we can give her all the support she needs." Then Isobell said, in the cruelest blow of all, "How are you going to tell the children that you're not going to be living with them anymore?"

"There's no way I could tell my children that," Ramez said.

"But there are so many children whose fathers die when they are still young," Isobell said. "Muriel has her own life ahead of her—here, with us. Why should she live with you if she does not love you? On account of the children? The children are better off here than in a home without love."

They argued through the night, with no progress. "They are stubborn people," Ramez said. "You don't get anywhere with them." When he asked for the children's passports, Muriel laughed darkly and informed him that they were hidden. "It was worse than I thought," Ramez said. "My wife knew how hard it was for me to be away from the children, and she'd never allow anything outside the house to interfere with our family life. She had a personality change—she'd become a totally different person."

The next morning Ramez postponed his flight and drove to the U.S. Consulate in Durban. Officials there told him there was nothing they could do about his "family problem," but if he brought the girls back with him, they could issue them new passports. Would they help him get the children to the airport and out of the country? That, they said, was out of the question.

The problem, as Ramez saw it, was that the new passports would not be ready until at least three days after filing. What if one of the girls let slip what they were doing in the meantime?

"I feared for my daughters," Ramez said. "I don't know what my mother-in-law would have done. She wasn't interested in my daughters—she cared only about *her* daughter—but she knew that the only way to keep Muriel with her was to keep my children there as well."

Not knowing where to turn, Ramez walked across the street from the consulate and chose an attorney at random—a young, earnest-seeming man who said he'd need to research the case before setting his course. Meanwhile, he advised, it would be best if Ramez returned to New Jersey and won standing from the court there as the children's legal guardian.

After delaying his flight several days and trying futilely to change Muriel's mind, Ramez took the advice—the hardest thing he had ever had to do. He would leave his children in South Africa and mount his fight to regain them from the States.

"I was tortured, torn to pieces inside," he said. For the children's sake, Ramez determined to compose himself. When Muriel told the girls that their vacation had been extended and that their father would return to fetch them two weeks later, Ramez didn't contradict her. He hoped to win his case quickly and whisk his family back home, keeping his children innocent and neutral. With hindsight, it was a decision he came to regret: "Maybe I should have told my daughters what was going on. It would have put pressure on my in-laws. . . . I feel very bad that I didn't tell them."

On the day he left, Muriel stayed in bed. "Her face was red like a tomato," Ramez recalled. "She was so tense that she couldn't even look at me or say good-bye."

Upon his return to the United States, Ramez contacted the South African Consulate in New York. In October he received his response. "If you do not want your children to stay in South Africa," wrote the vice consul for migration, "you may submit a sworn affidavit wherein you refuse permission for the renewal of their temporary residence permits"—the visas that were set to expire on December 4. "This will be submitted to the Department of Home Affairs, Pretoria, for their consideration."

The letter warned, however, that the department "cannot become involved in family disagreements," which must be resolved by "the legal profession." In a subsequent letter, the vice consul reaffirmed that Pretoria "does not wish to intervene in the domestic matters of the family."

In theory, the South African Home Affairs Office will refuse to extend a child's visitor's visa if *either* parent opposes the renewal. In practice, however, this policy is applied inconsistently, especially when the parent requesting a renewal is a mother with South African resident status, like Muriel.

In other words the government was offering no guarantees, nor even accepting responsibility for the matter—an all-too-common reaction that hampers left-behind parents throughout the world.

The fourth day of December came and went, and Ramez discovered that the children's visas had been renewed despite his written appeal. It occurred to him that the land of apartheid might favor Muriel over an outsider who hailed from the Middle East, though Lebanese people were legally classed as "white."

As the months passed, Ramez's life lost all shape and meaning. "My life revolved around my family, with my wife and children after work," he explained. "I was never out with the boys. Women would come and tell me that they wished their husbands were fathers like me. None of our neighbors expected this to happen."

In previous separations Ramez had kept in constant touch with his daughters. He'd call them every few weeks and ship tape recordings of his bedtime stories. The girls would talk back to the cassettes as if Ramez was in the room with them. Now he was cut off. Muriel was abusive on the phone—"very erratic, screaming, hateful. She says to me 'Suffer!' and she bangs down the phone." When the girls were put on, Ramez could hear Isobell prompting their responses: "I tell them, 'I love you,' or 'I miss you,' and they say, 'Uh-huh,' or 'I do.' I ask them, 'Are you afraid to say I love you?' and they say, 'Uh-huh.' "

Early on Ramez received three or four letters from his children, and then nothing more—not even a Christmas card.

On January 9, 1987, Ramez won temporary custody of his children from State Superior Court in Union County, New Jersey. His New Jersey lawyer called his new lawyer in Pietermaritzburg, at a firm Ramez had selected from a list provided by the U.S. Embassy in New York. In a return cable, the South African attorney confirmed that the custody order "will be enforceable by the officers of the Supreme Court of South Africa . . . provided the order and all supporting documents are properly authenticated."

Freshly armed, Ramez took a three-month leave of absence from Pan Am, flew back to South Africa, rented a hotel room in Pietermaritzburg, and prepared for battle.

Ramez became concerned when he realized he had been assigned a younger lawyer in the firm—"someone who had no experience with international cases." Ramez stressed that he wanted his case handled by the Department of Home Affairs and *not* in the South African courts. As far as he was concerned, the custody dispute was already settled, with jurisdiction properly asserted by the court in New Jersey; all that remained was diplomacy and paperwork.

The attorney told Ramez, however, that the case must be filed in a South African court as a fact-finding formality, to determine why Muriel was refusing to return to the U.S. Two weeks later the lawyer told him that they must withdraw the case without so much as a hearing. "He said, 'The courts here will always side with the woman. If we go forward they'll take all your money, your passport—and you'll have to pay your wife's lawyer.' "

According to Nathaniel Bloch, the Pretoria attorney who became the New Jersey man's legal advisor, Ramez's problem stemmed from the lack of any international law to determine the crucial question of jurisdiction—of which nation's court had the legal right to decide the family's custody case.

While South Africa will often defer to judicial orders from other countries, including the United States, its courts are not compelled to do so. In a domestic case, Bloch said, a person's declared intention to become a permanent resident of South Africa—regardless of current citizenship status—may lead a South African court to take jurisdiction, even when the case originated elsewhere. In the Shteihs' case, Muriel's resident status also might have moved the South African court to act. Finally, Bloch noted, the courts in South Africa, as in many places, strongly favored mothers over fathers in custody suits.

Feeling helpless and hopeless, Ramez took a chance. Home Affairs had told him that it would honor a formal request by the U.S. government for the children's return. Ramez asked for one, but the State Department balked. Without a formal agreement in place, there was no basis for such action. "I went to Johannesburg, I went to Pretoria, I went to Durban—no luck," Ramez sighed. On March 9 the consulate in Durban called to certify "that the U.S. Government has no objection to the return to the United States of Maya and Monica Shteih, both U.S. citizens, and Victoria Shteih, a U.S. permanent resident." Vicky was a British citizen because she'd been born in Scotland.

This wasn't enough to satisfy Home Affairs. Further, Pretoria now decreed that the custody case must be resolved in the South African courts because Ramez's own attorney had filed it there.

On March 12, 1987, the Supreme Court of South Africa awarded custody of the girls to Muriel and directed Ramez to pay

450 rands (about $220) per month for child support. The New Jersey order had been ignored. Even though the court also spelled out his visitation rights, Ramez felt crushed.

Up to that point Ramez's contact with his daughters had been tightly supervised by Muriel's family—"like in a prison," he said. When he drove up the dirt road to the farm for the first time, all three children rushed to his arms, "and we stayed about twenty minutes holding each other like this. My wife and her parents stood and watched us at the door to the yard, and would not move a bit. I walked in the house and they wouldn't talk to me. My children and I were sitting in the living room, and my wife and her parents stayed in the kitchen."

His voice tightening, Ramez said, "And then my oldest daughter looked at me and said, 'Do you want coffee?' She went directly to the kitchen, got a cup of coffee, and brought it to me."

By his second visit, however, Vicky was distancing herself, declining to sit next to her father. Oh no, Ramez thought. Now they've gotten to my daughter. After the South African court order was issued, Maya and Monica were thrilled at the prospect of a weekend with Ramez, but Vicky held back. She was tired, she said. She didn't feel well. She didn't want to go.

But as soon as she got into Ramez's car, Vicky relaxed—as if she'd been putting on a show to mollify her mother's family. When they reached the dirt road, she was asking about her friends in New Jersey. The younger ones quickly chimed in; there were so many things that they missed. Maya remembered the honey that came in bear-shaped squeeze bottles. Monica craved American peanut butter. Victoria wanted the Cabbage Patch doll she'd left behind. They all pumped Ramez for news of an elderly neighbor they'd always referred to as "Grandma," with whom they'd feast on cookies and sing nursery rhymes.

They couldn't call her Grandma any more, they told Ramez.

"Why not?" Ramez said.

"We have a grandmother now," Vicky explained—leaving Ramez to bristle at Isobell and the control she now wielded over his daughters' lives.

Most of all, the girls had missed time with their father. That evening in his room, where three extra beds had been added free of charge by the friendly innkeeper, Ramez resumed his telling of their favorite tale: the story of Anansi, a young heroine whose life moves from one adventure to the next, complete with birds and ants that change into airplanes and transport her to far places. "It combines reality and fantasy," Ramez explained, "as children like it."

The next day Ramez told his daughters, "You know, I love you very much."

"Yes, we know," Maya said, "but it's a secret between you and us." They were simply too afraid to admit their affection for him before their grandmother. Later that day, as they rode in a van Ramez had borrowed from a friend, Vicky began to sing along with a tape of Lebanese music. "Look," she said, "the buildings in Pietermaritzburg remind me of Lebanon."

They are not lost to me after all, Ramez thought happily. "They understood exactly what was going on—that they were there against my will," he'd say proudly, four years later. "I did not have to explain anything. Really, they are very brave children for their age."

At the end of the weekend, as Ramez turned up the dirt road to the farmhouse, Vicky announced, "Stop the car." Crying, she kissed and hugged her father while saying repeatedly "I love you, I love you." Then she composed herself and said, "Okay, let's go on now."

Just before Ramez dropped them off, Monica clung to her father's neck. "I want to go with you forever and ever and ever," she told him. "Don't go to Grandma's—just go to the airport and take us to America."

It was a poignant moment for Ramez, who had put his trust in the legal system and now found himself helpless to ease his daughters' pain. He sensed that his best shot was to somehow persuade Muriel to come home with him, if even for a visit—to get her thousands of miles away from her mother.

His wife, unfortunately, was less accessible than his daughters. At a birthday party for Maya in February, Ramez quietly cornered Muriel in the big front yard. He poured out his grief and longing, reminded her of all she'd thrown away. She began to stutter as she spoke, to look conflicted, as if caught in a lie. Ramez could see her old softness and devotion struggling to break through.

At that point her brother Gordon stepped in. He put his hands on Muriel's shoulders, turned her around, and pushed her toward the house. "We'll let the courts decide this," he told Ramez. "She's not coming with you."

Ramez had one more lengthy talk with Muriel, a four-hour marathon in her living room in March. He thought he'd brought her to the verge of saying she'd come home, that she was finally swinging back to him. Isobell glared daggers at him as he left and slammed, her hand on the kitchen counter. The next day Muriel refused to speak to him, and his campaign stalled.

Back home again, Ramez resumed his efforts to gain recognition for his New Jersey custody order. He gathered affidavits: from an old friend of Muriel's in England, to whom Muriel had confided "that her mother was difficult and . . . constantly interfered with her marriage"; from a family friend in Brooklyn, who vouched for the Shteihs' "very normal family life"; from a former New Jersey landlord, who remembered that Vicky "always greeted [Ramez] when he came home from work at the door" and that Ramez would take the family for walks in the park after supper.

All three attested to Ramez's qualities as "a very good family man," as the landlord put it, and to how his daughters obviously adored him.

It was during this period that Ramez also reached Muriel's oldest brother, David, now estranged from the family and living in Botswana. David confirmed that Isobell had tried to destroy his own marriage and that she held irresistible power on her home turf. "I sympathize with you," David told Ramez in a taped telephone conversation, "but as long as Muriel is under the influence of my mother, you haven't got a chance."

Meanwhile, the two governments involved hardened in their indifference. "When you get to these officials, it's not their children—it's not everything to them," Ramez complained. To the bureaucrats, he feared, he was is just another guy with a mother-in-law problem.

Ramez made his final visit to South Africa in August 1987, using a three-week vacation for one last personal appeal to Muriel. He showered her with invitations for dinner and weekend picnics with the children, but she would not—could not—accept. Ramez was thwarted at every turn. It was the ultimate frustration, for he *knew* he could bring his wife around if only he had the opportunity. One day he found himself alone in her bedroom and was struck by the photos pasted there. There were more than fifteen pictures, each one taken where Muriel had felt most at home, each featuring the woman who'd offered her the strongest kinship and keenest understanding: Ramez's own mother in Beirut.

Ramez had not surrendered, but as the months passed and his family remained seven thousand miles away, contact became more sporadic. Despite his instructions, the girls' schools failed to send him reports. In June 1988, when Maya underwent a tonsillectomy, Ramez heard nothing about it until the day before she was admitted to the hospital, after he happened to speak on the phone to one of Muriel's co-workers. He was becoming marginal to his daughters' everyday lives, and it seemed he could do nothing about it.

He last spoke to his children over the telephone in 1989, after the Dunlops had moved to the South African seaside town of Margate on the Indian Ocean, with Muriel and the girls occupying an apartment adjacent to that of her parents. Muriel had no phone, which meant that Ramez had to reach his family through his in-laws. When he was put through to his daughters, they were cool and cautious, and Ramez could hear Isobell telling them what to say. At other times Isobell would tell him they were out, a rejection that Ramez found unbearable. "I didn't want to talk to my daughters under those circumstances," he said.

His calls were further disrupted by a disagreement with Muriel over child support. For a time Ramez sent $220 a month, but he later scaled back. He estimated that his travel and legal costs had already depleted $10,000 in family savings and had put him another $20,000 in debt. Financial concerns had also prevented him from traveling to South Africa for his court-allowed visitations.

He persistently pressed on with his case. He dashed off letters to the State Department, to his congressman, and to Senator Donald Riegle of Michigan, who'd taken a leading role on the issue of international parental child abduction. Ramez pursued the question of Vicky's U.S. citizenship until he reached a dead end. According to government sources, Vicky's citizenship status would not impede her return to the U.S. anyway. He cultivated a contact whose father sat in the South African Parliament. "The only thing that keeps holding me is to keep the issue alive, even by bits and pieces," he said. "If I get rejection I will try again, until I knock on the right door."

The key, as Ramez saw it, was to get jurisdiction over his daughters' custody returned to the court in New Jersey. His great fear, Ramez said, was that his daughters would assume he had deserted them: "They'll say, 'Here is our father who was with us, day and night, who did everything for us, and all of a sudden he doesn't talk to us.' They will grow up to believe in nobody, to trust no one."

Nothing, Ramez insisted, could be further from the truth. He still writes his family twice a month and sends his daughters gifts on their birthdays, though he gets no response and cannot be sure his mail gets through. The girls are never far from his thoughts. He imagines them every time he glances at the yellow brick elementary school across the street from his house, every time he hears the sound of the neighborhood ice cream truck ("we're sitting and they're playing, and I see my oldest daughter standing like a rabbit with the ears, you know. 'Ice cream, can I have ice cream?' And *then* I hear the truck coming, and they run to the outside").

His last letter from Muriel came in August 1990, when she took him to task for missing visits and support payments. Inside the envelope lay a recent photo of the three girls, then twelve, ten, and eight—and Ramez nearly wept to see how much they'd grown up without him: "I'm missing the most important thing in life." Victoria's sweet smile was now tinged with the self-consciousness of adolescence. Maya stared straight ahead, fearless and confident as ever. Monica, no longer a baby, looked out hopefully from under a page-boy haircut.

That picture remains in its envelope, banned from his living room gallery. Ramez preserves the past by leaving everything as it was when his heart was broken. In his home his children are still little girls, frozen in their ringlets and overalls, just as he remembers them. He recalls anecdotes from their younger years in the present tense, as if they'd happened yesterday—or might recur tomorrow. I believe that he is reluctant to fly out to see them, as much as he misses them, for fear that they will outgrow his memories.

Ramez still aches for Muriel, five years after she left him. He's made no move to get a divorce. "I don't try to belittle my wife," he said. "I feel that she is a victim, just like my three daughters. Yes, she had responsibility, but when things go beyond your control, what then can you do?" He would take her back in a minute if she would agree to get therapy, to rid herself of Isobell's influence completely.

Occupying one end of a low-slung, three-family house, Ramez's home is an unlikely site for a shrine. It sits in a cookie-cutter development in New Jersey, a tiny bedroom suburb twenty miles southwest of New York City.

But the home is a shrine, nonetheless—a place to preserve past happiness. Out front there stands a tree whose apples Ramez's three daughters once reached to pick for the pies that his wife once liked to bake. It was June when I visited Ramez, months before apple season, and the tree bore a different, bitter fruit: four yellow bows nailed to its trunk. Beneath the bows he'd wound more yellow ribbon and inscribed in black "August 11, 1986," the date Muriel took their daughters to South Africa, where they remain. Underneath appears the inscription "Pray For Their Safe Return Home." Every six months, as the lettering fades, Ramez replaces the slim banner with a new one. But the message never changes.

Inside the home, time stopped on that day of departure more than five years ago. A living-room wall is padded with family memorabilia: studio portraits of Muriel and each daughter, with more yellow bows taped to their upper-right corners; a wedding picture of Ramez and Muriel in Scotland, he stiff and proud in his gray vested suit, she smiling shyly beneath her blond bangs and round cheeks, her white train trailing over a stone patio; a bright crayon drawing of a necktie—a Father's Day gift from his eldest daughter Vicky; a candid snapshot of Maya, the middle child, with a toddler's plastic golf club; and a close-up of Monica, the baby, looking out wide-eyed in her spot above the television set. Ramez once considered career in photography, and every shot is sharply focused, well composed.

On an adjoining wall Ramez framed one of Vicky's first-grade stories, penciled between horizontally ruled lines. Above the story's title—"My Flower"—was an illustration: a smiling girl, standing with her arms flung wide. Her right hand points to a swing set, like the one Ramez had recently erected in their backyard. Her left hand points to a palm tree, like the ones Vicky knew from visits to Ramez's native Lebanon.

"One day I went outside to play," the story began. "I saw my flower growing near a tree as cute as can be. Then a dog came out. Then he stepped on the flower and that was the end of my flower."

"She wrote this a few months before they left," Ramez told me meaningfully. "It prophesied their going to South Africa."

He mused constantly about his family, about the three disparate daughters who were so dear to him. Vicky, then seven, was "very gentle, very thoughtful, like an old lady," Ramez recounted, his voice warming to the memory. "She doesn't like to embarrass you or tell you that you're wrong. One day, when she was about three years old, we went to church, but we arrived late and everyone was leaving. I didn't want to disappoint her, so we walked inside. We sat in the church, and she could see that it was empty. She looked up at me and she said,

'Daddy, I think Jesus is not working today!' She has a lot of imagination."

Five-year-old Maya, with her reddish-blond curls, looked most like her father—"a carbon copy," Ramez said proudly, as he displayed a photo from his childhood. Maya was direct, tough, athletic—a girl who could hold her own with the boys on the block. "She's very sensitive, very emotional, very loving. When I went to visit them, my daughter Victoria would sit on my lap and go on for hours telling me everything that's happened. My daughter Maya would sit on my lap and just stare at me—like she is talking through her silence, through her eyes."

Monica, not quite three at the time, was "a combination of the two," both precocious and assertive. "You can put her in a group of grown-ups, and she'll sit and carry on as if she's their age," Ramez said. "If she wants something, she says it very loud to make sure you've heard her—being the youngest, I guess she has to speak up. Once she gets it, she is immediately calm and satisfied, she sits happy and relaxed.

"I imagine myself being on a battlefield, where everything is fired at you," he went on. "If you give yourself to failure, you can't help anyone."

Ramez mounts his battle at a white Formica table in his living room. There, deep into each night, he marshals his facts and intuitions and loads them into a computer. An accountant by trade, he is thorough by nature and habit. He has filled a file cabinet with his research data: countless legal briefs and affidavits; two custody orders, a New Jersey decree granting custody to him and a document from South Africa finding for Muriel; his wife's correspondence, and copies of his own letters to her; newspaper articles about similar abduction cases; and his intricate reconstruction of dozens of domestic incidents, many of them trivial at the time but ominous with hindsight. Everything is indexed, cross-referenced by date and subject.

As if to boost his morale he told me, "I'm not thinking of the problem, I'm thinking of the solution—nothing of failure, only of hope," he said in his Lebanese-accented voice.

Ramez refuses to weaken in this work. It is as if his life is an enormous puzzle, and his future hinges on the solution. Like a conspiracy theorist, he is obsessed with detail.

There are times when Ramez becomes discouraged. "By myself I'm just struggling in the mud," he said with a sigh. "I need a bigger organization to support me. On your own you have no chance—you just knock yourself against a wall." It is hardest at night and on weekends—family hours—and it's then that Ramez starts smoking his cigarettes, a habit he thought he'd quit for good before disaster struck.

But he never indulges in such pessimism for long. There is always the dossier to return to, the fat three-ring folders to feed. It is as if one more fact, one more perceived pattern, one more stroke of analysis will win his case and bring his family home to him. He still strives to write his own ending; he still seeks to reunite his family.

"It is very hard for me," Ramez said, "but I knew I must write about the situation in a lot of detail, even if it pained me as I write it. I mustn't write it in grief—it came as therapy, but the main object is that I want these facts recorded. I must be strong; I must not let myself down. I must push, push, push."

But there is no one to push on the red-and-beige swing set that sits rusting in Ramez's backyard. The pictures on his wall will never age, but across the sea three children keep growing older and ever farther away. One day they'll be too big for swings and ice cream trucks, and perhaps even for stories of girls who sprout wings.

Ramez originally wrote me in February 1991, after reading *Not Without My Daughter*. He drew parallels between our stories—that we'd both been deceived in connection with a family vacation and that our spouses had changed their behavior so drastically. Here was a man who had left his own country to become a U.S. citizen, and now he is alone, with his children in a third country.

I have seen other left-behind parents react to the trauma of abduction like Ramez. They get so consumed in building their case that they lose sight of their primary objective: maintaining a relationship with their children no matter what else happens. When I talk to these parents I advise them to exercise visitation, keep up their child support, send presents on birthdays—to do all they can to preserve their bond. Their ability to get their children back is, regrettably, often out of their control. Their expressions of love can help see them and their children through the trauma of separation.

6

Crossing the Border

Many left-behind parents conclude that it is hopeless to work through the courts, whether at home or abroad. They feel they have no alternative but to take matters into their own hands, outside the legal system.

As one who was forced to do the same when I escaped Iran with Mahtob, I well understand their desperation. In February 1988, a few days after my trip to Washington, where I'd heard the frightening news that Moody had left Iran, I received a call from a distraught Dallas woman named Cathy Mahone. "Thank you, *thank* you," she told me. "If it weren't for you I wouldn't have my daughter!"

In 1976 Cathy married Ali Bayan in a small Christian service. They settled in Dallas, Texas, where their lives seemed too good to be true. Cathy worked in real estate and Ali in a restaurant. When they visited Ali's hometown of Jarash, Jordan, Ali's family accepted and loved Cathy as willingly as her family had embraced Ali.

After Cathy became pregnant, Ali made another visit to his country. This time he came back a different person, with the "behavior change" I've seen in so many cases. He declared that the family was moving to Jordan, but Cathy refused. Their marriage deteriorated, and after their daughter Lauren was born they divorced.

Ali didn't leave for Jordan, but instead started a local business with his brother and remarried. He still spent a lot of time with Lauren; Cathy regarded him as a great father.

When the Texas economy fell apart, Ali lost his business. On November 1, 1987, while he had Lauren for an overnight visit, he took their daughter to Jordan, a betrayal Cathy never had anticipated.

The State Department gave her a list of Jordanian attorneys and advised her to go through the court system there. But Cathy had heard of the long delays and frustrations that other left-behind parents encountered along that path—and she knew she couldn't wait that long. Without Lauren her life had no meaning. She was willing to risk all to recover her daughter.

So Cathy went a different route: she hired a professional, who sent a team of commandos to Jordan to find Lauren. Cathy went along as far as Cyprus, where she waited at the phone for the commandos' report. She told me, "I took your book to Cyprus, and every time I doubted I could go through with this, I read further and got the courage to carry on."

Upon receiving word that Lauren had been located, Cathy joined the team in Jordan, where they were disguised as visitors to the Holy Lands. The commandos stopped Lauren's school bus and threw the vehicle's keys in the sand. Cathy boarded the bus to recover her daughter, then fled with Lauren to a waiting car. With mother and daughter hugging in the back seat, the commandos drove across the border into Israel, from where Cathy took Lauren home.

"If it weren't for your bravery in telling your story, I would not have my daughter back today," she told me, sobbing over the phone. But Cathy's crisis was by no means over: "Now I'm locked inside an apartment, with my daughter huddled in a corner and screaming each time someone comes to the door, 'Mommy, please don't let them take me!' I'm pacing the floor with a pistol in my hand. What do I do from here? What will the rest of our lives hold?"

I knew just how she felt. More than once I too had paced at home with *my* revolver, trying vainly to ward off my panic.

I had no satisfactory answer for Cathy. Until the world

comes to respect the rights of children, any peace for her and her daughter—or for Mahtob and me—will always seem temporary.

Cathy spent her whole life savings, roughly $200,000, for the counterabduction. Mother and daughter now live in hiding, with new identities. I have not heard from Cathy for several months.

After my story was aired on "20/20," a man who claimed to be a commando got in touch with me. He spent a weekend with us and told us the incredible story of his life. The man said that he'd been in the CIA for several years and that he wasn't proud of all that he had done there. Counterabducting children from foreign countries seemed to be a way to ease his guilt. After the man left, I asked Mahtob what she thought of him. "He doesn't look very tough," she said. She'd apparently expected him to have a physique like Rambo's.

These professional commandos are not always reliable. Some are honest; others are unscrupulous, even dangerous. In 1990 I met a Moroccan woman who'd married a Tunisian man in Belgium, where they raised their two daughters. Both parents were Muslim. After the father kidnapped the children to Tunisia, the mother hired a man to get the girls back, paying him 800,000 Belgian francs. The man she trusted to counterabduct her children never did the job. She had to redirect her efforts to locate him, and when she finally tracked him down he threatened her with a gun. At that point, thankful not to have been killed, but with her finances depleted, she turned her attention back to finding her children.

Given the erratic response of the domestic courts, the limits of international law, and the high cost and risks of hiring a third party, other victim parents are forced to rely upon themselves.

At times these parents are pushed into feats of high imagination. One such person was Gretchen, a German woman who'd just finished reading *Not Without My Daughter* and tried to reach me by telephone through my dad's doctor, Roger Morris, whom she'd traced through the phone book. She called in the morning, German time, which meant that she woke Dr. Morris in the middle of the night. We would learn that this was typical of Gretchen's impulsive nature.

133

I returned the call and Gretchen told me her intriguing story. At the age of fifteen she was studying French at the Sorbonne in Paris when she met a Tunisian diplomat who was several years older. "He was like Rock Hudson—very tall, very dark hair, very romantic and considerate," she said to me. After a whirlwind romance, they were married.

The diplomat eventually was called back to Tunis, where his behavior changed much as Moody's had. His outbursts became more and more intolerable. He wanted Gretchen to accept traditional Tunisian ways and suggested that she dress more modestly, even cover her head. She impulsively talked of divorce. His unwavering response was that she could do whatever she wanted, but she would never get their children. Gretchen would listen to him silently while burning inside.

One morning matters came to a head: the husband accused Gretchen of kissing the milkman. This was too much, Gretchen thought. She said nothing, but hatched a plan on the spot. She directed their chauffeur to take her and the children to the beach. On the way, she asked him to stop at the airport and wait while she mailed a letter to her parents. Wearing only a bikini, Gretchen ushered her children into the terminal . . . and then bought three one-way tickets to Germany. Tunisian law normally required a husband's permission for a wife to leave the country. But airport personnel recognized Gretchen as the wife of a diplomat and allowed her to board.

When they arrived in Germany, dressed for the beach, "everyone stared at us," Gretchen recounted. "It was really cold that day. And the chauffeur? He's probably still waiting at the airport."

One of Gretchen's genuine concerns was how Mahtob would feel toward her father as she got older. When Gretchen's daughter turned eighteen, she felt compelled to see her father and her childhood home, and went back to Tunisia without telling her mother. The trip resolved any lingering concerns, and fortunately her father did not attempt to detain her when she left to go home.

＊　　　＊　　　＊

Most counterabductions are considerably more harrowing than Gretchen's. They are acts of desperation, involving danger to both parent and child, as Craig DeMarr can attest.

In 1981 Craig DeMarr was a U.S. combat engineer stationed in Fulda, West Germany, a G.I. river-valley town of fifty thousand people about fifty miles east of Frankfurt and twenty miles from the East German border. Craig's job was to monitor seventy-pound blocks of "cheese charge"—plastic explosives—that were nestled under Fulda's main roads and bridges, just in case the Soviets decided to push through the nearby mountain pass and invade.

Off-duty, there wasn't much for a nineteen-year-old private to do in Fulda after he'd toured the thirteenth-century churches, except to visit the clubs that dotted downtown. In exchange for a token membership fee, a lonely enlisted man could drink with his buddies, hear ten-year-old rock songs, and meet young German women. Many of these liaisons were short-lived, but more than a few ended in marriage, with the brides following their soldiers wherever the U.S. military sent them, and eventually back to the States.

About six months into his hitch, Craig met Vera Hoffman at a large, low-lit singles club called the Overpass. She stood out from the crowd—a striking brunette with a knack for American slang and a weakness for the soldiers who used it. Craig asked her to dance, and she moved to American music as if born to it. He bought her a few drinks. He was hooked: "She just seemed like the right person to be with at the time."

I spoke with Craig in the paneled dining area of his living room, a place filled with bric-a-brac and family photos. Craig was a trim young man with dark-brown hair, grown out in the back since he'd left the military. There was more than a glint of mischief in Craig's straight-ahead hazel eyes and broad grin, but also an abiding gentleness.

Craig and the army never mixed. When he left the service in 1983 he told Vera he would be back for her. "Everybody says that," he noted, "and nobody believes them, because *nobody* ever comes back." Craig turned out to be different. He worked

135

for two months, until he could raise the fare to Frankfurt, and then the young lovers took up where they'd left off. They spent most of the next year hitchhiking through Europe, with no plan or agenda, just as Vera liked it. "Let's go to Spain today," she'd say, and they would.

Early one morning Vera slapped Craig awake, one of her less endearing habits.

"What do you want?" he moaned.

"Let's go get married," she said.

"Are you crazy?"

"No, let's go."

Craig pondered this development for a moment. "Then we're going back to the States," he said. He had tired of their vagabond life; he missed home.

"Sure," Vera said. She'd long dreamed of moving to the U.S.—the land of consumer plenty. Of course she would go.

They hitchhiked to Denmark and were married by a justice of the peace. They spent their wedding night in an abandoned windmill.

When they returned to West Germany there remained a problem: Vera couldn't bring herself to sever the cord to her homeland, to her friends and her father, a widowed crane operator. She kept procrastinating. Finally, almost a year to the day after Craig's return, just as his round-trip ticket was about to expire, Vera took the leap to America.

In Muskegon, a city on Lake Michigan about the size of Fulda, the marriage soon took a wrong turn. Vera tried to become a traditional woman and full-time homemaker. She even packed Craig's lunches each morning for his job at a local bowling alley. "She made a gallant effort to be human," Craig said wryly. But Vera couldn't resist Muskegon's late-night bar scene, her call of the wild. If Craig, now a working drone, couldn't share the fun with her, she'd find others who could.

"Vera adapted to the U.S. real, real well," Craig said. "She got Americanized"—he snapped his fingers—"just like that." She lost all traces of her accent, and new acquaintances assumed she was a native. She mused about becoming a U.S. citizen but never pursued it. She'd say, "I'm a German, I'll always be a German."

Late in 1984, despite the couple's ups and downs, Vera became pregnant with their first daughter. Craig was thrilled and hoped the baby would bring them closer, but his wife felt trapped, imprisoned. Vera herself had been raised by a series of "aunts"— her father's girlfriends, with whom she'd been left during his weeklong work trips. The idea of a nuclear family was simply foreign to her.

Vera suggested an abortion, which Craig rejected. Then she tried again to make the best of it. She quit smoking and drinking, watched her diet, took her vitamins. Stephanie was born in April 1985, and Craig was desperate to make the family work.

"I loved Vera dearly, and I'd do almost anything to make her happy," he said. When Stephanie was three weeks old they went to Germany for a two-week visit with Vera's father. On their first night in Fulda, Vera reverted to her old ways. She went out by herself and came home at 3 A.M., soddenly drunk—an acute embarrassment for Craig, whose parents had joined them for the trip. "I was still covering for her," he said, "and it was just gradually getting worse."

Back in the States they'd made a down payment on a modest version of the American dream: a small house with blue shingle siding on a busy Muskegon street. Craig felt proud to have a place of their own, but Vera was there only sporadically. She'd stay out all night two and three times a week, and her pace barely slowed when she became pregnant again early in 1987. This time there was no prenatal care, despite Craig's urging, as vitamins gave way to rum and Cokes. Craig would wait at the front door into the morning, cursing the light, until Vera returned home to "watch" Stephanie and sleep the day away. He was chronically late for work and got fired from more than one job as a result.

"I kept threatening to leave her, but I couldn't get myself to do it," he said. "I was losing jobs. I had ulcers. It was terrible . . . and it got worse." After a second daughter, Samantha, was born, Craig barely saw his wife. No sooner would he get home from work and walk through the back door than he'd hear the front screen door swing shut: party time for Vera. Craig would feed and bathe the girls, go to bed alone, then make sure his daughters had breakfast before he left the next morning. On those occasions when Vera returned before dawn, Craig suffered most. She would toss in her sleep and murmur things like "Dave, stop it!" or "Pete, quit it!" "It was just gut-wrenching," Craig told me.

There was one more family journey to Fulda after Samantha's birth. During their first trip Vera had scared Craig by declaring "I'm going to stay," then changed her mind. "And on the second vacation," Craig recalled, "she said, 'I'm staying—there's no doubt that I'm staying.' We almost literally had to drag her on the plane."

In November 1987 Craig made a last-ditch effort to salvage his marriage: a night on the town, with dancing and champagne. They both had a wonderful time—and when they got home, Vera walked off to her favorite bar. "I'm not done partying," she said. Craig knew he was beaten. He left his home the next day—and found himself pulling out of the driveway just as Vera's latest number-one boyfriend was pulling in.

Vera filed for divorce right away, "and she ended up getting almost everything I owned," Craig said with a wan smile. "I did everything wrong. I had never gotten divorced before."

Given Vera's track record, Craig's lawyer advised him to file for physical custody of his daughters. Craig held back; the responsibility seemed overwhelming. "At the time I said, 'Well, Vera's a woman, and here are two little, little girls. If she straightens out, she could probably do better than I would.' And my lawyers said, 'Keep an eye on it, and if she proves unfit and you change your mind, we'll get the ball rolling and get custody to you.'"

Craig took the counsel to heart. He organized a twenty-four-hour watch on the house, rotated among members of his family: "My mom would set her alarm for two o'clock in the morning, my dad would set his for four." A friend of his father's, a suburban police chief, ran license-plate checks on any visitors.

It soon became apparent that Vera was violating the custody order, which barred all non-relative males from the household.

Worse yet, she and her live-in boyfriend were brawling almost daily, according to blow-by-blow accounts that Craig received from three-year-old Stephanie during his weekend visitations. One fight left a hole the size of a man's fist in a paneled wall. In the spring of 1988, Craig obtained a revised custody order that specifically banned the boyfriend from the premises and prohibited Vera from taking the children out of state. Nothing changed. In the summer and fall of 1988 local police were called at least ten times to the house—usually after the boyfriend had assaulted Vera in front of the children.

Craig's concern switched to alarm after a teenage baby-sitter informed him that the boyfriend had sexually abused Stephanie. "That's when I bought a shotgun," Craig said, "and I was going to go sit in the backseat of his car and wait for him. But then I said, 'No, that's not going to get me anywhere. He'll be gone and I'll be in prison, and the kids will be there with her.' " Craig pulled back from the brink and decided to fight Vera through the system—to wrest physical custody of his daughters away from her. No longer running from responsibility, he knew that his children must be sheltered from harm and that no one else could do the job. A child protection caseworker told him there wasn't enough "physical evidence" to justify his petition.

In November 1988 police were called to yet another fight between Vera and her boyfriend—this time involving a gun. Vera had gotten hold of a .22 automatic, pulled the trigger twice, missed the boyfriend—she was a poor shot when she was drinking—and left two bullet holes by her bedroom door. The county ordered Stephanie and Samantha into DeMarr's care for the night. After Vera pledged that she would press charges against her boyfriend and never allow him back in the house (a promise she would soon break), her daughters were returned to her. Craig felt frustrated, helpless.

"The police were telling me 'There's nothing you can do.' And the Friend of the Court kept telling me 'You're the man, you have a job, and you're renting an apartment with a male roommate. This is the children's home. We can't throw her out and move you in.' "

At that point Craig formally filed for custody. While his petition was pending, he was ordered back into court—to surrender Samantha's passport and enable Vera to take the girls on a two-week trip to West Germany in December. Vera already had a passport for Stephanie in her possession. Craig was frantic. He'd heard that a narcotics squad was closing in on Vera and her boyfriend, and feared that she wouldn't dare return to the United States. But when he expressed his worries he received little sympathy.

"The Friend of the Court said, 'That's always a possibility and a concern, but until it actually happens there's nothing you can do about it.' And the judge said, 'You have absolutely nothing to back that up. She came here voluntarily. You will turn over Samantha's passport.' His tone was 'You moron! Why would you think that?'"

If Vera overstayed her two-week allotment in Germany, the judge continued, custody would automatically go to their father—a proviso that Craig found of little comfort.

Craig sent "maybe thirty letters" to his congressman, Guy Vander Jagt. The response was discouraging: There was no law preventing Vera from leaving the country. "I got nowhere real fast," he said.

As it turned out Vera did return, and on schedule. She called Craig Wednesday, December 28, and told him not to drop by that day—that the girls were at a birthday party. Would he mind waiting for the weekend to visit? Craig grudgingly agreed but sensed something wasn't right. He drove by the house and saw movement inside; they were home after all. As the day waned, the lights in his daughters' bedroom switched on. Craig figured that Vera was putting them to bed, that all was well for the time being.

No one answered the phone for the next two days. Saturday, December 31, Craig's mother drove by the house and called him in a panic. There was fresh snow on the ground—but no footprints or tire tracks around the house. "You better get over there," his mother said.

Within minutes Craig was at the back door. Within seconds

he had jimmied his way through. It was all too clear: No one lived there anymore. Bare wires trailed from where ceiling fans had turned. The kitchen appliances, the stereo, the dinette set Craig had recently purchased—all were gone. The few sticks of remaining furniture were gashed by long black cigarette burns. What hadn't been taken or sold had been ruined.

On the floor of the bedroom, dumped amid a pile of papers and a variety of drug paraphernalia, Craig found a discarded note from Vera suggesting that "maybe someday" he could visit them if he had money. Craig sensed an awful truth: his daughters were headed across the ocean, if they weren't there already.

He checked with an elderly neighbor known for keeping a sharp eye on the block. Vera and her boyfriend had piled several larger items into a pickup truck several days earlier, the neighbor said. That Thursday they'd loaded some remaining possessions into a rented car-top carrier.

In the days that followed, Craig clung to a faint hope—that Vera and her boyfriend would lay low near Muskegon for a time, then fly to West Germany after the heat was off. Craig took a leave from his job and vowed to track down his children. Barely sleeping, he watched his former home and four other local addresses that Vera and her boyfriend had frequented: "I'd just drive from house to house to house, twenty-four hours a day."

When Vera's phone bill arrived in the mail, Craig opened it for possible clues to her whereabouts. Vera was many things, as Craig would say later, but she wasn't stupid. She had attempted to cover her tracks with hundreds of long-distance calls, from television shopping services to dating hotlines. Craig crossed off all the 900-numbers, then those that he knew from their configurations to be pay phones. Of the remainder he looked for repeats, and found that fourteen calls had been placed to a number in Colorado Springs.

A private detective was hired, and he traced the number to a Cecil Blackburn—a G.I. whom Vera had known in Fulda. A contact at U-Haul confirmed that the fugitives had dropped off their car-top carrier in Colorado Springs. "That told me they're done traveling by car and they're getting on a plane," Craig said.

He called the local airport on January 2—and heard the numbing news that Vera, her boyfriend, Stephanie, and Samantha had departed for West Germany just one day earlier.

Craig believed that they were headed back to Vera's old friends and haunts in Fulda—a suspicion confirmed when he learned that a letter from the boyfriend to his mother bore a Fulda return address. Pinpointing the children's whereabouts did little good, as the U.S. State Department explained to him. West Germany was not a signatory to the Hague Convention, the international agreement that originated in 1980 to expedite the return of abducted children to their home countries (a reunited Germany would sign the accord in December 1990). Craig's only option, the department told him, was "to go there, hire a German lawyer, prove her unfit in Germany, and hope like crazy you win a court case in the next couple, three years." Craig lacked the patience, the bankroll, and the faith in German justice to try such a course. The U.S. judicial system had blocked him at every turn in his quest for custody. What chance would he have against a German mother with a home-court advantage?

Two weeks later, on January 13, 1989, the Michigan court awarded temporary custody to Craig. "I had everything I'd been fighting for," he said ruefully, "except now the kids were gone."

For three months Craig was cut off from his daughters. He heard nothing by phone or mail. It was the worst time of his life. "I freaked," he said, his eyes glistening in recollection. "I cried uncontrollably, it hurt so bad. I didn't eat, I didn't sleep. I was lost. No one could help me—and the people that *could* help me wouldn't."

Craig was broke all the time. He was paying rent on his apartment, plus payments on his family's house to avert foreclosure. He petitioned to move back into the house, but the court turned him down; he'd signed a quit-claim deed during the divorce proceedings, and Vera retained legal title. So Craig couldn't sleep there, but he'd slip inside and wander its rooms, remembering bath times and breakfasts and a thousand childish things. He'd leave everything just as he'd found it; he'd fantasize that Vera might return someday for some neglected possession. It made no sense, "but I was doing *something*. I had to do something toward getting the kids back." When he couldn't bring himself to leave, he'd sit at the top of the stairs, just outside his daughters' bedrooms, all night long.

Craig's parents couldn't stand it anymore and decided to go another route: they would hire mercenaries to snatch the girls and bring them home. They wrote to every would-be commando who could afford to advertise in *Soldier of Fortune*. The response was not encouraging. Virtually no one wanted to hazard West Germany and its tightly guarded borders at any price. The most positive response came from a professional who called himself the Fat Man. "I'll do it for $10,000 up front, plus you pay for my flights, my hotel, my food, and my car, the whole nine yards."

"Well, that's not unreasonable," Craig's father said.

Then the Fat Man added: "Craig has to go with me. And he has to slug her in the head or do whatever he's got to do. I'm gonna wait in the car, and I'll give him and the kids a ride to the border, but it ends there."

Craig rejected the deal as "a $15,000 taxi ride." He was fast coming to a fateful conclusion: the only person he could trust to rescue his children was himself.

It was about the same time, in April 1988, that Craig traced and called Vera's brother in West Germany. After an appeal to their common fatherhood, the brother confirmed that Stephanie and Samantha were in Germany and doing well, and agreed to ask Vera to contact Craig.

An hour later Vera phoned with a terse message: "We're here and we're fine. We're going to live here for the rest of our lives, and there's nothing you can do about it."

Craig played it cool: "As long as you're happy and everything's okay." Then he spoke to his daughters for barely one thick-throated minute, and was leveled by the fear he heard in Stephanie's voice.

"Daddy, when are you going to come and get us?" she pleaded. "We don't like it here—it's *icky*."

"I'm sorry, honey," Craig replied. "I can't come get you." He knew Vera was listening in. He knew that he didn't dare hint at his actual intention: to snatch the kids back on his own within the next month.

Craig's plan had been weeks in the scheming, but now it began to take shape with the aid of two helpers—one willing, the other less so. The latter was Vera's boyfriend, who had wearied of Fulda and was headed back toward Muskegon, a small city with an active grapevine. Craig obtained the man's flight schedule and waited that day near the home of the man's parents, around the corner from his house (the court had finally relented and allowed Craig to move back in).

When the boyfriend spotted Craig he stepped outside. Holding a bottle of whiskey in one hand and a glass of the stuff in the other, he might have intimidated someone with less to lose. He was shirtless, and his face and chest were etched by old, deep scars, trophies from a knife battle at a local tavern. He made it clear he was ready and willing to take Craig on.

"I don't want to fight," Craig said. "I want to talk to you." He knew the boyfriend was his best source of information, and he was determined to extract it by any means necessary. "He cooperated real well," Craig recalled. "Well, he knew I wanted to kill him."

The questioning began: What was the address of Vera's new apartment in Fulda? How did you get there? What floor were she and the girls on? What was the layout of the apartment—where did everyone sleep? Did Vera leave the kids alone there, or did she use a baby-sitter? Where was her favorite bar?

Craig got his answers, but he wasn't altogether happy with them. According to the boyfriend, Vera stayed at the apartment all the time—often with several friends—except when out partying every other weekend, when she left the children with her father. Craig stewed for days over various scenarios. How would he ever pull this off?

He received a needed boost of confidence from his second collaborator—a muscular, gung-ho ex-marine named Frank Corbin, whom Craig had met the year before. They'd become basketball and card-playing buddies, but Craig didn't know Frank all that well until one afternoon in April, as they labored over a

144

new transmission for Frank's 1967 Oldsmobile Cutlass. Craig was talking about his children when Frank, who had one son himself with another on the way, looked up and said, "You know, you ought to go over there—just take the kids."

"I am going over there," Craig replied.

Frank didn't hesitate. "I'll go with you," he said.

Craig tried to dissuade his friend. He explained that if someone—namely Vera—happened to be killed during the snatchback, they were staring at the electric chair. Even if the kidnapping itself went smoothly but they didn't make it out of West Germany, they were likely headed for life in prison. Craig had no money to pay a partner. Frank would be taking a huge risk for no gain.

"I don't care," Frank said. "Let's go."

After a family parlay, Craig's parents agreed to finance the plan with $20,000 of their savings. His father had opposed Craig's shouldering so much danger, but he could find no alternative and was impressed by his son's resolve. Craig wasn't famous for direction or stability, but now he felt wholly focused. He'd never been so sure he was doing the right thing.

"I had quit my job," he noted. "I got my house back in shambles—and I didn't much care about it anyway, unless I had the girls here to share it with. They were my life, and when that was stripped away I had nothing left—literally nothing left.

"At that point I was so mentally tortured that I couldn't care less for my own well-being, as long as those kids got what was coming to them: a decent life."

Now they were plotting in earnest. Craig placed a sobering call to a woman at the U.S. Consulate in Amsterdam—the destination of their escape route. He explained the situation and asked if he'd be able to get new passports for his daughters upon reaching the Netherlands.

"We won't get involved in a custody dispute," the official said, "but if you bring your custody papers with the children, along with their birth certificates and Social Security cards, we'll give you the passports." More to the point, the woman continued, "How do you plan to get across the West German border?"

145

"I can't tell you that," Craig said.

"I suggest that you don't even try," the woman said. "No one makes it."

Undaunted, Craig and Frank assembled their disguises. Frank's code name would be Brad Madison and he'd dress in military fatigues, the better to blend into Vera's G.I.-oriented social set. Craig's new identity was Bob Servo and he'd wear loose-fitting, Mexican-style clothing and mirror sunglasses; the civilian dress would allow him to stay at a Fulda hotel without arousing suspicion. Both got military crewcuts, and Craig dyed his brown hair and mustache black.

On April 30 the two flew to Amsterdam, then boarded a train to Frankfurt. Craig had ruled out a direct flight into West Germany. Vera's father, according to the boyfriend, had alerted German immigration officials to block Craig from entering the country. The train was safer, but there would still be passport checks on either side of the border. If the border guards were to log Craig's passport number into their on-board computers the game would be up. To avoid them, Craig held his passport in his lap while feigning sleep, hoping he would slide through. The ruse worked on the first go-round. "He's sleeping," Frank offered. "We haven't slept in twenty-eight hours." But the guards returned for another check at the next stop.

"My palms were sweating," Craig recalled. "They came back and I acted like I was sleeping again, and one of the guards nudged me twice. There were these little old ladies playing cards across the aisle and one of them said, 'Leave him alone, he's exhausted. He has a passport, you checked him last time.' " Craig was saved.

After staying overnight in Frankfurt Craig redyed his hair, and the pair drove a rented Peugeot the five hundred miles to Fulda. They found a serviceable hotel, which was no small trick in Germany, where G.I.'s are widely viewed as destructive deadbeats. They hailed a cab to Vera's apartment on Berthold Strasse, as per the boyfriend's instructions, to give Frank a feel for the crucial geography. On the road back to their guest house, they passed the Green Goose, Vera's tavern of choice. Then Craig sent Frank out shopping, "just in case" they encountered resistance at a delicate moment: two switchblade knives, a large wooden maul handle, thirty yards of rope, and several rolls of duct tape.

On their second day in Fulda they took the Peugeot back out to the Netherlands border, some five hundred miles away—about four hours' drive time on the *autobahn*, the federal highway that has no speed limit. Their goal was to find an unguarded crossing, but their prospects dimmed as the day wore on. "We got out of the car and walked through woods and over two railroad tracks, but the path always stopped—you couldn't get through for one reason or another," Craig recounted. "And the whole way there were guards on motorcycles, guards on horses, guards walking with dogs."

Finally they picked up a young hitchhiker and asked him where he'd go if he wanted to get "some illegal stuff" out of the country. No problem, the young man said. Just ten kilometers down the road lay a crossing that was guarded only twelve hours each day. There was just one catch: you wouldn't know in advance what time the guarding started on any given day.

Craig and Frank drove to the designated point for practice. "When we got there it was guarded, and we just drove through," Craig said. "We waved at the guy and he waved back. He was in a little guard shack off an itty-bitty, two-lane cobblestone road. You couldn't even believe it was a border check." With growing excitement, the pair mapped out the route to the crossing. This might not be so tough after all.

Their third day in Fulda was a Friday—time for action. After a day spent poring over their maps and dwelling on worst-case scenarios, they drove to the Green Goose at 7 P.M. Frank strolled inside wearing a bright red nylon windbreaker for future identification; Craig waited around the corner in the Peugeot, his eyes glued to the tavern's door.

Plan A relied on Vera's love of drink—and the disabling combination of alcohol and a sedative pain reliever called Tylox, which Frank's father took to combat a crippling case of arthritis. Before leaving the U.S. they'd called a friendly pharmacist, estimated Vera's body weight, and asked him how many capsules of Tylox would be required to knock her out.

At the Green Goose that evening, all seemed in order. Vera surfaced at 8 o'clock. Frank introduced himself, struck up a conversation, and began buying her brandy and Cokes. After an hour or so he showed her the drugs, which had been transferred into two unlabeled antihistamine capsules, and told her that their high compared to that of cocaine, a rare commodity in West Germany. Vera readily gulped the capsules down, kept drinking—and was utterly unaffected. Frank and Vera left the Green Goose on foot and proceeded to close several other bars. Twenty-eight brandy and Cokes later, Craig's ex-wife was still standing—swaying slightly, perhaps, but quite conscious. "She was tough as nails," Craig later acknowledged, not without a trace of admiration.

At some bleary hour the next morning, Frank followed Vera back to Berthold Strasse—along with three other American men, two German men, and two other German women. Vera's two-bedroom apartment, it became evident, served as the group's flophouse. The party rolled on with five cases of beer—on through Saturday and into the next day, until Vera fell into a peaceful sleep Sunday afternoon.

Craig, meanwhile, was frantic. He'd lost sight of Frank and Vera on their way out of the Green Goose (Frank had shed the red windbreaker) and hadn't heard from his partner for almost forty-eight hours. Back at the guest house, too wound up to sleep, Craig paced and waited, his mind racing to dark places. Frank's wife had sworn she'd leave him if he went ahead with this adventure; his friend had little to look forward to back home. Had Frank gotten violent and been arrested? Had he double-crossed Craig, told Vera what was going on, and been paid off by Vera's father? How well did Craig *know* this guy, after all?

By 6 P.M. Sunday Craig had exhausted his patience. He drove to Vera's apartment, rang the outside doorbell and waited, his heart pounding, holding his maul handle and a gym bag with the duct tape inside. He was ready to cold-cock Vera or anyone else in his way.

148

One of the men leaned out the window: "Who is it?"

"It's Bob Servo," Craig called. "Is Brad Madison there?"

Frank peered outside. "Oh my God," he breathed, and the next sound Craig heard was Frank hurdling the banister on his way down from the third floor. He threw open the front door and hissed, "What are you doing here?"

"I'm going to club you to death," Craig said. "Where have you been?"

"I got it under control," Frank insisted. "I got her house keys; she wants me to come back tonight." Partly mollified, Craig left, but he gave Frank a stiff tongue-lashing when his partner stopped by the guest house to change clothes an hour later. Since they'd packed as lightly as possible, Frank simply exchanged his shirt for Craig's to give Vera the illusion of a normal-size wardrobe. Frank pledged to keep in better touch, and they devised a new plan.

The immediate obstacle was that Vera never seemed to be alone—her party friends stayed on through the week, leaving only to replenish their stock of alcohol. Vera's father had dropped Stephanie and Samantha back at the apartment on Sunday. While both girls seemed in good health, Frank never saw them go outside to play, nor get a bath, nor eat a single structured meal during the week he was there. Every so often Vera would slice pieces of bread, meat, and cheese and leave them on the kitchen counter; whenever the girls were hungry they'd simply grab what they wanted. For all of her neglect, however, Vera kept a keen eye on the children, as if she were waiting for something to happen.

"She never bonded with the girls," Craig observed. "It's not that she didn't want to—she had no idea how to do it. It was like 'Here's food, you need food; here's clothes, you need clothes.' Other than that she did her own thing."

The party lasted two days, three days, four. From dusk to dawn Craig sat outside the apartment complex in his rented car with Dutch plates. He began to attract attention, and it wasn't particularly friendly. Two people wrote down his plate number. A third took his picture.

Thursday Frank finally persuaded Vera to shuffle her friends out the door and give the two of them some time alone. They would stay home that weekend—with the girls. Back at the guest house, Craig urged Frank to get Vera out as well, leaving Frank alone with the kids and allowing the snatch-back to proceed without physical confrontation. "Give her a pocketful of money and send her to the bar," Craig said. "She'll go in a minute."

Vera stalled. She'd kept her routine for four months, and she wasn't eager to change. Craig had moved his vigil to a nearby Greek coffeeshop, his anxiety rising. His hair was getting longer, and too many people might recognize him in this town. He knew that Vera and Frank were sleeping together and that Vera was happy with the status quo—a G.I. with cash in his pocket. Craig feared that Frank might be having a better time than he was letting on: "He was procrastinating, he kept putting it off. I was beginning to wonder if he was starting to like her and planned on staying there. . . . I was holding his passport and his plane ticket because I wasn't real sure what he was up to."

Friday, May 4, Craig delivered his partner an ultimatum: he was taking his girls on Sunday, ready or not.

Several days earlier, while they'd been hiding out at the guest house, Craig had reminisced about his Boy Scout days. His troop once studied an Indian tribe where the braves would awaken each morning and declare, "Today is a good day to die." At about 8 P.M. Saturday evening Craig was called to the phone at the coffeeshop. The voice on the other end was taut and alive—the voice of an old leatherneck in his element. "It's Brad," the voice said. "Today's a good day to die." Craig laughed; his palms started sweating.

Craig raced to Vera's building. He hurtled up the two flights to her apartment and burst through the front door: he was about to see his daughters for the first time in four months. Frank intercepted him and laid a light hand on his chest. "Calm down," he said. "They're both here and they're fine." Craig took a deep breath, stepped into the bathroom, washed his hands and face. This was no time to alarm them, he told himself. Then he followed Frank into the living room, where the children were

150

watching a German cartoon. They were slim and fine-featured. Stephanie, the elder at four, had straight blond hair and a ready smile; Samantha, only two, still had her baby face and light-brown curls.

"Girls," Frank said, "There's someone here that wants to see you. He's a friend of mine."

Stephanie turned and stared at the black-haired man in the baggy clothes for two or three seconds, an aching eternity for Craig. "Daddy!" she screamed, and then her tears flowed and she threw up her hands and ran at him. Craig squatted to catch her and was nearly bowled over. Samantha wasn't sure what was happening, but she followed her sister's lead, and quickly Craig's arms were filled with the two people for whom he'd risked all. The girls looked thinner than he remembered them. Their pink-and-white cotton nightgowns were frayed. Their hair needed a cut and shampoo . . . and they were the most beautiful children Craig had ever seen. He felt suddenly buoyant, as if a great weight had been lifted from his shoulders. It was, he'd say later, "like every roller coaster ride you'd ever had, like all of them combined."

"Can we go home now, Daddy?" Stephanie asked.

Craig had rehearsed this line in his head countless times. He said, "Yes, honey, your vacation is over. It's time to go home."

They moved fast; while Vera wasn't expected back before the wee hours, Craig didn't want to push their luck. Frank instructed each girl to take along one favorite toy. Samantha chose a stuffed red-vested rabbit, a present from Vera during a recent bout with pneumonia. Stephanie picked her security blanket, the green baby bunting that Craig's mother had knitted when she was tiny. Craig added a large teddy bear—a pillow for the ride ahead.

In the spirit of subterfuge Frank left his windbreaker at the apartment, along with his last pack of American cigarettes, his lighter, and a note: "I took the girls to my friend Bob Servo's house. If they fall asleep there, we'll spend the night and I'll bring them home in the morning." Frank grabbed two disposable

151

diapers—enough to cover Samantha's immediate needs, but not so many as to make Vera wonder. Then the men scooped up the girls and carried them down to the Peugeot. Craig climbed into the backseat to play with his daughters while Frank took the wheel. By 9 P.M. they were off: the Netherlands or bust. When they reached the *autobahn*, Frank notched into fifth gear and pressed the accelerator to the floor, pushing the four-cylinder compact for all it was worth. They would average better than 135 miles per hour that night.

The two men had planned this trip in intricate detail. They would try to keep the girls awake to within one hundred miles of the border, then let them fall asleep. Just before the crossing Craig and the children would move into the Peugeot's roomy trunk, already outfitted with foam rubber and blankets. With luck, the girls would sleep through to the Netherlands. To be safe, Frank would tap the brake pedal if a border guard approached—alerting Craig, who could see the brake light from inside the trunk, to cup his hands over the mouth of any child who had awakened.

They also had a contingency plan. If something went wrong and they were stopped, Craig would slug the nearest guard, then tackle as many others as he could while Frank took off in the car with the girls. He was to keep going until he reached the U.S. Consulate in Amsterdam and to remain there until Craig's parents showed up with their lawyers. The main thing, Craig stressed, was that his children must not go back to Vera, no matter what.

The trip was swift and, through its first three hours, uneventful. Craig was "very scared—apprehensive and excited and relieved all at once." To pass the time, Craig and his daughters played patty-cake. He gave both of them a lollypop, in hopes that the sugar high would keep them up a bit longer. The girls were tired but in high spirits; they were thrilled that they'd soon see Craig's parents and a cousin who'd been their playmate in Muskegon. Samantha, not yet two, was still learning to talk, and she babbled away in German. Stephanie, who'd just turned four, had retained her English. At one point she looked up at her father and said, "I *knew* you'd come and get me." Craig, striving to keep both of them from crying, replied, "Well, I just couldn't *leave* you there."

After a brief stop at a rest area, where Craig changed Samantha's diaper, the girls dozed off and Craig moved to the front seat. The night had grown cold. The men covered the reclining children with their jackets, and then with their flannel shirts, leaving themselves in soiled T-shirts. Craig knew they were roughly half an hour from the border. Without the girls awake to divert him, his nerves intruded. Would they make it across? What would happen when they got to Holland? They drove on in the night through the wooded marshlands, the two men barely speaking, each alone with his skittering thoughts.

It was about this time that they realized they were lost. Horribly lost. They'd been following the map they'd made on their second day in West Germany, which called for a right turn just before the highway ended and became another road. They must have turned too early or too late. As they approached the crest of a hill, a white sign they'd never seen before now loomed: GRENZE ZOLL, 1 KM. The border was barely half a mile away. Craig's pulse quickened. He knew they were headed toward something more formidable than the friendly cobblestone crossing.

"Get to the top of the hill and stop," Craig said. He and the girls would get into the trunk, and they'd proceed as planned. As Frank squealed to a stop from sixty miles per hour, the Peugeot was abruptly bathed in floodlights. The sign had lied. They weren't half a mile from the border. At most they were seventy yards away—within hailing distance of a major crossing. It was eight or ten lanes wide, with a glass booth for each lane and spotlights between the booths. The Peugeot was the only vehicle in sight, and every guard on duty was surely staring at it. The trunk plan was dead. Worse yet, there was no way out; the road they'd come in on was one-way.

Craig was reeling with adrenaline. He pointed to a parking lot to the side, where trucks were inspected, and urged Frank to pull in. In no small frenzy himself, Frank stopped in the middle of the lot and shut down the car's lights and engine—a move that could only tighten the guards' grips on their pistols. Then Craig spied a pay phone toward the guard shacks. "Go to the phone and act like you're making a call," he told Frank. "I'll try to figure something out."

There wasn't much to figure. They were stuck. They could either forge ahead or turn themselves in—and Craig was not about to give up. Frank got back behind the wheel and said, "Well, what are we gonna do?"

"You got a wild hair?" Craig said, with a thin smile. "Drive through."

Frank digested that one. "You want me to just hit first gear and blow through it?"

"No," Craig said, "if they shoot at the car they might hit the girls. Just come to a rolling stop by the booths and wave your passport, and see if they wave you through." Up to that moment Craig had been consumed by panic. He'd been visibly shaking; even his lips were twitching. As soon as he'd decided what they must do, long shot that it was, both men relaxed.

Craig had used the rolling-stop method successfully before, but it wouldn't work this time. Their behavior had been too eccentric. "*Halt!*" screamed the guards, as half a dozen of them scrambled out of their booths, their hands on their guns. They were now within twenty feet.

Two guards approached either side of the car and demanded passports. Frank complied, but Craig froze in his seat; he'd left his papers in a bag in the trunk. " '*Raus, 'raus!*" the guard in charge shouted. "Out, out! Get out!" Praying that his daughters wouldn't wake up, hoping that they'd somehow be overlooked under the litter of shirts and jackets in the back seat, Craig took the car keys, rummaged through the trunk, and casually presented his passport. His spirits sank when he saw that the guard held one of those portable computers that had almost snared him on the train to Frankfurt. Craig *knew* all was lost when a third guard leaned forward and played his flashlight over the back seat. Stephanie's straight blond hair gleamed in the midnight blackness.

154

The guard opened his mouth as if about to ask a question
. . . when Craig distracted him by taking three quick backward
steps. "Halt, *halt!*" Two of the guards unsnapped their holsters
and gripped their 9-mm semiautomatics, West Germany's answer to the Colt .45.

Craig put on his best straight face. "Nothing, nothing," he
said. "Go look through the trunk."

"Do you have anything to declare?"

"We don't have anything," Craig said. *Except for two little
girls without any papers in the back seat.*

The guard returned both men's passports to Frank, but he
still wasn't satisfied. The pair didn't fit the standard tourist profile:
"Where are your souvenirs? Where is your camera?" Craig didn't
respond. He slid back into the passenger seat, replaced the keys
in the ignition, and said softly to Frank, "Go slow. Don't stall the
engine, don't squeal the tires, just casually drive away."

As Frank accelerated, several guards walked alongside for
three or four steps, as if they weren't finished. Then they fell
back, and the Peugeot was through. The entire episode had
lasted perhaps seven minutes.

Craig wasn't yet ready to celebrate. He couldn't be sure
that they had made it into the Netherlands, or that a second
crossing point might not lie ahead. They drove on for another
two hours, long after West Germany's white license plates had
given way to Dutch yellow, until they reached the outskirts of
Amsterdam early Sunday morning. They grabbed a nap in a
parking lot, then looked for a hotel close to the U.S. Consulate, which would reopen Monday. "We wanted to be very
near it," Craig explained. "We still weren't positive if they [the
Dutch] could make us go back to Germany, so we wanted to
stay out of sight."

They also needed to conserve their cash, as Craig had but
$80 left from his $20,000 fund. They found a single room in a
seedy hotel and snacked on dry cheese and toast with warm
Coca-Cola. Monday they had the girls' pictures taken, then returned to the consulate for the precious passports. With the
children in tow, Craig and Frank were ushered to the head of a

155

long line. Finally, Craig thought, they'd found a place where they'd be treated with respect, as *Americans*. Then he found himself face to face with the official he had phoned from the States the month before.

"How did you get across the border without passports?" she sternly demanded.

"It doesn't matter—we're here," Craig said. "Here's the pictures, here's the birth certificates, here's the Social Security cards, here's the court order giving me sole custody."

The official wanted to know everything: "Did you smuggle them? Did you hurt anybody? Did you kidnap these kids?"

"Listen," Craig said, "they're here, and they're American citizens. Here's the paperwork, give me the passports. It's really none of your business how we got here."

They sparred for a quarter hour before the official relented; she had done her duty, and she could see that the children seemed happy with their father. A few minutes later she walked back to Craig and said, "Here are your passports, Mr. DeMarr. Congratulations." Several other consulate employees stood up and applauded. One of them loudly relayed the news to the waiting applicants, and soon everyone in the room was clapping. The sound washed over Craig like a warm bath.

There were other wonderful encounters, such as the one with the two Northwest Airlines employees who gave up their reserved seats on an otherwise booked transatlantic flight the following day. Others were not-so-wonderful: a customs official in Boston yanked Craig out of line, ripped open his bags, and pressed for the whereabouts of the girls' mother ("I told him that she had family in Germany and was staying over a week or two") before letting them pass.

Craig had been through too much to assume they were home free. He and Frank had remained tight-lipped through the flight from Amsterdam, sipping their welcome Budweisers and watching the girls gorge themselves on complimentary peanuts. Even after they'd touched down in Detroit and were waiting for Craig's family outside the terminal, he kept his guard up.

"I was bent over tying Stephanie's shoe," he recounted, "and I didn't know they had pulled up behind us. I heard footsteps slapping pavement real fast and someone screaming. It was coming right toward me; I turned around and I was going to hit whoever it was because my nerves were shot. I figured I didn't come all this way to be turned back or get caught now."

The footsteps belonged to Craig's girlfriend, who jumped into his arms before he could do any damage. Stephanie hurled herself at Craig's mother, wrapping arms and legs around her; Samantha toddled straight to her grandfather. Amid the tears and round-robin embraces, the two exhausted heroes were presented with prizes for the van ride home: two cartons of Camel cigarettes, two six-packs of American beer, and, best of all, two custom T-shirts. Craig's shirt read "Superdad" on the front, with the names of his daughters on the back. For Frank Corbin: "The best friend any man could ever ask for."

In Muskegon there remained the task of healing—and, in particular, of allaying the girls' fears of their once and future home, where they'd seen so much ugliness. Each morning Craig would bring Stephanie and Samantha to the house he'd reclaimed in disarray. While the children played, their father worked on the plumbing and the walls. Craig's mother and girlfriend had already made over the girls' bedrooms with new wallpaper, carpets, and frilly curtains, as if to blot out the past.

Most important, Craig installed new windows and doors, front and back, complete with dead-bolt locks and steel frames for the door jambs. At that point he asked his daughters to lay down their toys and help him: "I would have them hand me hammers and nails, and I'd say 'Watch.' And I'd pound the nails in and say, 'See, no one can kick in this steel door. No one can get in here to get you.' "

Despite Craig's efforts, the old hurts died hard. Once back in their home, Stephanie would wake up screaming about Vera's old boyfriend: "Icky David's gonna get me! Icky David's breaking in! He's smashing the windows, he's gonna get me, he's gonna hurt me!" Craig would run upstairs to flick on the light and

157

reassure her. If the nightmare was especially bad, he would carry her downstairs and show her that the doors were locked, that her world was shut tight and safe.

During those first months his daughters were reluctant to let Craig leave their sight. They would cling physically to his side. When he entered the bathroom to take a shower, they would sit just outside and talk to him through the door: "You still there?" "I'm still here." The girls were shy around strangers, and especially around strange men. They'd be unnerved by normal household tension, and so Craig took pains to make "everything smooth, no big rush, no yanks." They were horrified by people yelling, convinced it was a prelude to violence, and Craig laid down the law to his friends: no loud arguments were allowed in his house.

Over the next two years, Stephanie and Samantha would demonstrate the resilience of the very young. These days they are sociable, well-mannered, apparently well-adjusted kids—so much so that a child protective worker advised Craig that they need no therapy, at least for now.

Still, their childhoods may never be normal. Craig recognizes that their security hinges on his unceasing vigilance—just as I am always watchful with Mahtob. At Stephanie's school the principal has agreed to keep doors and windows locked. At the end of the day Stephanie waits in her classroom with her teacher until one of three designated people—Craig, his mother, or his sister-in-law—collects her. If Vera were to surface there the staff—armed with photographs and detailed descriptions—would call the police. Although the school is just blocks away, Craig's first-grader never walks home with her mates nor even steps outside unattended.

At home the same rules apply. He allows his daughters to play inside the home of one next-door neighbor, a person who knows their history. "I have windows in every room of the house that are always open," Craig noted. "I'll watch them go over there and I'm always watching them out the window." He lets Stephanie ride her bicycle with friends on a quiet road behind the house, as long as she stays within sight. He feels safe when the girls are at his parents' house, where the star attraction is an

158

in-ground swimming pool. Those are the bounds of his worry-free universe.

When running errands with his daughters, Craig carries a .22 Magnum Derringer. Inside the house he has hidden a loaded gun, beyond the girls' reach, in every room. Three times a week he calls Vera in Fulda. If she answers he hangs up—feeling better for the knowledge that she remains six time zones away from them.

There are times when Craig wonders if he is being overprotective. He said, "I can't believe I'm doing this. Sometimes I think I don't have to sit here and watch. . . . But what if Vera got on a plane? What if she's in the park across the street, watching me in a rented car, and I go in the house and leave the kids out there? It only takes a minute." He leaves nothing to chance. If a teenager smashes a pop bottle on his sidewalk, he will climb out of bed to investigate. If a strange car loiters near the house in the evening, he will call 911.

"It's never really done," he told me glumly. "It just keeps going and going."

The hard fact remains that Vera is the mother of his daughters, and she appears unlikely to fade away. At last word she was working at a Fulda kiosk, selling cigarettes and beer. Every two weeks or so she calls her children. Stephanie usually resists getting on, but Craig coaxes her to the living room phone: "I remember what it felt like, to be totally shut out—it's a horrible, horrible feeling. I look back and I cry when I remember how I felt. I can imagine how it would feel to have your child come on the phone and say, 'I don't want to talk to you.' So I say to Stephanie, 'Just tell her hi, and that you're in the middle of a cartoon, and she'll understand.' "

Although Vera has threatened Craig's life more than once over the last two years, he still has "a spot that feels sorry for her. But I don't want that in my life or my daughters' lives."

Stephanie has forgotten most of her German vocabulary, save for one nursery rhyme phrase: "*Augen, nase, und mund*" ("Eyes, nose, and mouth"). Her fear of returning to Germany, however, is longer lived—as is her longing for her mother. During a recent chicken-nugget lunch at a local Burger King, Craig

159

asked the girls if they'd like Vera to visit, and both of them nodded.

"Would you want her to move here and stay with us?" he went on.

Stephanie screwed up her small face, the picture of ambivalence: "Kind of, kind of not. I'm a little bit scared."

"Would you worry about her trying to take you back to Germany?" Stephanie shook her head. "Why not?" I asked.

"You're here," the six-year-old said. "She can never take me back."

"And what would Daddy do if some icky people tried to get in our house?"

"You would *kill* 'em!" Stephanie shouted, with the sureness that comes from an oft-recited lesson.

In a singsong voice Samantha piped up, "And we'll never, ever see mean David."

"That's right, honey," Craig said, and he wiped some catsup from the little girl's mouth.

A single parent's life is a demanding one, and Craig's is no exception. To spend more time with his girls he has put off looking for full-time work. Jobs in Muskegon are hard to come by, in any case, with the city's reported unemployment rate hovering at 12 percent. Craig pays the bills with free-lance auto repairs, irregular work for his father's Bayview Detective Agency (a direct outgrowth of the ordeal), and some help from his family and church. When his nerves "get a little ragged," he waits for the girls' nap time, carefully locks the front and back doors, and joins a friend for a game of pool on the basement table. An hour later he is at peace again, ready for whatever comes.

"You get a little harried sometimes, but you know it's always worth it," he said the other day. "I wouldn't trade my life for anybody's."

When the sledding gets toughest, Craig remembers the magical calm that blessed him at the West German border, when he and Frank Corbin sat in the parking lot with the most dubious of plans—when the odds were slim to none that they would get through safely.

"I've always been a firm believer in God," Craig said. "But

I think now, more than ever, that I have a guardian angel. There was something there when we crossed that border, and it wasn't just my adrenaline running. It was like God put his hand on my shoulder and said, 'Hey, you're all right. You're doing the right thing. I'm here.' "

Despite our constant worries, Craig and I are among the lucky ones. The great majority of left-behind parents are not so fortunate. They spend their days in empty houses, with memories and old photographs for company, with dusty toys and rusting swing sets. They generally lack the resources or the opportunity for a counterabduction—and when they try to regain their children legally, through another country's courts, they are typically rebuffed.

In Iran I lived in a society that gave me no standing before its courts. A woman and her children were owned by her husband; it was as simple as that. Even if I'd been able to persuade Moody to divorce me (an unlikely development), he would have been granted custody of Mahtob.

Although Islamic law places children with their mother until they reach the age of seven, everyone I questioned in Tehran said I would be sure to lose in court there. There were too many strikes against me—my non-Muslim status and, even more damning, my U.S. citizenship. I believed I had no chance for a legal victory against a native Iranian doctor (to this day, Christy Khan is the only Western woman I know who has won permission through an Islamic court to take her children out of a predominantly Islamic country).

When a man is the left-behind parent, he may encounter yet another obstacle, whether at home or abroad—the perceived bias against fathers in custody battles. One of every five international parental abductors is a mother—which means that one of every five left-behind victims is a father. Stories like those of Craig DeMarr and Ramez Shteih illustrate that our cause is neither maternal nor paternal, but *parental*. It also reminds us that gender alone cannot determine which parent is best suited for custody—and that a child's right to stability and security must come first.

161

7

Hoping, Praying

After numerous consultations, Chris Korest, Arnie, and I realized that no region, no state, no socioeconomic class was immune to international parental abduction. The problem was much bigger and closer than most had suspected. To promote greater awareness on this subject Chris suggested a public workshop, with special invitations going to judges and attorneys.

Following her emotions as a woman and a mother, Lori Hansen Riegle, the U.S. senator's wife, was drawn into our circle of supporters. She came to Lansing, where our first workshop was staged, on a snowy night in November 1990.

Representatives came from the National Center for Missing and Exploited Children and the State Department. In addition to these professionals, two left-behind mothers—Christy Khan and Jessie Pars—shared the podium.

I talked about my experience, and Jessie Pars, a woman from Philadelphia, told how she had convinced her husband to bring their two children to Turkey from Iran for a visit, where she was able to recover them. Then Christy Khan spoke of her two sons, who at the time were still in Pakistan.

There were few dry eyes in the audience at this point. The audience was clearly moved to discover that this problem was so common in our own area. We had a new group of willing supporters.

We met again in August 1991, when Mrs. Riegle and One

World : For Children (the organization Arnie and I had co-founded to respond to the issue of international parental child abduction) co-sponsored a fund raiser for Christy, who had incurred heavy expenses in retrieving her children earlier that year. Having been so close to the case, I found it tremendously rewarding to see mother and children together again, this time—we hoped—for good.

In my brief remarks that evening I felt compelled to remind Christy's well-wishers that her case was regrettably atypical. "Christy and I are the lucky ones—we have our children," I said. "But most of these cases do not have a happy ending."

In a distressingly large majority, in fact, the left-behind parents remain just that. Some can't even locate their kidnapped children, or are denied permission to enter the abductor's country. Others are rejected by the country's court system because of national or religious differences. A few manage to gain custody, but then are blocked from leaving the country; they pay for their parenthood with their freedom.

As I made my brief speech, my eyes fell upon another victimized parent. Mariann Saieed, I told my audience, had returned just the week before from Iraq—leaving her two children behind with the father who had abducted them. "After being promised that she could bring her son home," I continued, "he had his bags packed—and then her husband changed his mind again and said no."

Mariann had shown great bravery in coming that night—to join all the well-wishers in watching Christy's sons cavorting while her own children remained so far away.

For Mariann Saieed, the Ohio antique show was a disappointment. She usually fared well with her collection of pre-1970 games, toys, dolls, and books. "You can buy your childhood back from me," went her motto, and many did. But not so on this balmy Saturday in June 1990. By 7 P.M. Mariann was restless. She called home to her apartment in suburban Detroit, where she'd left her husband Khalid with their eight-year-old son and four-year-old daughter the day before.

No one answered the phone. In another family that might have implied some harmless diversion—a trip for ice cream, perhaps, or a movie. But for Mariann the rhythmic ringing signaled a calamity. Khalid never took the children *anywhere*, especially not at night.

As she replaced the phone on its hook, she'd later recall, "I knew in my heart he had taken them to Iraq."

Mariann kept calling on the hour, and with each unsuccessful try her anxiety swelled. It would be no great surprise if Khalid were to leave her without warning; he'd left half a dozen times over the past ten years, and recently he'd longed to return to Iraq, his homeland. Mariann had always imagined that he'd go solo—the same way he'd traveled before, the way he lived his life. Until now she'd never dreamed that he might take the children along with him.

Mariann started her long drive home the next day, forcing herself to take it slow, to fend off the panic that might cause her to have an accident. She couldn't help thinking about her husband's recent suspicious behavior. Khalid had always resented her passion for antiques, and in particular her business trips. The first time she stayed overnight in Ohio, he refused to accept her collect call. The second time he sulked for a full week after she came back. Before this third trip he'd been uncharacteristically supportive, saying "Go, please go. And if you're too tired, why don't you stay over till Monday?"

When Mariann arrived at their apartment that evening, she found everything just as she'd left it—except for an empty suitcase box on the living room floor. She kicked the box in frustration: "That's when I knew for *sure* he had gone." On the dining room table she found a note, scribbled on a scrap of computer paper: "We are on vacation. We'll see you when we get back."

None of the children's clothes or toys was missing. Khalid had gone all out in his attempt to "throw me off as long as he could," Mariann concluded, "so that he could get the kids settled in before I had any chance to contact him." As the credit card bills rolled in over the next month—Khalid had secretly piled up

164

$30,000 in purchases, cash advances, and bank loans—it became clear he'd bought the children new clothes the day before they left.

Mariann's fears were confirmed when she pored through a mound of papers that Khalid had left behind in a garbage bag and pieced together his itinerary from flight numbers and reservation codes. She eventually traced his route: a drive to Toronto, followed by flights to London, Vienna, and finally Baghdad.

After a sleepless night Mariann called the juvenile division of her local police department, who referred her to the National Center for Missing and Exploited Children. "They took my name and address," she recalled, "and said they'd send me a book, and directed me to the State Department." She called the Office of Citizens Consular Services and received "a big, long booklet from them about international parental abductions, which basically tells you there's nothing they can do."

The worst, of course, was yet to come. Two months after the kidnapping Iraq invaded Kuwait. Five months later her children's new home was bombed relentlessly by her own nation. It would be a very long time before Mariann could establish whether Adam and Adora had survived.

Mariann and Khalid met as students at a community college near Detroit in 1980 and were married six months later. She was twenty; he was twenty-three. Khalid, who'd come to the U.S. two years before for an engineering degree, was a man without apparent vices; he didn't smoke, or drink, or gamble. Aloof and ambitious, he would routinely log fifteen-hour days in the campus library.

Mariann had just concluded a relationship with a more tumultuous young man, and Khalid's undemanding ways seemed a relief by comparison. "I have no idea what attracted me to him," Mariann said. She is a tall, strong-featured woman with green eyes and shoulder-length brown hair; her voice is melodic and animated in conversation. "I just remember the first time that I saw him, it was something instant. I knew right away. I said, 'He's the one for me.' "

The first serious trouble came six months into their mar-

165

riage, when Khalid returned from a six-week visit to Iraq, and Mariann informed him that she was pregnant with Adam. Khalid was furious. He accused Mariann of violating their "agreement" to delay having children for at least five years, until he'd finished his schooling. "You did this on purpose," he said heatedly. "You've ruined my life." Shortly after that Khalid moved into his own apartment, leaving Mariann without a car or enough money to pay her bills. "There were days when I had nothing to eat, or when the only thing I ate was a candy bar," she said.

Three weeks before Adam was born, Khalid moved to Texas to attend school. After he returned to Mariann several months later, he seemed uninterested in his baby; he never bathed or changed Adam, nor so much as fed him a single meal. All household chores fell upon Mariann, who had also taken a full-time job as a mail carrier. "I took Adam to the sitter's, picked him up after work, took care of everything at home, and paid the bills while Khalid went to school," Mariann recounted. Her stress was compounded by the fact that she could "never trust him again," especially after Khalid went AWOL a second time when Adam was eighteen months old.

During that second separation Mariann's mother expressed concern that Khalid might someday leave the country and take Adam with him. To reassure her Mariann said, "There's no way—he would never do that."

The family dynamics changed after Adora came into the picture. When her daughter was born, Mariann had a disturbing premonition: "I *knew* there was going to be big trouble down the line."

Khalid was, if anything, more irate about the second pregnancy; with two children he realized he'd have to cut short his work toward a master's degree and start to earn some money. An expert at the silent treatment, he stopped speaking to Mariann for months. In May of 1986, when Adora was three months old, he disappeared yet again, this time to enroll in a college in California.

Between her job and her children's chronic illnesses—both had developed asthma—Mariann had reached her limit. Over the phone she gave Khalid an ultimatum: "If you don't get back here soon, you're not going to have a family to come home to." Khalid came back and found work with an electronics firm called Perceptron. Mariann quit her job with the post office. For the next three years she was to be a full-time, stay-at-home mom.

The family still had problems. During their harshest arguments Khalid and Mariann would threaten to leave one another. The word "divorce" had surfaced more than once, though Mariann doubted she could ever muster the courage to follow through with it. Her premonition about Adora was borne out; as soon as their daughter was out of diapers, Khalid began to reveal an extreme puritanical streak. He was distressed by stories of sexual activity and drug use among teenage girls in the United States. When Adora turned three, he'd get upset when she wore a bathing suit or anything else that bared her midriff. When the family was out together, he'd make a scene out of the most innocent circumstances.

"Adora is a very open, gregarious girl," Mariann related. "From the time she could talk, she'd talk to anybody. When she was a year and a half old, she'd go up to strangers in the grocery store and start talking to them: 'Hi, how are you?'

"Once we went to a restaurant, and she started talking to the busboy—he was a kid, not even eighteen. Khalid got very angry and told her, 'Turn around and be quiet!' And I could tell by the tone of his voice exactly what he was thinking—he didn't want her talking to a strange man. He gave her this look—which she, of course, never understood. But I did."

Khalid's involvement with his homeland seemed minimal, aside from monthly calls to his family. He hadn't seen them since 1980. Though a Muslim, he was neither devout nor observant, and he rarely spoke to Mariann about the culture in which he'd been raised. By 1988, as the Iran-Iraq war began to wind down, he occasionally pressed Mariann to move to Iraq— "for a year," he'd say, to allow the children to get to know his family, to see if life might be easier there.

Mariann knew that Khalid felt "stuck" in the States, without friends or extended family. She was adamant in rejecting the

167

move. She and Khalid had long before agreed that they would raise their children in America, and what if they were to arrive in Iraq and he decided to prevent her and the kids from returning? She simply didn't trust him enough.

"I kept encouraging him to go, or to get some of his relatives to come here for a visit. His brother almost did, but he backed out at the last minute, and I think that was the last straw that made Khalid decide to go ahead. He wouldn't normally show any emotion, but I could tell he felt really bad that his brother wasn't coming."

In March of 1990 Perceptron laid Khalid off. The loss of his job cut another tie in a life that already had little stability.

In retrospect, as Mariann sifted through her husband's papers and phone bills (most of them directed to post office boxes), she realized that Khalid had been planning the act for at least two years—from the first time he'd proposed the trip and she had turned him down. He'd studied articles on international abductions at the local library. He'd obtained work-permit papers from the Iraqi Embassy in 1988. Khalid waited until just before he left, however, to make the final, critical preparation: adding the two children to his Iraqi passport.

"The last time he came back, when Adora was little, he told me several times: 'I'm never going to leave the children again,'" Mariann said. "That was his firm state of mind. No matter what happened, or whom he hurt, he wasn't going to leave the kids. In his mind he's done the right thing now."

That was all hindsight. "Looking back on it, I see the signs," she said. "But anyone who knew him never thought he would take the kids."

The loss of her children plunged Mariann into a state of shock and grief for months. "People would say they couldn't imagine how difficult it was, and I'd tell them, 'You wouldn't *want* to imagine how I feel. Because if you imagined that, it would just tear you up so much inside.' Because this is the absolute worst thing you can go through.

"It was like you feel after you find out the IRS is going to audit your taxes, or just before your car crashes—that feeling in the pit of your stomach that something terrible is going to happen. And I felt that way every day."

Mariann began vomiting after every meal she ate. She couldn't leave her apartment without crying. She'd drive along for a bit of fresh air, and some memory of Adora—who'd always accompanied her in the car—would bring about uncontrollable weeping. She'd have to go home, as she could barely see the road.

At other times Mariann would no sooner get out than she'd be seized by the irrational conviction that Khalid and the children had returned to the apartment. "I'd think, what if they came back and I'm not there? So I'd race back home, and of course they weren't there."

She lost interest in her antiques and canceled buying trips. Mariann knew she needed a job—Khalid had emptied their small savings account—but couldn't begin to pull herself together for an interview. A life that had revolved around children was now empty at its core. She reached the point where Lee Ballas, her best friend, would call her each morning to make sure she got up.

"Lee would say, 'What are you going to do today?' And I'd say, 'Nothing.' And she'd say, 'No, you're not going to do nothing, you're going to do this. First you call the State Department, then you take a shower and get dressed. Then you go to your post office box [which Mariann kept for her business], and then you come over here and we'll decide what to do for the rest of the day.'"

At least once a day Mariann tried to reach her children by phoning the home of Khalid's brother in Mosul, a large, sprawling city in northern Iraq. It was clear that Khalid was avoiding her. Most of the time no one would answer the phone; occasionally a child would answer before the call was cut off. Mariann also phoned her State Department caseworker, Dawn McGlynn, as often as she could afford, but McGlynn was having no more luck.

Finally, on July 31, 1990, with the active cooperation of Iraqi officials, a nervous Khalid was persuaded to attend a meeting with U.S. Embassy representatives in Baghdad. Six weeks after the abduction Mariann had some word: her children were all right.

Although no law or power could compel Khalid to return Adam and Adora, Mariann had reason to be encouraged. Joe Wilson, the embassy's chargé d'affaires and the second-ranking officer after Ambassador April Glaspie, had taken a personal interest and seemed dedicated to doing whatever he could to help.

Two days later, on August 2, Iraq invaded Kuwait, and Wilson, among others, was attending to other problems. Mariann felt even more disconnected than before, as she could no longer get a phone call through to Mosul: "I thought, *it couldn't get any worse*—and, of course, it did." Stunned, she sat in her apartment and watched Cable News Network (CNN), her staple activity for the next six months.

As word got out about her plight, the Detroit news media, and then CNN itself, came calling. At first Mariann felt reticent, but Lee prodded her to cooperate: "You need help, Mariann, and maybe there's somebody out there who will hear your story and be able to help you."

The CNN exposure would indeed prove helpful. Besides putting Mariann in touch with other women in similar situations, it gave her a contact at the network. When CNN cut off one of Saddam Hussein's anti-American speeches, Mariann—starved for news of any kind—called their office in Atlanta to protest: "We want to hear *whatever's* being said, and decide for ourselves."

Joe Wilson hadn't forgotten her. In September, during a trip to Mosul, Khalid's hometown, he tried to reestablish contact with the man on his own. "It wasn't something he had to do—he'd never gotten involved in a case before—but he looked at it as a humanitarian mission," Mariann explained. Khalid, though impressed with Wilson's manner and high station, refused to meet with him except through "official" Iraqi channels—an impossible demand at the time.

Later that month came a breakthrough. Khalid wanted to

register the children in school in Mosul, but needed copies of their birth certificates authorized by the State Department. Wilson struck a deal: the embassy would provide the authorized copies if Khalid agreed to call Mariann.

A few days later Mariann picked up the phone to hear Wilson's voice: "I have your husband here and he wants to talk to you." Khalid's tone was maddeningly casual—"Hi, how are you?"—but Mariann reined in her anger. The State Department had given her strict advice: "Be as nice as you can be, and keep the conversation open. If you antagonize him, he won't call again."

After learning that the children were healthy and in school, Mariann asked if she could join them in Mosul. "Of course," Khalid replied; that was what he'd wanted all along. They agreed that Mariann would try to obtain a visa through the Iraqi Embassy in Washington, then still in operation, and that Khalid would help on his end if she hit a snag.

Now Mariann had a purpose in life. To finance her trip she sold all her belongings, then auctioned her antiques for $5,000. She moved out of her apartment and in with her brother and sister-in-law, Tom and Mary Ann Smith. She bought her airline tickets to Baghdad, but in October her plans were dashed. The Iraqi Embassy informed her that it needed "a formal invitation from Baghdad" before it could issue a visa. She later found out that, because of the crisis, no visas could be approved without the authorization of an Iraqi citizen—in her case, her husband.

Khalid got through to Mariann in late October from the U.S. Embassy in Baghdad and assured her he would "work on it from here. Just wait for me to call again, and get ready to come."

So she waited . . . and waited . . . but the weeks crawled by, and there was no word. As the United States geared up for war and President Bush's deadline for an Iraqi withdrawal loomed, Mariann sank to a new psychological low. "Christmas was coming, and there were TV commercials with kids on all day long, about how wonderful the season was. I don't do too well around holidays anyway, and I felt so terrible that I didn't know how much longer I'd be able to take it."

At last, on December 21, Khalid called again, with good news: her visa had been approved. Mariann asked if their children were there, and Khalid said that Adam had just gone out to play. "And I started screaming 'Go get him! Please, please, go get him!' I hadn't talked to either of the kids since they left—it had been six months. Adam came back to the phone and just said, 'Hi, Mommy.' And I started crying. He said he was fine and Adora was fine—I could hear his dad telling him what to say in the background—and that he wasn't having any problems with his asthma, and that he loved me and missed me, and wanted me to come there as soon as I could. I got to talk to him for ten minutes before we were cut off."

On December 25, at three in the morning, Mariann was awakened by a call from an Iraqi consular official in Baghdad. "Merry Christmas," the man said. "We're giving you your visa." As he recited a telex number for her to use in Washington, Mariann stared at the phone and thought "this must be a joke."

In fact it was quite real—but the sands of Mariann's reality were constantly shifting. She bought a ticket for the next available flight to Amman, Jordan, on January 12, but she had so little money left that she feared she might be stranded there, five hundred miles short of Baghdad. The Amman-Baghdad leg of her trip had to be reserved and purchased in Jordan, as no one in the U.S. was issuing plane tickets into Iraq. And she knew she was cutting her schedule perilously close to President Bush's January 15 deadline for Hussein and his troops to withdraw from Kuwait.

On the day Mariann was scheduled to leave for Jordan, the U.S. closed its embassy in Baghdad. There was no point in going now; all commercial air traffic into Iraq was suspended. Khalid, who was calling more frequently now, told Mariann, "You can wait until the war is over—it's going to be over in a couple of weeks, anyway. Don't worry, the kids are in the safest place they can be." Mariann couldn't believe what she was hearing—*He's telling me they're safe, and they're in a war zone.*

What Khalid didn't tell her was that Adam and Adora, with about fifty of his relatives, had moved to a family farm outside Mosul for the duration of the war, not that the truth would have

172

been all that reassuring. For forty-three days the farm lacked electricity, running water, or kerosene for light and heat—while winter temperatures dropped into the forties.

As she sat glued by the nineteen-inch Hitachi television in her bedroom, Mariann felt more helpless than ever. With diplomatic relations severed, there was nothing any official could do—not even Joe Wilson, who'd been forced to leave Baghdad with the rest. Mariann could only watch the flickering screen and wait. She slept fitfully, a few hours a night at best.

Early in the evening of January 16, Mariann awoke and turned on the TV, which she'd switched off just half an hour before. She was greeted by the sights and sounds of the first Allied bombing raid on Baghdad. She went to her friend Lee's house, and the two of them stayed up watching all night. From that point on Mariann tried to stay within earshot of an operating television twenty-four hours a day.

"I *had* to watch everything," Mariann said. "I had no choice. Because if I didn't watch it, my imagination just went wild, and I would start to think about the kids and everything terrible that might be happening to them."

With all contact from Khalid severed, Mariann determined to find out everything she could about Iraq—although, as she discovered, the body of available knowledge was limited. Despite the fact that suburban Detroit had the largest Arab-American population in the United States, the Detroit Public Library offered no books about Iraq written since 1972, before Saddam Hussein came to power. Mariann did find a detailed map there, which she photocopied and posted on a bulletin board in her bedroom, along with copies of newspaper and magazine articles. "I made my own information center," she said, "so I could keep track of what was going on."

There was little information anywhere about Mosul, though it was the third-largest city in Iraq—a vacuum that Mariann would find even more unnerving later that spring, when the Kurdish rebellion unfolded within fifty miles of where her children resided. One day, while flipping through the television channels, she came across a syndicated Christian Science Monitor program about the nearby Nineveh ruins. There she caught

173

her first glimpse of Mosul: a sprawl of low-slung cement buildings on the Tigris River, with no discernible downtown or city center. "It looks," she told Lee, "like your basic ancient civilization." Mariann felt better, more connected with her children; though she couldn't hold them or even talk to them, she could now begin to picture their daily lives.

Mariann's typical day was disheartening at best, desperate at worst. When Iraq sent SCUD missiles into Israel, she worried that Israel might respond with an even more indiscriminate attack on Iraq's civilian population—or the opening rounds of World War III. Adam's ninth birthday passed on January 30, and still the bombs rained down. Adora's fifth birthday fell on February 24—the day the ground war began.

"That was probably my worst day," Mariann recalled. "I had no idea if they were safe, if they were alive, if they were bombed. I drove around in a daze, just to find something to do. I cried so hard the entire day, and all night long."

By March Mariann's "temporary" stay at her brother's house had stretched to half a year. She had no job, no children, no home of her own. To make matters worse she felt estranged from her country, repulsed by all the flags and yellow ribbons. While no fan of Saddam, Mariann saw herself "on the Iraqi side, because my kids were in Iraq. I felt very, very alone during the war. Everybody was saying how right it was, and I'm thinking 'What if my kids are killed by these American bombs?' "

Ever since the abduction, Mariann's life had consisted of one crisis after the next: the Iraqi invasion, her visa problems, her money woes, the bombing, the ground war, the civil fighting between Iraqi troops and Kurdish guerrillas. Several times each day, whenever CNN showed its latest footage of the war's devastation, Mariann feared that she'd see her children's broken bodies carried out of some rubble. It reached the point where she confessed to Lee "that I wished my kids were dead instead of over there. I felt terrible feeling that way. But I said, 'If they were dead, at least I could grieve, and eventually go on. As long as I don't know how they are, I'm grieving with no end.' "

Even as Mariann despaired for the future, there were other, more positive developments that kept her afloat. The first of these occurred back in November 1990, when Mariann attended the seminar on international parental child abductions, sponsored by Senator Riegle's office. As she listened to the speakers, she became aware that the problem was far more common than she'd thought. She was most impressed by Christy Khan, who stressed the importance of reaching out to the local Muslim community for support.

It had been an especially tough day for Mariann, and she cried most of the way through Christy's presentation. Afterward Christy approached her and said, "I wanted to come out there and just hug you, and to say to heck with this speech." They exchanged phone numbers, and a week or so later Christy took Mariann to see Imam Mardini, the Detroit-area Muslim leader, with whom Christy had taken her Islamic vows.

"I was afraid to go by myself; I'd never talked to an *imam* before," Mariann said. "But he was very nice, real down to earth, and the most peaceful man you could ever meet." The *imam* had his own problems; anti-Arab sentiment in the area was cresting, and his Muslim center had just been broken into for the second time. He took time to hear Mariann out and said he would try to contact some people in Iraq on her behalf. He stressed that Khalid's actions were "not the Islamic way," that their culture valued a stable family life above all.

In January CNN drove Mariann to my home, to conduct a joint interview. Mariann had read *Not Without My Daughter* shortly after the abduction, skimming over some details for her emotional self-protection. "When I met Betty, I said I felt like I already knew her. Everybody put us together because our stories were kind of similar; everybody always confuses Iraq with Iran, anyway. When I started doing the local news programs, every single one of them said, 'Do you know about Betty Mahmoody?' "

Mariann noted that both Christy and I tried to emphasize the positive in the midst of difficult times. I had demonstrated the value of trusting my husband's compatriots, the friends who had helped me and Mahtob escape. I never stereotyped Iranians nor tried to deny Mahtob's heritage.

"All that had a big influence on the way I dealt with the

175

whole problem," Mariann explained. "Because you can go any number of different ways. You can get angry and fight, or you can get real nasty and vicious, or you can be complacent. When Khalid first took my kids, I was as angry as anybody, and I could have said a lot of things about him to the media. But I held back because of people like Betty and Christy, who kept telling me that lashing out wouldn't get my kids back."

I tried to encourage Mariann at that meeting with CNN. When the reporter asked me whether I had any advice for her, I replied, "If it were Mahtob over there, I would go." That support spurred Mariann onward—as did the January world premiere of *Not Without My Daughter*, both in its happy ending and its frightening depiction of the status of girls in fundamentalist Iran.

"The thing that hit me the most is when they said that girls in some parts of Iran are ready for marriage between the ages of nine and ten—that completely sucked the wind out of me. I kept thinking about *my* daughter, and I was very afraid, because I didn't know who was raising Adora, or what ideas they had. I later found out that they didn't do that in Iraq, but I had to go over there and see for myself." As tough as it was to bottle her anger, it was harder still for Mariann to make ties with the Iraqi-American community: "They were the last people I ever wanted to see, because they just reminded me of Khalid." In March 1991, after Operation Desert Storm had ended, after she could no longer watch the Iraqi children on CNN begging soldiers for food, Mariann told herself, "I have to try something—I just can't sit here any more, waiting every day to hear." When she saw a TV news report about a Detroit-area Iraqi-American group called Victims of War (VOW), which was raising money for food and medicine, she called to volunteer her help.

The group was shorthanded, Mariann was told, because three of their volunteers had recently left for Iraq, taking supplies and letters from relatives in the States. Could she answer the phone in the office?

At first Mariann stopped in once or twice a week, but by April she found herself at the phones Monday through Friday, seven hours a day. The demand for information was enormous, and Mariann felt good to be at the center of things, privy to the latest reports about conditions inside Iraq. Nonetheless, the work had its drawbacks. Though they could also speak English, everyone else in the office spoke Arabic to one another (or Chaldean, a dialect spoken by Iraqi Catholics), and Mariann felt left out. "But I remembered Betty and Christy's advice, and I forced myself to show up each morning."

With time Mariann experienced something remarkable: a deepening empathy, despite the language barrier. Every person she met at VOW agreed that Khalid had been wrong to take their children, and it was soon apparent that Mariann and her office mates had much in common: relatives in distress; a sense of horror at what the bombing had wrought; and a reluctance to voice their protests against the recently concluded war for fear they would be viewed as less than loyal Americans.

As the weeks passed, Mariann's volunteer work became a source of mutual revelation. When the Iraqis realized that Mariann bore no hostility toward their people, they accepted her as one of them; when she stopped stereotyping them as so many Khalids, she was ready to meet them halfway.

In one conversation Wala Kachaco, a woman who worked across the hall from VOW for the Chaldean Federation, told her, "During the war, if I would have seen you as an American, I would just as soon have run you off the road." To which Mariann replied, " 'You know, before the war, I felt the same way about Arabs.' But we got over that, and got to know each other, and we all became really good friends."

One of her best friends was the group's vice-president, Shakir Al-Khafaji, a quiet, tireless architect who arranged and oversaw VOW's trips to Iraq. In May Mariann had received a letter from Khalid, postmarked in March, which informed her that he and the kids had survived the war in good health. It wasn't enough, not nearly enough. She needed to *be* with her children, and she felt prepared to live the rest of her life in Iraq if that is what it would take. She pleaded with Shakir to help her get into the country, and he readily agreed: "I'll get you there, no problem." She was added to a delegation set to depart in late June.

177

A State Department attorney did her best to discourage her: "You can't go to Iraq, you've got to be crazy to go there. And if you get there *and* you get out, I will fall out of my chair."

After that Mariann stopped consulting with the State Department. "I couldn't take anything negative," she said. "It was hard enough to decide to go. I had no idea whether they were targeting Americans over there, or whether my husband had changed his mind about my coming, or whether I'd be held there, like Betty—or even whether I'd be able to see my children. If I had listened to negative people, I would not have gone."

On March 26 Christy Khan returned to the U.S. after being granted custody of her two sons in the Pakistani courts. It *could* be done, Mariann thought, no matter what the State Department lawyers said.

Still, Mariann waged a daily struggle with her fears and uncertainties. "The news media made it look like a fairy tale—that this mother loved her kids so much that she was willing to risk everything and go to live in Iraq. It wasn't like that at all. I had to be pushed in a lot of ways to do this—and a lot of it was from the media coverage. I'd said in the beginning that I wanted to go, and now that I had the chance, I'd *better* go, because that's what everyone expected.

"For a whole year I really had no idea what to do, or if what I was doing was right. That was really hard for me, because I grew up in a family that was very organized, very planned. It wasn't a fairy-tale ending—it was a nightmare, all the way through."

Shakir was as good as his word. Not only did he get Mariann a visa under the auspices of the Iraqi Red Crescent, a chapter of the International Red Cross, but he raised $300 to help pay her expenses during a five-day layover in Amman. After a seventeen-hour bus ride, including a four-hour delay at the Jordanian border checkpoint, the VOW group reached Baghdad on Monday, July 1. Tuesday Mariann set about her task: locating her family. Her only lead was a Baghdad rooming house that Khalid had told her he frequented on business trips. The clerk recognized Khalid's name and promised to try to get a message to him in Mosul.

During this errand, and in comparing notes with other

members of the VOW delegation, Mariann began to appreciate the impact of Desert Storm upon Iraq's capital city. Four of the five bridges across the Tigris River were still out, clogging traffic in the overwhelming heat. Every major building around her hotel, the famous Al Rashid from which CNN had broadcast, had been bombed. Countless homes had been wrecked as well—including an entire neighborhood that was destroyed when a bomb missed a nearby bridge. According to Shakir, five hundred people were killed in that one strike alone. Several hospitals along the river had met a similar fate; the shambles of former shops and restaurants were everywhere.

Late that evening Mariann joined her friends at a downtown restaurant, which was candlelit because of a power outage. It was after eleven when a man approached their table and asked for her by name. Speaking in Arabic, the mysterious messenger told her, "We got hold of your husband, and he's coming down tomorrow with the kids to pick you up." The message she'd left at the rooming house evidently had gotten through. Mariann was overcome by the thought of how close she was to seeing her children. She started to cry, and her companions—even the Iraqi men, who rarely show such emotion in public—wiped their eyes as well.

At 10 A.M. Wednesday Mariann sat anxiously waiting in the mammoth lobby of the Al Rashid Hotel. Suddenly she turned . . . to find her family right behind her. She clutched her children to her for the first time in a year. The buzzing lobby hushed, with all eyes drawn to the reunion. Adora, a stunning little girl with a heart-shaped face and thick black hair, seemed slightly uncertain, but readily returned her mother's hug. Adam, a thin boy with a sweet smile—now filled in with new adult teeth—stared at Mariann and grinned.

Mariann was shocked at how the children had changed. While both of them were well dressed and groomed, the normally high-spirited Adam seemed subdued. Adora, meanwhile, had forgotten nearly all her English and responded to Mariann's emotional questioning—"How are you? How *are* you?"—with a quizzical stare.

"She's not speaking English," Khalid explained apologetically. "I tried to speak English to her, but everyone else speaks Arabic."

"Well, that will change now that I'm here," Mariann said firmly. She wasn't pleased, and she hadn't forgotten her anger toward Khalid, but she couldn't deny that she was happy to see him. He was a familiar face in this new world, a link to home and her past. It wasn't clear where the two of them stood—Khalid had never been demonstrative, and Mariann didn't expect him to change now—but she dared hope that their marriage might have a new beginning.

"If I'd wanted to, I could have sent you divorce papers in the mail, and you would never have seen the children again," he told her early on. "But I didn't want to do it like that. I know that they need you, but I wanted you to come here."

After the children played in Mariann's hotel room while Khalid took a nap, the four of them squeezed into a Toyota Corolla with Mariann's luggage and Khalid's brother and niece, who'd come along for the occasion. Adora, who had grown four inches and weighed at least fifty pounds, perched on Mariann's lap, where she stayed sleeping for the rest of the trip.

Four hours of parched and desolate road later they arrived in Mosul. Mariann's first impressions were less than positive. Unlike Baghdad, the city was devoid of greenery; any plant life had burned off after the spring rains passed months before. While everyone had told her that Mosul, due to its higher elevation and more northerly latitude, was cooler than Baghdad, Mariann now understood what they meant; when Baghdad melted in 115 degrees, Mosul might swelter at 100. She thought of the black slacks and blouses she had packed and cringed.

As Khalid approached their rented house, the neighborhood was pitch dark, except for a few scattered homes lit by private generators. "Oh, damn," Khalid muttered, "the electricity is out." He drove up to a steel gate and stopped. Mariann passed through to a small, tile-covered patio behind the cement house, which Khalid and the children had been sharing with his mother, and was warmly greeted by a welcoming party of ten or twelve people. Mariann sat on a mattress pad and tried to acclimate herself by the dim light of a kerosene lamp. Ten minutes later Khalid rose and said, "I'll be back in a few minutes." He was gone for an hour and a half—leaving his wife to field a rush of questions in Arabic, too fast for Adam to translate. He's running out on me again, Mariann thought glumly.

Hot and exhausted, she asked Adam to direct her to a bathroom. "Mom," Adam said, as they used the lamp to guide themselves into the cement house, "the bathrooms aren't like they are at home."

"What do you mean?" Mariann asked.

"They're not like they are at home," Adam repeated.

Nothing could have prepared Mariann for what greeted her: a foul-smelling hole in the ground, lacking even the flush system that was standard for Mosul's middle class. She stumbled out without using it.

When Khalid finally returned, Mariann could contain her rage no longer. She told her husband to take her inside, and then she exploded: "I can't believe you can live like this! How can you go from our house in Michigan, where you complained that I didn't dust enough, to this?"

Khalid was crying. This was not how he'd imagined their first night back together. He knew the house wasn't much; he'd been looking for something better for the past month, but money was short. The United Nations embargo had ruined his plans to enter the import-export business. The Toyota was borrowed; he couldn't afford to own a car. In better times his brothers and sisters had helped him, but they too had been devastated by the last ten years of war—first with Iran, then the Gulf War. Hardpressed to make a living, Khalid had spent all his time trying to revive a video store that he'd bought for next to nothing.

Mariann awoke the next morning under a hazy, cloudless sky that would never change, and got her first real look at Mosul. In contrast to Baghdad, the city had sustained relatively light damage from the U.S. air attacks, although a bomb had demolished a house down the street from Khalid's brother. One of Khalid's young nieces, watching the night flashes with several other children, had been wounded by shrapnel.

Even after the fighting had ceased, the war continued to disrupt almost every aspect of Mosul life. The city's electrical system would go out one to three times a day, for up to six hours at a stretch. Public water supplies would also be shut off daily, from three to five hours—a special torture in the summer heat. On one memorable occasion, an unusually long power outage was followed immediately by a water cut-off that lasted into the night. As a result the hydraulic air conditioners were disabled all day and all night.

"We washed the patio off with cold water, and then lay mattress pads down there for the kids," Mariann recounted. "There were probably 150 kids on the block, and it was pitch black, and all the babies were scared and wailing—it was the most miserable sound you ever heard."

The war had also suspended another vital municipal service: the draining of the reservoirs underneath people's bathrooms. As a result sewage overflowed into the streets and flooded some of them: a putrid, green current that pedestrians did their best to jump over.

For Mariann there was also a smothering sense of isolation. Her companions from VOW were all based in Baghdad. The mails were almost useless, and Iraq's telecommunications grid had been wrecked; there was no way for Mariann to reach her family in the United States. The TV news, of course, was all in Arabic. "I was suffering from CNN withdrawal," Mariann said. The radio stations were noteworthy only for their periodic offerings, in various arrangements, of Frank Sinatra's "My Way"—Saddam Hussein's favorite song. Western newspapers were unavailable; there was no way for Mariann to assess the constant rumors that the war might resume.

Her husband's work schedule didn't help matters. Khalid was no less driven in business than he had been in school. He'd go to the video store by 8 A.M., come home for a two-hour lunch break during the inevitable midday power outage, then return to work till 10:30 at night. When he quit for the night, he was tired and cranky, and as close-mouthed as ever. He followed this routine seven days a week; Khalid was no more religious now than he'd been in the U.S., and didn't observe the Muslim sabbath.

In a sense, Mariann thought ruefully, their family life in Mosul all too closely resembled the setup she'd come to hate in the States.

On Mariann's third day in Mosul, Khalid told her he'd return with food at lunchtime. The afternoon came and went, and no Khalid. The only food in the house was some frozen pita bread and grape leaves, which the children rejected. Mariann knew that Khalid never cooked and that Adam and Adora had been eating elsewhere before her arrival—generally at the home of Sageta, Khalid's sister-in-law. She had no idea where Sageta lived, and she'd been warned against walking in the city on her own, anyhow. The war had produced a rising criminal element, and Mariann's conspicuous Western dress—though covering was optional in Iraq, she saw only one other woman wear slacks there—might have drawn unwelcome attention.

"We all lay on the bed," Mariann said. "None of us had eaten anything all day. The kids were crying, and I was crying, and we fell asleep." After Khalid came home late that night and Mariann took him to task, he apologized and promised to correct the problem. He never did stock the house with food, but his relatives—ten or fifteen of them at a time—began visiting every day, from early morning till midnight. Meal preparations were still erratic; there was no real planning, and rationing left everyone short of rice and flour by the end of the month. At least Adam and Adora weren't crying from hunger.

For Mariann, however, the family's attention became too much of a good thing. With two hundred relatives within a radius of five miles, she and Khalid rarely had a minute alone together. "We need some time for just you, me, and the kids, to get to know each other again," she told him.

"I don't invite them over," Khalid replied, "but you can't tell them not to come, because that would be rude."

The exception was Sageta, who was unfailingly considerate and limited her visits to an hour. She was also the only one of Khalid's relatives who spoke English. Sageta would look through

Mariann's family pictures from Michigan and try to cheer her up by saying "You miss your family, but I'll be your sister now."

Even this relationship was bittersweet. Sageta had taken the lead in caring for Adam and Adora while Khalid was at work. Adam had never forgotten Mariann, but Adora was young enough to be confused and had taken to calling Sageta "Mama."

"When I first got there, Sageta said, 'She has a mama in Iraq and a mama in America,' " Mariann related. "And I said, 'No, she doesn't. She only has one mama in my mind, and she doesn't have a mommy here.' But Adora really loves Sageta too, because she took care of her like a daughter, which was better for Adora. But it hurt me a lot."

Toward the end of Mariann's first week Khalid proudly announced that he'd rented an apartment for a week in a "tourist city" by the newly renamed Saddam Dam fifteen miles north of Mosul. Mariann was delighted with the modern apartment, Western plumbing, and best of all, hot running water and a shower—until she heard the drone of U.S. fighter bombers buzzing the dam on a reconnaissance mission from Turkey. The planes flew so low that the vacationers could read the numbers on their sides. Everyone stopped to watch, even the small children in the swimming pool. These incidents were especially traumatic for Adora, who was so frightened of planes that she would close her eyes when she saw one on TV. Adam revealed that U.S. bombers had flown daily raids over the farm before she came. "What did you do then?" Mariann asked him. "I'd count the planes," her son replied. At the time there was widespread fear that the United States might resume the bombing. After two helicopter gunships appeared within a few hundred feet of their apartment's windows, the Saieeds cut their stay short after three days.

Back in Mosul Mariann resettled into an unvarying daily routine. Boredom was her chief enemy—to the point where she read a 500-page novel, the only book she had with her, twice. To shorten the day she and the children awoke together as late as they could, usually around eleven (as the kids' room wasn't air-conditioned, Adam and Adora slept on mats by their parents' bed). With few toys available, Mariann and the children would sing songs and play made-up games, such as pitching clothespins into a bucket.

Another attraction was the set of photographs from home that Mariann had brought out cautiously, so as not to annoy Khalid. Adam was particularly struck by a picture of his six-year-old cousin Andrea, his favorite playmate. "She's so beautiful, Mom," he said. "I wish I could see her." He couldn't believe how big Andrea's little sister Christina had grown.

Adam's strong feelings for his cousins were reciprocated. A year after the abduction Andrea was discovered in her bed by her mother, sobbing "I miss Adam and Adora."

It pained Mariann to see how little continuity her children had retained in their lives. "What did you do on your birthday?" she asked Adam.

"I don't even know when it is, Mom," he said. Neither child had been so much as told about their last birthdays. When Mariann protested this neglect to Khalid, he responded, "There wasn't any reason to celebrate."

In the midafternoon, when the electricity was cut off and the air-conditioning conked out, they would seek relief from the dead indoor air and move outside, to the minimal shade of the overhung patio. Here was the day's main event: doing the laundry by hand. Mariann ran a hose from the kitchen sink, through an open window, and into a large bucket. Adora manned a smaller bucket, while Adam rinsed. Since the children had few changes of clothes, they did the wash every day for ninety minutes—or even longer, until the all-purpose soap ration ran out toward the end of the month.

The children's other daily highlight was their father's return for lunch and late dinner, though Khalid frequently had little patience for them. Although Adora could do little wrong, Khalid was hard on Adam, and even held the nine-year-old responsible for any misdeeds by his baby sister. "You're supposed to be watching her," he'd growl. At one point Adam told Mariann, "Mom, remember when we were back in America? Daddy never spanked me. You know what? He spanks me all the time here—all the time."

If the impatient Khalid had to ring the bell twice at the

locked front gate, Mariann noted, "he'd yell at Adam for not getting out there after the first ring. As soon as the doorbell rang, Adam would go—I made sure of it, because I didn't want him to get yelled at either. I'd say, 'Go, go, go!' And he'd jump up, put on his flip-flops, and run out to open the gate."

Khalid's erratic discipline aside, day-to-day handling of the children fell to Mariann—and it was no easy task. Adora, perhaps overwhelmed by her mother's presence, became wild and hyper-active—climbing bookshelves, hanging from door frames, often falling and hurting herself. Adam, meanwhile, regressed into screaming temper tantrums and outright defiance. Mariann found herself in a no-win situation. If she tried to get the kids under control, Khalid would rebuke her for yelling at them. When she showed the children affection and enjoyed a close moment with them, he might seem equally displeased. "You only came here to see the kids," he'd say. "You don't care about me."

Though Mosul would always seem strange and uncomfortable to Mariann, her experience there also confirmed something positive: a deepening admiration for the people she'd once feared and distrusted. "The Iraqis are the friendliest people on earth," she said. "They'll do anything for you. If you go to somebody's house, and they only have a little food, they'll give it to you—or they'll run to the store and get what you want while you're sitting there. Compared to Americans, they're ten times more warm-hearted and generous. In fact, it was hard for me to adjust when I got back here."

Hospitality has its limits when the guest cannot eat—which was Mariann's problem throughout her stay in Mosul. Whether from the stress or from differences in the food ("all the vegetables tasted bitter to me"), she had no appetite for anything Sageta prepared. When Mariann forced herself to eat, she couldn't keep anything down—save for an occasional bite of watermelon, which Khalid sporadically remembered to pick up on his way home from work. Even then, she was often disappointed to find the melon unripe; because of the drastic reduction in imported food, Iraqi farmers were meeting demand by harvesting their crops prematurely.

186

By the third week it got worse, "to the point where I couldn't even swallow anymore," Mariann said. "I went to a doctor, and she said it was all psychological." The effects were all too real: in a little over a month in the Middle East, Mariann would lose forty pounds.

Toward the end of July, she barely had the strength to get out of bed: "Since I wasn't eating, things started getting really fuzzy. I didn't know what was going on. . . ."

As usual, Khalid had little sympathy: "Do you know how many invitations I've turned down because of you? Because you didn't want to do anything."

One morning Mariann awoke, and in foggy half-consciousness came to a terrible realization: she would have to leave Iraq or likely die there. She was too weak to cook or even to play with the children. I'm a burden, no good to anyone, she thought. Yes, she would have to go. There was only one question: would she be able to take Adam with her?

Before her trip, Mariann refused to entertain the thought that Khalid might permit her to take one child home but not the other. If pushed to the wall, she thought then, she'd have to choose Adora, the baby. When faced with the reality of Khalid's stubbornness, her attitude changed. While Adora had adjusted relatively well in Iraq, Adam was miserable. His arrival in that country had been "the worst surprise of my life," he told her. In Mariann's absence, he'd begun to forget what his mother looked like. "I just wanted a picture of you," he'd say, crying passionately. Adam missed everything from the U.S.: his grandparents, his friend from across the street, all the toys he'd left behind.

"Why didn't you bring my bike?" he demanded. "Why didn't you bring my G.I. Joes?"

"Adam," Mariann reminded him, "I really didn't think G.I. Joes were a good idea."

Mariann told her son she would do everything she could to get him back home, and it seemed she had grounds for hope. After all, Khalid's primary concern had always been for Adora. Her husband had said more than once that he wanted Adam to go back to school in the States. He told Mariann to "get ready," to "go ahead and pack"—that he and Adam would accompany her to Amman, where the U.S. Embassy could grant Adam a passport. Khalid implied that he and Adora would follow them to America after he sold the video store, though he left that for some vague future.

For the rest of the week Adam was brittle with anticipation. Mariann obsessively planned their welcome-home-party menu: "Wendy's hamburger, and meatloaf, and hot dogs, and sloppy joes, and corn on the cob. When you don't eat, food is all you can think about." Her sense of urgency was heightened because the United States set an inspection deadline for Iraq's military sites on the day they were set to leave. (Mariann later found that 300,000 fearful Iraqis had fled the country that week for Jordan.)

"How does it look?" she'd ask Khalid, regarding the threat of renewed warfare. "It doesn't look good today," he'd reply, or: "It looks better than yesterday." He would not elaborate, and Mariann was left to her imagination—which ran wild every time a cruising U.S. bomber broke the sound barrier.

Several days before their slated departure Khalid changed his mind: Adam would have to stay. In a panic, Mariann called Shakir in Baghdad, who interceded with her husband over the phone. It turned out that Khalid and Shakir knew each other from student demonstration days in Washington, D.C. Shakir said he'd arrange for a Red Crescent letter of safe passage, to make sure they'd have no trouble at the border, and Khalid agreed to let the plan go forward.

Thursday, July 25, the day they were scheduled to leave for Amman, Khalid came home from work and postponed the trip to Friday. Friday, he pushed it to Saturday. "I knew he was stalling, and I knew it was bad," Mariann said. "That Saturday he came home, and I said, 'What's going on, when are we leaving?' And he said, 'Let's go talk about it,' and I knew right away what he was going to say. We went into another room and he sat there and said, 'I've made a decision. I'm not going to split up the family. If you want to stay and be a proper mom, you're welcome to stay. If you want to leave, you're welcome to leave. It's your choice.' "
He'd never promised Adam could leave in so many words, Kha-

lid insisted. Besides, he added, in the lowest blow of all, Mariann no longer had the financial means to support their son.

"I was hysterical," Mariann said. "How could he be so cruel? I started screaming at him, and I picked up a pillow to throw at him, but he got up and said, 'Don't you dare,' and started toward me, so I just sat back down. I was literally beating myself—I was so angry that I *had* to hit something, and there wasn't anything there except him and me."

The children, who'd been playing outside within hearing range, were terrified by their mother's loss of control. They had never seen her like this. As Mariann's weeping gradually subsided, Adora entered the room and asked if her mother was leaving.

"I just kept telling her 'I love you, I love you, go out and play.' And then Adam came in, and he kissed me on the cheek, and he said, 'Don't worry, Mom, when I grow up I'll come back to you.' He said it matter-of-factly, and then he walked out."

In retrospect, Mariann would conclude that Khalid had manipulated the situation in a last-ditch effort to make her stay—that he'd never intended to let Adam leave. As she saw it, "He wanted me to become a traditional Iraqi housewife—to stay home, be with the kids, do what he said, live the life that he wanted to live. But I wasn't a typical housewife at all, and he knew it."

At that point, despite her anguish over Adam, Mariann felt she was in no position to delay her departure. All of her VOW companions had already left Iraq, and her exit visa was about to expire. Had she stayed beyond that point, she feared that Khalid might prevent her from leaving, just as Moody had entrapped me seven years before.

There was no point in attempting an escape with the children. Iraq's northern border area was studded with mines and laced with barbed wire—and even if they made it to the checkpoint alive, she had no passports for Adam and Adora.

Mariann was, in a word, resolved. "I'd had to live without my children for a year," she explained, "and that's probably the only way I was able to come back here without them—because I'd learned how to live without them."

She was still crying at 4 A.M. Sunday, when she and Khalid boarded a taxi bound for Baghdad. There he reneged one more time; he would not accompany her to Amman, after all. The cab driver was reliable, he assured her. It would be business as usual at the video store that day, Mariann thought darkly. Then Khalid made one last stab: "Why don't you stop being so stubborn, and just stay, like you had planned?"

When Mariann refused, her husband's tone turned harsher. "You asked me if you could come here—I never asked you," he said. Then he was gone, a stiff, unbending figure receding from the cab's rear window, in the white afternoon light of Baghdad.

Throughout the thirteen-hour drive to Amman, Mariann dwelled on many things: How were her children coping with her disappearance? Would she make it on her own, past the Jordanian checkpoints? How would her friends in VOW react to her leaving? As it turned out, Shakir was mildly disappointed. He thought that Mariann should have "toughed it out" and stayed a month longer by getting a new visa through her husband, to see if Khalid might have relented before the start of school: "It's better to be miserable for a few more weeks than for the rest of your life."

The others, however, simply welcomed her back as would her family and friends back in Michigan. Especially kind were two single Iraqi-American women her age, Kawkub Daoud and Nadia Sukkar. "Nadia was very sweet to me," Mariann said. "I poured my heart out to her, and she listened to everything. She said, 'I know you're suffering, and you don't deserve this.'

"And Kawkub gave me some advice. She said, 'Mariann, I know it didn't work out exactly how you wanted. But I don't want you to sit here in Amman and feel bad about what happened. I want you to look at it as a chance to spend thirty days with your kids that you wouldn't have had otherwise.' That picked up my mood completely—I was able to relax and not feel so bad."

The three women became inseparable during the five-day layover in Jordan—to the point where Nadia and Kawkub shared one bed in their room, so that Mariann, by that time strapped for funds, could have the other. Nadia had her reasons for gloom. Her father had been hospitalized in the U.S. for a heart problem, and her hometown of Basrah, Iraq's second-largest city, had been hit especially hard in the air war. The situation was so bad—people living in the streets, the ancient mosques destroyed—that cab drivers there had refused to take Nadia to her childhood home.

The women had two choices: they could sit in their hotel room and count the hours till their plane took off, or they could make the most of Amman and try to forget their worries. They chose the latter—and Mariann managed to have some fun. They lounged by the hotel pool and went out to the city's best Arab restaurants, some featuring live entertainment. Khalid had never exposed Mariann to any of this, and she found that she loved it all: the food, the music, the whole ambiance of this different culture.

Mariann would return to Michigan as she had left, without her children. In another sense she had not left empty-handed. Her viewpoint had been altered forever. She could no longer brush aside the suffering of faraway people; she had become a citizen of the world.

"Every person I met in Iraq had someone in their family bombed or killed," she said. "But that isn't the big story to the Iraqis. The big story to them is that their entire economy is falling apart because of the sanctions. People haven't worked for a long time, and they know things are getting worse. Women are selling their gold jewelry; girls are selling their bodies to buy food.

"They can't get milk, or food, or medicine. Seventy percent of their medicine was imported from the West, but now they're only getting 10 percent—and they need three times as much. The anesthesiologists are quitting because they don't have any anesthetics to give the patients. The vaccines that need refrigeration spoil and babies in incubators die because the power goes out overnight. We had people in VOW who went to hospitals and held dying babies in their arms."

Despite the devastation of Desert Storm, Mariann en-

191

countered no hostility in Iraq. "They made a big distinction between the U.S. government and the American people," she said. "They had no stereotypical American in their mind—and they wanted to convince me that the Iraqi people were not our enemies."

The current sanctions, she added, were not costing Saddam Hussein "one ounce of sleep over this, but the people are being hurt. The middle class has become poor, the poor have become desperate. And they're all sliding down this great deep ravine, and they're wondering why. They don't have a voice in their government; they didn't do anything to deserve what's being done to them. They just want to get back to a normal life, but the sanctions won't let them. And so their suffering goes on and on and on, through no fault of their own."

On August 31, a month after she'd left Iraq, Mariann called the clothing shop next to Khalid's video store in Mosul, and the proprietor answered—as simply as that. The phone lines were finally open for incoming calls. Within seconds she was speaking to her husband. The conversation was all business. Khalid asked about his pending U.S. citizenship (he had passed the test but missed his swearing-in before leaving the country) and about the children's U.S. passports, which would make it easier for all three of them to reenter the country. Mariann said she was working with the State Department on both counts. After ten minutes the line went dead.

Although Khalid still couldn't call out, Mariann could call her husband—and, with some prior arrangement, her children—whenever she wanted, for the first time in fourteen months. A year before she might have been elated. Now she felt oddly depressed.

"Now it's a problem to keep myself from calling all the time—I could call them every day, and it wouldn't be enough," she said. "But it's ridiculously expensive, and I can only afford it once a month. And now that I know I can talk to them, I think about them all the time. The only way I can get through the day is to *not* think about them—and now they're right there, at the other end of the phone."

Before they were cut off, Khalid renewed his invitation for Mariann to return for another visit, at his expense. "But I'm scared to do things on his terms," Mariann said, "because I figure if I do, I won't have a choice of whether or not to stay." As an alternative, she is saving money on her own. It is a slow and frustrating process, as she is "deeply and forever in debt." To raise funds she took two full-time jobs in mid-September: a paid position in the VOW office and a cashier's job at a video store owned by an Iraqi-American businessman.

The future is uncertain. Within the next year Mariann hopes to see Khalid and her children again—in Iraq, or on neutral turf in Jordan or Austria. There is a chance, according to Khalid, that he might bring Adam and Adora to the United States for a visit, or even for good. He would not say when he might come, and Mariann has learned to keep her hopes in check.

In some ways her life is more difficult than before her trip. There are days when she feels overwhelmed by guilt and loneliness. "I still battle depression a lot," she said. "It's still back there, the part of me that just wants to go hide somewhere, to just lie there and not get on with what I have to do."

But the events of the past year have tempered Mariann, and she no longer gives in to paralysis. In her worst moments, she remembers what she told Adam and Adora in Mosul: *If something really bad happens and I have to leave without you, I will come back and fight for you. Mommy loves you and Mommy will always love you, and I'll be back.*

Mariann will be true to her word—that much, she knows, is certain. She also knows there can be no happily-ever-after ending to her story. "No matter what happens," she said, "I'm going to be living with this for the rest of my life."

Part Three

8

Mothers of Algiers

After I'd been to Europe in 1988 and met the Mothers of Algiers, the French women whose children had been abducted to Algeria by their fathers, I realized that a book was needed to awaken the world to the dimensions of this truly global problem. My new project received a huge boost from Arnie Dunchock, who'd already expressed keen interest in the issue of international parental abduction. Once he recognized there really was something to write about, he wanted to be part of it. Over the next three years he would devote countless hours toward making this book a reality.

I'd already seen firsthand how Arnie could get wrapped up in a project he cared about. He'd invited me to assist him on a case involving a Mexican-American named Frank Garcia, whom Arnie believed had been wrongly convicted and jailed in 1985 for murder. As I learned more about the case, I found it compelling. I felt a kinship with Frank; I knew what it felt like to be confined unjustly.

I also developed new admiration for Arnie's dogged (and unpaid) work on an appeal. In November 1988 Frank was granted a new trial.

In 1990, two years after my first meeting with the Mothers of Algiers, Arnie and his sister Joan accompanied Mahtob and me to Paris to meet them again. We were convinced that their story would be an important part of the new book.

Shortly before we left for Paris, Mahtob said, "You are going to be working, so why can't I learn French?" Quite an ambitious request for a ten-year-old on summer vacation. Antoine Audouard, my French editor, arranged for an instructor, for both Mahtob and for Joan, who teaches English as a second language to elementary students.

My literary agent, Michael Carlisle, had an actor friend who was willing to rent his Paris apartment to us while he was off doing a movie. This was a treat for my daughter and me. We'd made four trips to Paris, but we'd always stayed in a hotel and were always escorted by a driver provided by my French publisher, Fixot. This time we would see Paris from the inside. We would learn to find our own way around town by using the Metro, the efficient Parisian subway—a proud new experience for two people from Michigan, the automobile state.

When we arrived in Paris on a Sunday evening, we didn't have a city street map, but Mahtob wasn't worried at all. "Tomorrow morning just take me to Hotel Balzac," she said. "The man there speaks English, and he'll give us a map."

"Do you know how to get to Hotel Balzac?" Joan asked.

Mahtob replied, "Just get me to the Champs-Elysées, and I'll find it." From that point on Joan and Mahtob became a great team. They saw more of Paris those two weeks than I have in six trips. Meanwhile, Arnie and I met with some of the most inspirational people I have ever encountered: the Mothers of Algiers.

In August 1980, when Amar and Farid Houache left their home in France to visit their father's family in Algeria, it was in the spirit of adventure. The trimly built boys had visited Ghardaïa, a north-central city 250 miles from Algiers, once before, in 1976. They'd been a bit jittery about that first trip, but now they were older—Amar was thirteen, Farid almost twelve—and they knew what lay in store. They looked forward to seeing their grandparents and other relatives—especially the many cousins they'd played with four years earlier. Besides, their father would be with them, and they'd always trusted and revered him. They'd be back in a few weeks, in time for the start of school. Vacation would be finished all too soon.

In September, when Brahim Houache told his sons that he was "sick" and that they'd have to postpone their return to France, Amar and Farid were glad their vacation wasn't over. As the days passed, however, they began to wonder why their father showed no symptoms. During his "recovery," when Brahim enrolled them in an Islamic school, they soon became restless. Amar and Farid couldn't speak a word of Arabic; some of their teachers translated for them, others didn't bother. The boys weren't especially interested in learning a new language. After all, they'd be leaving any day for their own school in France.

Back in the Paris suburb of Massy the boys' mother, Marie-Anne, got word of Brahim's illness and her sons' delayed return. She too became skeptical. Her marriage had been shaky for years, ever since Marie-Anne had left the shop she and Brahim co-managed to take a clerical job and, eventually, to become an administrative secretary. Brahim felt threatened by Marie-Anne's independence; he hated the idea that she would go into the outer world to work. When his shop was bought out by a supermarket, his resentment deepened.

On the surface Brahim seemed thoroughly assimilated. He and Marie-Anne had married in a Catholic church, where their sons were later baptized. Although he always spoke French, never Arabic, and spent all of his time with native French people, he actually felt victimized, excluded, out of place—much like Moody, who'd endured repeated harassment by American doctors. Brahim had taken to railing against the land he'd adopted in 1962. France was "a garbage can," he said. Like Moody and Khalid Saieed, he was convinced that Western culture corrupted children; Amar and Farid would grow up drugged and delinquent. Brahim feared he would lose control of his sons, just as he'd lost control of his wife.

Four days later Marie-Anne received a second letter: Brahim was staying in Algeria, and the boys would stay with him. At first she couldn't believe it; the bomb had dropped out of nowhere. Marie-Anne's second reaction was *denial*—that there was no way Brahim could get away with it. Surely, she thought, French law would require the immediate return of her French sons. She held to this conviction even after a phone call to the

French Ministry of Justice resulted in no encouragement and little information, except the fact that they were overwhelmed with similar cases. Marie-Anne was amazed; she had never heard of such parental abductions before.

In early October Marie-Anne traveled to Algiers, where the French Embassy had organized a meeting with Brahim. She had come to talk to him, she said—but first, "I want to know what the children think about this." They took a taxi to Brahim's apartment, but Marie-Anne had to wait several hours more to speak to her sons, who'd been staying at their grandmother's house 120 miles away.

When they saw their mother, Amar and Farid were both excited and fearful. Why was she there? Had something terrible happened?

Then they saw her pained expression—and they *knew*, before she'd said a word. "Your father wants you to stay here for good," Marie-Anne began.

"But Mom, we want to go home!" Amar protested. "We have to go to school!"

Marie-Anne did her best to calm them: "You can't come back just yet, but I'll do everything I can to get you home."

It was a promise, as future events would prove, that this mother would not take lightly.

The boys asked Brahim what was happening. Why did he want to keep them here? What were his plans? Amar, who was generally more assertive (and louder) in confronting his father, said, "Dad, we want to go back to France."

"Shut up!" their father replied. "It is none of your business!" Since they'd arrived in Algeria Brahim had grown harsher, more dictatorial toward his sons—and more frustrated. He'd convinced himself that he was doing the right thing for Amar and Farid— and that it was only a matter of time before they would understand and thank him for it.

Brahim had miscalculated badly. The boys were caught up in a storm of emotions, none of them good. In part they felt guilty for their earlier pleasure at extending their stay; they'd been, in effect, unwitting collaborators to their father's scheme.

Mostly they felt a burning, adolescent anger toward Brahim. He'd lied to them. He'd torn them from their home, friends, and French family under false pretenses. Even after they'd arrived in Ghardaïa, he'd continued to lie by feigning an illness and putting off the moment of truth.

The whole family was in on it, the boys realized. Ever since they'd arrived, they'd been shuttled from one house of relatives to another. Up to that point they'd enjoyed the constant companionship of their cousins. Then it hit them: these people were their guards. They concluded that Brahim probably planned the abduction during a previous family visit in April. "Why don't you come back?" Brahim's relatives had coaxed. "The sun is always out. You'll have your home and your boys, and life will be easier."

The fact that Amar and Farid hadn't been coerced to go to Algeria—that they'd joined their father voluntarily, even eagerly—made them feel even worse.

Like incest and sexual abuse, parental abductions violate a child's sense of self. Amar and Farid had trusted their father. More than that, they idolized him; they wanted to follow him, to be like him. By taking them without asking, by crushing their will, he had robbed them of their budding manhood—their very beings.

Marie-Anne stayed on in Ghardaïa for two weeks. She considered moving there to watch over her sons, but soon rejected the idea. In Algeria she would have to convert to Islam. Brahim showed her the place she would stay—alone, apart from her children ("They have to get used to their new life," her husband told her). Moreover, she knew she had no chance to regain her sons under Algerian law—and she still clutched the illusion that she might prevail in the French courts.

As they tearfully parted from their mother, Amar and Farid clung to the hope that they would soon be rejoining her in France—perhaps as early as the next month. This began the period when they planned and waited for that *day*, always thinking it was just around the corner. They even thought about which Algerian mementos they would take back with them.

201

It would be some time before Marie-Anne realized that neither country protected the victims of international parental child abductions—and that only new laws, respected by both sides, could set matters right.

France and Algeria are separated by a mere four hundred miles of Mediterranean Sea, a one-hour flight. For centuries the two cultures have intertwined—passionately, often furiously. Once partially conquered by Muslims, Algeria was later ruled by France from 1834 to 1962, when the Algerians won their struggle for national liberation. That war was France's Vietnam—long, bloody, and for no clear purpose. It left both winners and losers with a lingering sense of unease and resentment.

In recent years France has drawn increasing numbers of immigrants. The largest incoming group—800,000 strong—is Algerian. These mostly young North Africans are battered by an unemployment rate estimated at 40 percent—and by racist politicians who stoke anti-immigrant sentiment. There is much distrust in the country, on both sides of the cultural fence.

The gap becomes especially acute in the home, in marriages between Algerian men and French women (it rarely happens in reverse; Muslim women are forbidden to marry non-Muslim men, on pain of ostracism by their families). Under French secular law, husband and wife are equal in status; their children's education and future is their joint responsibility. This ideal of shared custody extends even after a couple's divorce. Algeria's Code of the Family, adopted in 1984, is both patriarchal and imbued in Islam. Polygamy is allowed—but only for men. A woman needs permission from a male guardian before marrying—and then must obey her husband's wishes.

According to the code the mother feeds her children's bodies, but the father feeds their minds—by teaching them the customs and meanings of his faith, and by raising them as good Muslims.

In France, the Algerians' attempt to transplant their paternal dominance often clashes with another Muslim ideal: the importance of a stable and harmonious family unit. In condemning the wave of parental abductions to Algeria (a total of three thousand by the mid-1980's), Sheik Abbas, the grand rector of the Grand Mosque in Paris, stated: "That these children are not raised by their mothers troubles me infinitely. The mother is irreplaceable. No one can deny that. One must understand, though, that the father, as the head of the family, bears responsibility for the future of the child. That child is called [by] his name and [has] his religious identity."

Once a couple divorces in Algeria, the father remains the children's sole guardian. While a mother may retain custody, she has no decision-making power and must raise the children within the father's religion, namely Islam. In France (where one of three marriages, mixed or otherwise, ends in divorce), Algerian men saw that French judges routinely awarded custody—and with it parental authority—to the mother. This placed the fathers in an impossible position. Rejected by French society, further wounded by the loss of their wives, they typically embraced Islam with renewed fervor. Many concluded that they had but one choice: to snatch their children away to Algeria. They had no moral qualms about what they were doing—and once they were home, they were backed by church and state.

In this light Brahim Houache may be seen as a representative abductor. There is no question that he felt bitter and mistreated in France. When his marriage soured, there was little left to hold him there. For Brahim it seemed natural to retreat to the security of his native culture, to cling to it more closely than before he'd left—and to bring along the two boys for whom he felt responsible.

For Amar and Farid, however, a happy adjustment to their new life in Algeria was impossible. Under the best of circumstances the transition would have been difficult. Everything was so strange to them: the language, the traditional garb (including a small hat for school), the religion, the social dynamics. The only uncovered female faces they saw belonged to their grandmother and aunts.

These, then, were far from the best of circumstances. The boys never lost their sense of displacement. They held desperately to their hope that they would escape from Algeria, even as one year melted into the next. Marie-Anne visited nearly every six months, and they anticipated each visit as the one that would spring them back to France. Why should they adapt to the temporary?

Every day Amar and Farid would be reminded of their otherness. At school they were monitored closely by the principal, who was related to their father. While accepted by their classmates, they were referred to as "those who have crossed the sea"—as people from a different place. Except Arabic, in which they gradually became fluent, they found their courses—in the Koran, English, and French—boring, slow-paced, taught mainly by rote. The brothers knew they were falling behind their French classmates back home.

In January 1981 Marie-Anne saw a television program on counterabductions. She contacted two of the women on the show: Gabrielle Barton, who had retrieved her two children from Saudi Arabia, and Jocelyne Bany, whose seven-year-old son had been kidnapped by his father to Algeria. Though she still held out hope for a legal solution, Marie-Anne began devising a plan that excited but terrified her: the escape of her sons.

In March she traveled to Ghardaïa to see the boys. She made up a code to communicate with her sons and warned them to be ready for anything. She took snapshots of the boys for fake passports—and then she realized she had no chance of success. For one thing, Brahim was suspicious of Marie-Anne's every move and prevented her from spending any time alone with Amar and Farid. For another, Marie-Anne discovered that she would need written permission from Brahim to get the boys out of the country, even if the bogus passports passed muster. In addition, there were 250 miles of Sahara desert between Ghardaïa and coastal Algiers, the point of exit from the country, with no way of getting there.

The boys resented their restricted access to their mother, this violation of their most intimate relationship. They also resented Marie-Anne's low status in Brahim's family. She was treated as a lesser person, as someone "unclean" because she was

Christian, and for the outrageously cruel justification that she'd lost her children. Brahim went so far as to order her to touch nothing in the house.

Mother and sons would play endless games of Scrabble, just to be able to sit close together and pass silent signals. They took to sneaking out to the yard to grab a few conspiratorial moments free from Brahim's inhibiting glare . . . to exchange hugs, kisses, and whispered dreams of escape and reunion.

Shortly after the two-week visit ended and Marie-Anne returned to France, she received a letter her sons had somehow managed to smuggle out. "Mother, be careful, beware," it read. "Father is going to be married again." Marie-Anne then explored the route taken by so many left-behind parents: her country's legal system. She obtained a divorce and went back to her maiden name of Marie-Anne Pinel. She gained custody of Amar and Farid through the French courts—only to find, like so many before her, that these pieces of paper were meaningless. Despite the longstanding relationship of the two nations (or perhaps because of it), a French ruling had no force in Algeria.

When Marie-Anne attempted to win custody in an Algerian court, she was rebuffed. The country's Islamic law was clear: the boys belonged to their father. However, the court ruled that Brahim must provide monetary compensation to Marie-Anne— money that would help pay her legal fees.

In 1982, when Brahim remarried, the boys stopped living with other relatives and moved into their father's house. There they found themselves under the thumb of a stepmother, with predictable conflict—especially while their father was jailed for two months for political activity. One night, after Amar came home at 10:30 P.M. (past his strict curfew), the stepmother ended an argument by slapping him.

Following Brahim's orders, Amar and Farid halfheartedly followed the major Islamic rituals, including sunup-to-sundown fasting during the month of Ramadan. They had no interest in the religion's meaning; for them it was all pretend and empty show. As they watched their father perform his daily devotions, the boys became increasingly cynical. Brahim had destroyed his family, lied to his sons, coerced them to stay in a place they hated. How could he—or the relatives who supported him—call themselves good Muslims? As Farid saw it, "People would say black and do white, or say white and do black."

The boys' attitude toward their surroundings was rooted in their emotional distance from their father. With time Amar and Farid came to stop fearing Brahim, but they also stopped respecting him, just as Mahtob had lost respect for her father the day Moody said "we're not going home." The boys' idol had fallen—hard. They felt only scorn and pity for this man who claimed to be so righteous, yet whose life with them was built on a central, unforgettable lie.

From the start Brahim discouraged all contact between his sons and their mother. At his directive the local post office workers (who were his friends or relatives) intercepted all mail in either direction, even Marie-Anne's birthday parcels and Christmas cards. He even ordered the stepmother to search the boys' schoolbooks for hidden pictures of Marie-Anne and to tear them up. But Brahim couldn't stop the mother from striving to get her boys back.

After I met Marie-Anne, I was struck by the similarities in our stories—our initial feelings of helplessness, our frustrations with the legal system, our low status in the Muslim world. There were also significant differences, however. I was fortunate to remain with my daughter after our abduction, to be able to carry out an escape and, as it turned out, to resolve the situation in a relatively brief period of time. None of this was possible for Marie-Anne. To her advantage, however, she had the comforts and reinforcements of her native country. To her credit, she was years ahead of me in grasping the need to work with others rather than as an individual.

Annie Sugier was a five-foot-five bundle of inexhaustible energy, the kind of person who gets things done by sheer force of will. Her voice was gentle and high-pitched, but her confidence and determination always rang through.

Annie was an engineer for the French Atomic Energy Commission. She had lived abroad and had some understanding of other cultures. Her passion was for feminist causes, and it was through them that she met Jocelyne Bany in 1981. Moved by the woman's plight—to have one's child trapped so far away and to be powerless to help—Annie referred Jocelyne to a friend of hers, a feminist lawyer named Linda Weil-Curiel. Discovering that Jocelyne's case was but one of many, Annie and Linda founded the Solidarity Collective of Mothers of Abducted Children, nicknamed the Mothers of Algiers. They drew in three other friends to help them: Chantal Hanoteau, a publishing researcher; Odette Brun, a retired physician; and Anne-Marie Lizin, a member of the Belgian Parliament.

These women referred to themselves as "shepherds," rather than leaders, of the left-behind parents, but they might better be called godmothers. None had children of her own. Yet they all felt a burning zeal to prevent international parental child abductions. They were feminists, but they came to the issue from a broader tradition as well—from a concept of equality and universal human rights that stemmed from Voltaire and the French Revolution.

In November 1983, at the time of a state visit to France by Algerian president Chadli Benjedid, the godmothers led a protest demonstration outside the Algerian Embassy in Paris, where police roughly intercepted them. Several of the women were arrested and ushered into a police wagon, where Annie met Marie-Anne Pinel for the first time. This demonstration marked the official birth of the Mothers of Algiers.

Undaunted by the arrests, the Solidarity Collective proposed to up the ante. Their next action, they declared, would draw unprecedented public attention to the issue: the mothers would take a boat dubbed *Liberté* to Algeria, where they would try to meet with officials and see their sons and daughters. The *Boat to Algiers*, as the media called it, enlisted about thirty mothers (including some ethnic North Africans residing in France) on July 6, 1984.

As they gathered on the dock in Marseilles, the mothers were both exhilarated and nervous. Marie-Anne had continued to visit her sons every six months, but other mothers had not seen their children for years. What if we're arrested in Algeria—or don't get to see the children after all? Are my children eating? Are they crying at night? Have they accepted their new lives—and will I be disrupting them? Will they even recognize me? How will I support them if I *do* get them back?

In the days leading up to the trip both the French and Algerian governments, feeling the heat, had approached the god-mothers with offers of open negotiations if the protest was called off. Annie was undecided; which course was best? She worried that the group was too large to organize properly, that it might fall apart once it reached Algeria and was faced with arrest.

The mothers were about to board *Liberté* when Annie called out: "No, we are not boarding! The *Boat to Algiers* is canceled!" Despite their consternation, the mothers respected Annie and abided by her decision.

Almost as soon as the words were out of her mouth, Annie regretted them. "I made a mistake in 1984 when I stopped the boat," she confessed later on. "I couldn't accept this mistake." Here were all these women whose expectations she'd built, who had changed their lives and kept the faith, and now Annie had let them down. She had relied instead on the governments, which continued to stall on the promised negotiations. "This was a great error, and therefore a great responsibility," she told herself. From that point on she would redouble her efforts to win for these women the only thing that mattered: a renewed relationship with their children.

The first order of business, it was decided, was to select a core group, five representative mothers who could be counted on in any circumstance. "Only women who would fight were trust-worthy," Annie decided. They must be of impeccable character, unquestionably loyal, committed to working together, and ready to sacrifice all to achieve their common goal.

"We know we shouldn't ask people to be perfect," Linda Weil-Curiel noted, "but we knew to succeed, these mothers had to be perfect."

Annie never doubted that Marie-Anne Pinel should be one

of the five. "I liked Marie-Anne from the beginning," she said. "She was always on time, she did what she was asked to do, and she didn't talk much. She was just what I was looking for."

As political people in the best sense, the godmothers knew that any struggle worth fighting would not be won quickly; they were in it for the long haul. Over the next seven years they would make tremendous sacrifices of personal time and money (for quite some time they'd support the organization almost entirely out of their own pockets).

The godmothers also understood the need for cooperative group action, for reasons of both principle and practicality. They were entirely loyal, unselfish, and dedicated to the cause, rather than to any individual. Annie, the leader, discouraged talk about particular cases. If the mothers were to attain their goal, she knew that they must remain unified and focused.

As word spread of the godmothers' activity, dozens of mothers with children stranded in Algeria clustered to their side. For the mothers, this work was the most positive kind of therapy: funneling their energies, relieving their tensions, helping them cope.

After the boat fiasco, "we decided to do things together, actions that seemed logical to us," said Jocelyne Bany, another chosen representative. "We can't demand the return of our children; we're aware of that. So we try to negotiate and ask for things we know we can get."

"We wanted to castigate the government, to underline its weaknesses," Annie said. "When we went to the Human Rights Commission of the United Nations and met with the French representative, he said, 'It is not the moment and not the place.' I couldn't bear to hear that."

The basic demand was for visitation rights, along with some system to enforce those rights. The wheels of government, both French and Algerian, were maddeningly slow. Once again the Mothers of Algiers raised the stakes. On June 17, 1985, nearly five years after Amar and Farid were taken to Ghardaïa, the core group traveled to Algeria, caught a secretary off guard, strode into the French Embassy compound in Algiers, sat on the grass with their knapsacks and refused to move. At first the embassy officials tried to coax them into leaving: "Do you realize this is an embassy? What is it you really want? You can't stay here." But stay they did. Then the officials tried to scare them. Come nightfall, they said, the compound would be patrolled by watchdogs.

The mothers were unimpressed. "We're not leaving," one of them said, "until you solve our problem."

The French ambassador was in a delicate situation. He didn't want to encourage these women and their embarrassing protest. At the same time, he couldn't leave them exposed to the elements overnight. Since he had to give them shelter, he reluctantly directed that a small one-story building in the compound—an empty facility that had once been used as a snack bar—be opened to house them.

The occupation had begun. The mothers, who'd left their jobs for the cause, had no idea how long they would be there or whether their bold step would bear fruit, but they felt bound to see it through. The French government was paralyzed. As awkward as the occupation might have been, any attempt to remove the mothers would be a public relations disaster. As luck would have it, a hijacked plane had just landed in Algiers, drawing the international press behind it. When the hijacking ended after only a few hours, all those reporters had nothing to report— except for the mothers' soon-to-be-famous occupation.

Accommodations were less than deluxe. In the one large room, the women slept in sleeping bags on a bare tile floor. In a small adjoining room there were kitchen facilities, including a gas stove and a small refrigerator. There was also a bathroom with a cold-water shower.

The first few nights had the air of a pajama party. Each woman shared her story to general excitement and sympathy. Later, as the anecdotes were recycled, the excitement wore off; their stories, the women realized, were depressingly similar.

The days settled into a bland monotony. There was no television, nor any incoming calls, and their radio sometimes could receive only one station. Annie, Linda, and several others—including a priest—worked as couriers, bringing in everything from soup and dishes to books and toothpaste. Marie-Anne had one welcome break from the routine when Amar, in Algiers for a sports event, managed to break away to the embassy for a brief visit.

"We will not move from here," the five wrote to Annie on June 21. "Morale is excellent even if we end up being here six months . . . we are ready to suffer the worst. Hang in there! We know that we can count on you."

Four months into the occupation, one of the mothers faltered. Helene Montetagaud decided she could not bear one more day in the embassy. To protect the group's image, the others announced that Helene would be leaving them to become the group's "ambassador" in Paris. She spoke to the French Parliament about the mothers' commitment and their life inside the embassy. Beginning that day Helene delivered forty white roses every Wednesday to the French president, the prime minister, the minister of justice, and both houses of the Assembly. At first the flowers were fresh; after a time Helene switched to withered rose petals, to symbolize the mothers' wilting hopes.

Thanks to enormous international publicity, the occupation was making its mark. Those rusty wheels of government were beginning to creak in the right direction. French and Algerian officials proposed a deal: if the mothers would end their protest, each government would appoint a mediator to expedite visitations and devise some "judicial ruling" to resolve the issue and ensure the children's Christmas visits.

On November 24, five months after they'd entered the embassy, the four remaining mothers walked out. Their adventures were by no means completed, but they would look back at their spartan experience in Algiers as the high point of their work together.

The mothers were tired of waiting. As the holidays approached their children remained in Algeria, as inaccessible as before. The Chadli government had agreed conditionally to implement transborder holiday visitations but was holding out for an official French guarantee that the children would be returned.

211

On November 25, 1985, Marie-Anne Pinel wrote to French president Mitterand:

We have returned after five months of peacefully occupying the French Embassy at Algiers, but without our children.

We are at the eve of Christmas, and it is insufferable to me to think that once more my children, Amar and Farid Houache, will be deprived of the love of their French family. . . . If you contact President Chadli, Amar and Farid can come to France for Christmas vacation, December 20th till January 3rd.

I solemnly promise to return my children at the end of this period, and not to take advantage of this occasion to use French law to obtain custody. . . .

Marie-Anne's parents, her boss at the National Office of Navigation, and the mayor of Massy sent similar appeals to Mitterand. The president replied that he could offer no guarantee without a formal treaty. Not to be deterred, the Mothers of Algiers enlisted a wide range of political and religious authorities—from the French Communist party to the Protestant Federation to Muslim leader Sheik Abbas—to provide their individual written assurances. Annie pledged personally to escort the children to the plane back to Algiers, "so that they take off without difficulty." Finally, to lay to rest any last reservations, the mothers swore before a French judge that they would return the children at holiday's end.

With its conditions met, the Algerian government set about enforcing the agreement. When the fathers balked, they were visited by police, who pointed to the children in question and demanded: "Now, you come."

The first transborder visit did not involve many: only six children, including Amar and Farid, crossed the sea. Even as the French families celebrated their return, no one could relax entirely. Everyone knew that the holiday was but a brief respite from the pain of their separation.

Two weeks later the mothers were faced with their most agonizing challenge—tougher than risking arrest at a demonstration, tougher than sleeping for five months on a floor. To prove they would not abuse the parental power the fathers had shared with them, to stand by their "word of honor" deemed so critical by the Algerian government, and to demonstrate their solidarity with one another, they returned every single child on schedule.

The mothers' anguish cannot be overstated (one child professed that he would rather be killed than return to his father). Had the mothers decided to renege and keep the children, the Algerians would have been powerless to compel them. Yet these strong women overrode their maternal instincts and gave their sons and daughters back, when everything in their nature screamed to do the opposite.

Amar Houache was a special case. At eighteen he was legally an adult in France, but he was still a minor in Algeria, where the age of majority is nineteen. He had to sign his own "Declaration of Honor" in Ghardaïa, promising to return. Still, he could have stayed in France had he so chosen. He never considered breaking his word. "He was very courageous and mature," Linda noted. "He saw that it would endanger the negotiations if he stayed, so he went back to Algeria. He sacrificed himself for the others."

It was about this time, in January 1986, that one of the godmothers embarked on a mission that would jeopardize her future and even her freedom. As a non-French national, Anne-Marie Lizin had become a trusted intermediary between the mothers and the Algerian government. Back home in Belgium her own government had ignored the mothers' issue—a fact that Marie-Anne, the Belgian representative to the European Parliament, found intolerable.

Anne-Marie's assistant, Ginny, had been made aware of a Belgian woman with a story similar to both mine and Marie-Anne Pinel's: the year before, her husband had lured their three teenage children, two boys and a girl, to Algeria, ostensibly for a weekend visit to attend a wedding. When they arrived, the father left them with his relatives in a small city near Algiers and cut off all contact with their mother. When the father returned to Belgium for the children's school documents, he was arrested and jailed. There the case stood: the father in jail, the children stranded with their grandmother and without money.

When the teenagers went to the Belgian Embassy and appealed for help in getting back to Belgium, they were informed that the diplomats' hands were tied. Anne-Marie got much the same response from officials in Brussels. "I really cannot do anything," the minister of foreign affairs told her, "because we have no agreement with Algeria." Absent a treaty, the Belgian government was disinclined to pressure the Algerians on the case—especially because a natural gas contract between the two countries was pending.

Privately, however, the government delivered a different message to Anne-Marie. "We have to do something," said one highly placed civil servant, "but we can't do it officially."

Anne-Marie had had her fill of bureaucratic foot-dragging. "If you wait for official action, you wait for years," she complained. These children could not wait that long; one of them had already lost a year in the university. Anne-Marie decided to put the state on trial, to make this a test case. With a journalist in tow she would travel incognito to the Algerian city of Annabas, near the Tunisian border. The children would be picked up at their home by a Tunisian driver and taken to meet her. Anne-Marie and the journalist would pretend to be the children's parents and get them across the border, where her husband was waiting, and they would all fly back to Belgium.

The plan backfired. Someone had informed the Algerians of Anne-Marie's intentions, and she was arrested while deplaning in Annabas. The Tunisian driver was stopped by police a few minutes after he picked up the children, who were returned to their relatives. They had no idea what was happening, and would get no word until much later.

Anne-Marie and the journalist were jailed for one night, then transferred to a hotel, where they remained under house arrest for six days. They were treated with civility ("Don't beat this woman!" the Belgian ambassador pleaded), but they had no contact with the outside world. Anne-Marie feared the worst: that

214

the resulting scandal would ruin her political career and that she might be detained for a very long time.

Throughout her questioning, she kept asking the Algerian authorities about the children, insisting that they must be freed to return to Belgium. The Algerians were open to negotiating the point—but not before the father was released from jail in Brussels. A deal was struck: charges against Anne-Marie and the journalist were dropped, the father was freed, and the entire family got together in Algiers to discuss a reconciliation. The mother, who still had ambivalent feelings about the father, agreed to take him back.

In an effort to save face, the Algerians insisted that the mother return to Belgium by herself, with the father and children following together a week later in front of the TV cameras.

Anne-Marie was delighted that the children were going home; as she flew back to Belgium, she thought ruefully that it would be her last political act. When a friend met her as she stepped out of the plane in Brussels, she asked, "Am I going to prison right away?"

"Are you kidding?" the friend said. "You are queen of the day." It was true: Anne-Marie's arrest had made headlines throughout Europe. In her absence she'd become a cause célèbre. She was admired as that rarest phenomenon: a politician with a heart. Far from ending her career, her "vigilante" rescue attempt would boost her to higher office. Shortly after that she was named Belgium's secretary of state to Europe 1992, the body that would formulate the continent's unification.

When I asked the repatriated teenagers what they thought of Madame Lizin's bold act, they promptly replied, "Good."

Back in France, the Mothers of Algiers found themselves stalled yet again. It had appeared the time was ripe for France to negotiate a bilateral treaty with Algeria on parental abductions. But in March 1986 the French Socialists lost control of the government to the Neo-Gaullists, and momentum was stalled.

On the first anniversary of the embassy occupation, Marie-Anne Pinel joined the other mothers for a celebration in Paris.

When a reporter openly questioned whether Amar really wanted to leave Algeria, Marie-Anne put a call through to the music shop where her older son worked. Amar answered and said, in one breath: "We are leaving."

Amar had always told his mother that he and Farid would leave together. When he turned nineteen, he purchased airline tickets for the two of them to Algiers. After reaching the capital, Amar and Farid attempted to enter the French Embassy. Now it was their turn to occupy—to seek refuge, justice, and home. The youths had no papers and were turned away at the door. Their French citizenship was denied; as far as the embassy was concerned, they were Algerians. They had no place there. It was a jolting letdown—as it had been for Mahtob and me when the Swiss Embassy in Tehran denied us haven.

For the next two weeks Amar and Farid stayed in the capital, at the beach houses of various Algerian friends. Soon word was out that their father had gotten warrants on them—for seventeen-year-old Farid as an illegal runaway, and for Amar, who had passed the Algerian age of majority, on the more serious charge of corrupting a minor. At one point, when the police came to their door, the brothers had to hide in a bathroom while their friends denied having seen them.

"If they are caught here there will be trouble—deep trouble," the police warned.

At that point the brothers, the closest of allies for so many years, made a painful choice: to protect their friends they would have to separate. Amar would avoid arrest by flying on to France—with the aid of a French Embassy guide and Linda Weil-Curiel, who happened to be in Algiers at the time. Farid, meanwhile, would return by bus to Ghardaïa, where Brahim would take him to the police station for questioning. When asked where he'd been, Farid answered, "I was where I wanted to be."

Amar couldn't help feeling that he was betraying his brother, who tended to suppress his emotions and endure his pain. Farid's life actually improved back in Ghardaïa. Perhaps Brahim, knowing time was running out, had given up trying to control his younger son. Farid was left free to see whomever he wanted and

216

to do mostly as he pleased. He lived with Brahim in a state of belated truce, counting down the eighteen months until he reached the age of freedom.

One day Farid's stepmother told Brahim that she wanted to visit her parents overnight. Brahim refused to allow her to take their two young children, and the next day he refused to take his wife back. He divorced her and kept the children, who never saw their mother again.

At that point Farid tried to intervene on behalf of the stepmother. He knew just how painful it was to be cut off from one's mother, and hated the idea that these children would repeat his and Amar's lonely history. Despite Farid's pleas on her behalf, she was not allowed to see her children again.

There were no transborder winter visits—Sheik Abbas had suggested that the mothers stop calling them "Christmas visits," so as not to offend Muslim sensibilities—in 1986. The Algerian fathers refused to let their children go, and this time the unwritten agreement was not enforced.

The Mothers of Algiers were devastated, infuriated. They had done everything they'd been asked, and still their children were kept from them. The godmothers hatched a new plan: a three-week protest march from Paris to Geneva. The core group would walk 375 miles in the nastiest winter weather of the year.

"I'm on this march because of rage," one mother explained.

"We were without much hope for a long time," added Margaret Hughes, a British woman who had joined the core group, "but now we're doing it because we think it's possible. We're marching in order to negotiate."

At a press conference in Paris Anne-Marie Lizin explained, "It's a march that stems from despair, but it's also so that other nations will not be accomplices to the violence done to children. It's so that children can see their fathers and their mothers across borders."

In a communiqué, the godmothers issued an eloquent appeal: "At a time when fathers and mothers tear at each other through their children, they [the marchers] want to make clear that an abduction is never a proof of love, but always an act of violence which destroys the child. . . . The law of the strongest must not govern the private relations at the heart of the family."

The mothers issued an ambitious set of demands: free movement of children and free right of visitation for both parents; the appointment of a European mediator; the naming of a new French mediator, a post then vacant; official recognition by the United Nations' Commission on Human Rights; and, not least, a formal and permanent accord between France and Algeria.

The Algerian government, about to take another bruising before the court of world opinion, did its best to stop the march. Annie had learned her lesson, and the mothers rejected an invitation to go to Algiers to talk. They received a warm sendoff from French president François Mitterand, who had finally climbed onto the bandwagon and who promised "to deal personally in this affair with President Chadli."

On February 10, 1987, escorted by a battalion of television cameras, the mothers left Paris. Six days later they detoured into Strasbourg, where the Algerians staged an impromptu reunion by flying in several children for a forty-eight-hour visit. When the mothers met the children at the airport, they had an unwelcome surprise: the fathers had come as well, with other men the mothers resentfully perceived as bodyguards.

The meeting of mothers and children was a moving, bittersweet sight. Some of them hadn't been together for years—and couldn't even recognize each other. Greetings were difficult, as they no longer spoke the same language. The mothers desperately wanted to smother their children with hugs and kisses, but had to hold back because the children were frightened.

The Algerian mediator had hoped that the parents might reconcile, or at least resolve their differences, by spending the night together—an impossibility for most of the women, who'd been separated or divorced for years. The fathers refused to allow the children to stay alone overnight with the mothers.

"We feel like we've been had," said Jocelyne Bany.

"The problem," added Helene Montetagaud, whose daughter was not on the plane, "is that the fathers think that once the children are in France, they will not return to Algeria. The mothers are afraid that if they let them go, they won't return. So it's a vicious circle."

Her analysis would turn out to be prophetic.

Before the group left Strasbourg, suffering yet another painful separation from their children, Annie announced that the mothers and fathers had signed private agreements for transborder visitations. Although these contracts were unenforceable by any court, the Algerian government promised that they would be respected.

The protest, Annie made clear, was not over: "The mothers are fighting not only for themselves but for all the others, and for the signing of a convention that will allow the children real and continuous relations with both parents." The group would press on to Switzerland.

When the mothers reached Geneva, the media storm had grown until it threatened to sweep away all resistance. In a warm welcoming speech Leonid Emenov, the president of the Commission on Human Rights, declared, "The suffering of mothers is the suffering of humanity, because mothers are the source of life, the source of peace. . . . We believe that the international community will finally solve many problems, including yours."

The Algerian ambassador to the UN offered more specific encouragement: "We have a very sad problem and we are all conscious of it. We say in Algeria that it goes both ways, so please excuse us, we think that fathers have a heart like mothers do. That said, nobody is trying to complicate your problem, and I believe that it can be solved."

The Mothers of Algiers had gained acceptance of most of their points: formal recognition by the UN, a renewed commitment by Algeria to foster visitations, and a resumption of negotiations toward a bilateral pact. After so many setbacks, however, the mothers remained skeptical. "The children are being used like chess pieces," said Marie-Paule Meziani, a core-group marcher. "Everyone speaks of rights, but nobody even mentions the children's sufferings."

The Geneva negotiations continued. The key issue, Annie

observed, was to define the principle of "competent jurisdiction"—to decide which country holds the authority to award custody in a given case. This principle, she noted, must be framed not by nationalism—the idea that either France or Algeria was an inherently superior place to grow up in—but by the best interests of the child. It must reflect a child's right to continuity and to be protected from the rupture of abduction.

The French were careful to stress that they were not asserting cultural superiority, an understandably sore point among the Algerians. As the French delegate to the UN Commission noted, "These children have the right to the love of their fathers as well as their mothers, to the love of their paternal family as well as their maternal family, even to benefit from two distinct cultures."

There was the heady smell of hope in the air, and the mothers began to allow themselves to breathe it in. "Two humanists," said Claude Allaer, the new French mediator, "can always work out an agreement."

In July 1987 twenty-six children made the second transborder visitation, which concluded without incident. In December forty-four more made the trip to France.

These events were a mix of joy and crushing disappointment. At the winter visit one child hadn't seen his mother for ten years, and their reunion moved all who witnessed it. But many other mothers had come to Orly Airport fully expecting to greet their children, only to discover that the fathers had broken their agreement at the last moment. Some had sent sons but not their daughters; others had resisted altogether. Ten of the mothers immediately began a hunger strike at the airport.

For the rest the visit passed all too quickly . . . and then the unthinkable happened. One French mother refused to return her seventeen-year-old son to Algeria. When Annie heard the news, she exclaimed, "It's always the dishonest who get their way."

In March of 1988 there was a second betrayal—and this one was even more demoralizing. After a specially arranged visitation with her young daughter, the first since the girl had been abducted several years before, another mother decided to break her word and keep her. The other mothers knew that she was the most fragile member of the core group and that her story was especially tragic. The Algerian father worked in Saudi Arabia and lived in France, and had dumped the daughter with his family.

The two defections appeared to be catastrophic. From the outset of the negotiations the Algerians had stressed the importance of dealing with people of integrity. Given the cultural differences between the two countries and the absence of any legal framework to lean on, the mothers' word of honor was the only lever that could move the other side. The Algerians believed that they were already making the lion's share of concessions. The fathers had physical control of the children, as their society deemed proper. Why should the Algerians relinquish the power they seized unless they could trust the mothers at their word?

That word had proven reliable in the great majority of cases. But in two cases it had failed—and the godmothers feared that those two cases would destroy their credibility. They feared that the defections would torpedo their movement at the brink of its ultimate goal: a bilateral treaty that would above all protect the rights of children.

But the godmothers, though heartbroken, were indefatigable. Annie, in particular, refused to surrender, or even to retreat. Instead, she resolved to turn this huge negative into a positive (as Anne-Marie Lizin once said, "I think Annie is the most clever person I ever met"). Marshaling the public support the Mothers of Algiers had garnered over the years, she and Linda returned to Algeria in April to meet with a highly placed official.

First of all, the godmothers said, the mothers' effort had been essentially honorable, and the world cried out for Algeria to return the honor by signing a treaty.

Second, the transborder visits were unwieldy and, in the long run, impractical. Next year the mothers would ask for two hundred children; the year after that, for four hundred.

Third, the two defections were a painful reminder that people were fallible and that it was unfair to make mothers—or fathers—choose between their heart and the larger cause. Private

221

moral agreements were inadequate. A *treaty* was needed—for its enforcement power, and for its stamp of legal and social approval. Neither side could allow the least scrupulous among them to determine their destiny.

The crisis "actually helped us a great deal," Linda said. "We always wanted a convention. This showed that we were not going to solve the problem without a legal instrument."

When she and Annie left, Linda recalled the Algerian official saying something like "we must come to an end."

"After we returned to France and spoke to an advisor to the prime minister," she continued, "he told us these words have a special meaning in diplomatic language, that they were very significant. 'Maybe we can start new discussions,' he said."

And so negotiations toward the treaty were renewed, more vigorously than before. There was, however, one casualty: the highly respected Claude Allaer, the French mediator who had personally guaranteed the children's return to Algeria, was forced to resign after the first defection.

By way of contrast, it is worth noting Farid Houache's behavior during this period. At the time of the third transborder visit he was almost nineteen years old—a legal adult in France, and just shy of his Algerian majority. Had he chosen to he could have remained in France, and no one could have forced him to go back.

But Farid did just the opposite; he did what parents always wish their children will do. He had internalized the values of his mother and of the group in which she'd played such a prominent part. He understood the value and importance of sacrifice. Like his brother, he wanted to help free *all* the children, not just himself.

The mothers knew they needed to keep up the pressure. With Claude Allaer out of the picture and the treaty still in the realm of theory, they had little hope of seeing their children during that summer's vacation. To dramatize their enduring torment, six of them staged another hunger strike beginning on Mother's Day, at Orly Airport. That strike would last more than a month, leaving one mother gravely ill. As a measure of the movement's growing influence, President Mitterand flew in by helicopter to visit the strikers.

As the negotiations entered a critical stage, the godmothers passed the ball to Georgina DuFoix, Mitterand's minister of immigration. The first French official to make the mothers' cause a top priority, Georgina had organized the charter flight in 1985 for the first transborder visit. Like Annie Sugier and Anne-Marie Lizin, she gained the Algerians' trust by acknowledging the importance of personal integrity over protocol. "I don't want your word as a diplomat," she said once, to inspire an official to take the high road. "I want your word as a man."

The Algerians would pay Georgina their highest compliment: "She is so persistent, she must be a man."

Although Allaer was gone, his ideas lived on in the treaty's working draft that he'd authored. What remained was the necessary if mundane task of revision and haggling. The negotiators realized that the document's final language needed to be painstakingly precise—both for the treaty to be passed and for its authority to be respected as law by both sides.

Above all, the treaty must be compatible with the Algerians' cultural sensitivities. As Linda noted, "You can't tell an Algerian father that he's not the head of his family and that he won't have control over his child." Or as the Algerians put it: "You can't compel a dignified father to give up his child." With this in mind, Linda added, the treaty must avoid using the words "mother" or "father." No agreement could possibly mesh with the legal traditions of both countries. The treaty would skirt the issue by referring to "the parent who is in charge" and by focusing on what was best for the child. It would be realistic rather than legalistic.

On the treaty's two basic principles there could be little question, much less opposition. The first held that children have a right to stay in the place they consider home and that neither parent may tear a child away from that place. The second affirmed children's right of access to both parents, including regular visitation with their noncustodial parent.

Taken together, the godmothers felt certain, these principles would deter most international parental abductions. If parents understood that any abducted child would be sent back home swiftly, they would be discouraged from trying it. And if those parents believed their parenthood was not threatened, regardless of their marital situation, they'd have less incentive for such a desperate act in the first place. As long as children kept moving freely—between parents, cultures, and continents—there would be no reason for anyone to stop them.

As it evolved, the treaty sold itself. World opinion had become an irresistible force for enactment. The catch-as-catch-can transborder visits were too erratic on their face. Most important, the treaty was presented in a way that allayed Algerian fears. It was not a French ploy to wrest all parental power from the fathers. Rather, it provided that both parents *share* power through custody and visitation—and that both be held responsible in assuring their children's rights.

After seven years of grindingly slow progress, the historic breakthrough came suddenly. "Come now," the Algerian caller urged Georgina DuFoix in June 1988. "It is the moment to sign. It has to be done now. Come quickly to Algeria."

Three days later, on June 21, the Franco-Algerian Convention was signed, sealed, and delivered. A temporary binational commission was appointed to advise on all abduction cases already in dispute, including those of the Mothers of Algiers. Future cases would go directly to the courts.

This was, I am convinced, a significant event in the history of human relations. It was the best kind of victory, for there were no losers. The godmothers had seen their vision through to the end. The Mothers of Algiers were no longer severed from their children. The Algerians won new respect from the world by breaking the chains of mutual bad faith and by accommodating the values of another culture. They could no longer be cast as the villains.

Best of all, the children won—all the children who now had two parents instead of one, all the children who would avoid the trauma of abduction in the future. And in this ringing affirmation of their rights against such formidable odds, the winners were all the children of the world.

In its definition of "competent jurisdiction," the Franco-Algerian Convention overcame the judicial nationalism that protects parental child abductors throughout much of the world today. An Algerian father can no longer assume he will be favored and protected by an Algerian court—nor, by the same token, can a French mother assume an automatic advantage in a French court. According to the convention, jurisdiction over international custody disputes belongs to the country where the parents were married, where they lived together and raised their children—the place, in short, that the children consider home.

In practice, the vast majority of cases under the convention have seen children returned from fathers in Algeria to mothers in France. However, the accord has also kept children in Algeria in cases where their age or length of stay there made that appropriate.

Once competent jurisdiction is established, the court rules to return the children to their homeland. At the same time, it mandates visitation rights—as an indivisible corollary to custody—for the noncustodial parent.

Under the convention, enforcement powers are lodged in the countries' respective ministries of justice. Court rulings are taken seriously—on each side of the Mediterranean. Both French and Algerian officials are authorized to search out and find the children in question; to furnish any information that might assist the judge; and to physically return children to their custodial parents, as decided in court. Delays are not tolerated. Once a court has ruled on custody, children are generally returned within a few months.

The convention has teeth—and needs them, given the Algerian fathers' continued resistance, especially in such hard-line Algerian Muslim strongholds as Constantine. Any custodial parents who block legal visitations are subject to criminal sanctions. And if noncustodial parents fail to return their children on time after a visitation, local authorities round the kids up and get them home.

Although French mothers have done well by the accord, they do not have a blank check. To guard against a second disruption (the "ping-pong" syndrome) to a child's home environment, the mother usually must invoke the convention within a year of the abduction. If she waits too long the French court will rule that competent jurisdiction has passed to Algeria. And if the mother herself was lured by her husband to Algeria under false pretenses, she must first return to France, divorce the husband, and *then* file to recover her children. If she visits them in the meantime, she must stay in a hotel or some other neutral ground; a resumption of married life with her husband may forfeit competent jurisdiction to Algeria.

The Franco-Algerian Convention is not flawless. For the sake of Algerian ratification, it excludes several worthy groups: illegitimate children, parents who married in France but are citizens of other countries, French-born mothers of Algerian fathers (under Algerian law, citizenship is passed through the father and dual citizenship does not exist; a woman whose father is Algerian is Algerian as well, and therefore can make no charge of international abduction against an Algerian father).

But no loophole can tarnish the phenomenal, unprecedented achievement of the Mothers of Algiers. They achieved what no group or government had ever done before: an effective agreement on child custody between Christian and Muslim states. With their deep commitment, their willingness to risk body and soul, and their ability to enlist the people in power, they truly moved mountains.

Since the Franco-Algerian Convention was ratified, parental abductions between the two countries have been reduced to a trickle. Its shining success is a model for other agreements between Islamic and non-Islamic states, and for other nations with significant differences.

Amar and Farid are today young men of twenty-four and twenty-three. They will always be marked by their traumatic years in Algeria; they are cooler, more guarded than they used to be. "I feel that I was cheated out of my adolescence," Farid told me, when I visited his family in 1990.

Their story is one of triumph but also of tragedy. There is little doubt that Brahim Houache had good intentions when he tricked his sons into going to Algeria in 1980. He obviously felt compelled, for a host of complex reasons, to return his children to the land he knew best. And he certainly hoped to instill in his sons an appreciation of their father's heritage, culture, and religion.

But Brahim's tactic backfired. The father's coercion would taint all that followed; his sons immediately lost all respect for him and all interest in learning more about his homeland. In fact, they resented everything about their new home, just as inmates resent their prison. Among older abducted children this is a common and especially sad syndrome. In one blow they lose both of their parents—the one who gets left behind, the other whom they reject.

But while their resentment still smolders and the breach with their father may never be healed, it would be wrong to call Amar and Farid unhappy. They spend as much time as they can with Marie-Anne, as if to make up for lost years. I have never witnessed sons who so visibly admired and cared about their mother. Nor have I seen brothers quite so proud and attuned to one another, their acknowledged sibling rivalries and squabbles notwithstanding. These are people, I thought, who will never take one another for granted. They truly have bridged the generations; the values of the mother will live on through her sons.

Of all the stories I've heard throughout the world, this one holds special meaning for me. After meeting Amar and Farid, my hope is that my own sons will stay as close to one another and to me. There is nothing more important than the family bond, as we who've seen it threatened know best of all.

9

Fulfilling a *Nasr*

*I*n March 1990 Mahtob and I traveled to Tel Aviv, where our movie *Not Without My Daughter* was being filmed—a new and exciting experience for us.

After landing at Ben-Gurion Airport Mahtob and I went directly to the set, where our arrival in Tehran five years earlier was being re-created on film. As we approached Moody's film family, they all stood to greet us. At first I felt as if I were seeing things; some of the actors looked very much like the real characters. Immediately they began apologizing for what happened to us in Iran.

Sheila Rosenthal, the six-year-old actress playing Mahtob, was adorable—Mahtob and I both loved her as soon as we laid eyes on her. She was confused, thinking that we had *just* escaped. She was happy that we made it, she said, but wondered if we weren't "tired from riding that horse?"

Before we had time to catch our breath we were introduced to Sally Field, who was playing my character. I didn't have time to prepare what I would say to her. I told her how much I appreciated her taking the role; she said she'd been drawn by "the incredible story."

I spent three weeks on the set in Israel with Mahtob, who landed a role as an extra in the school scene. Mahtob had been traumatized each day in Iran when she was forced to be separated from me to attend a school that was strange and frightening to her. Now that it was just make-believe, she enjoyed dressing up each day in her *macknay*, or scarf, and in the waistless coat known as a *montoe*.

One day three hundred young female extras, dressed in their Iranian garb, stood on the school's balcony and chanted "Mahtob, Mahtob" as we approached. They all were eager to talk to the real Mahtob.

Sheila was great. Already a pro, she gave Mahtob acting tips. After a scene she'd always say, "Mahtob, you were really good." She took pride in translating the Hebrew she'd already learned. Sheila would introduce Mahtob as "the real Mahtob" and then add: "I'm just the pretend Mahtob."

Mahtob also struck up a friendship with Lee Harmon, Sally's makeup artist. Lee spent hours on the set with Sheila and Mahtob, making and flying paper airplanes. He reminded Mahtob of her grandpa; he was a jokester and loved fishing. Long after the filming concluded, Mahtob remembered and asked about him.

One day Lee said to Mahtob, "Come on, let's go to the trailer. I'm going to give you a black eye." He did just that. It looked so realistic, and so painful. He followed that up with a big burn "scar" on her hand.

Jaffa, the old Arab section of Tel Aviv, bore an uncanny resemblance to Tehran. For the film, posters with Farsi graffiti were imported from Iran. Street signs were changed. Huge pictures of the Ayatollah Khomeni were displayed on the sides of the buildings. Cars were painted white to resemble the Iranian Pakon, or orange after Tehran's taxis, and bore mock-Iranian license plates. Iranian consultants were called in to assist the wardrobe department in creating authentic-looking clothing. The Israelis were curious about what was happening, and so many people gathered to watch that the police came to investigate. The Uflands issued a press release stating "This is only a movie. The spirit of the Ayatollah has not invaded Tel Aviv."

The similarities reminded me that we were only six hundred miles from Iran, too close to Moody for comfort. Between that proximity and the longstanding Israeli-Palestinian problems, I'd been apprehensive about our going to Israel. The Uflands, Michael Carlisle, and the State Department had assured me that security in Israel was the tightest in the world. I believed them after I was held at check-in for our El Al flight out of Chicago, where airline officials stopped me because of my Iranian last name. They refused to accept my explanation for my trip until after they phoned the producers in Israel. The El Al people later apologized, but I felt relieved that they were so conscientious.

Anyhow, I was soon caught up in the day-to-day activities on the set. It was fascinating—and more than a little eerie—to watch my life played out before me. I enjoyed most of it but could barely force myself to watch certain scenes. When Sheila screeched in terror upon being left at school for the first time, it tore at my insides—I felt a compulsion to rush out and comfort her. Toughest of all were the dramatizations of Moody's abuse toward us. They were so realistic that I relived the horrors we had endured in Iran.

Months before I had spent several hours with John Goldwyn and Chris Bomba on the script. After our session they paid me a high compliment: "After meeting you, whoever plays your role should come across as a *real* person—an ordinary person with whom everyone can relate."

Sally Field had been my choice for the lead role from the start. I'd found her moving and believable in the movies I'd seen her in. As it turned out, Sally was perfect for the part. She didn't consult with me about her characterization, but I felt we'd communicated through the script I'd worked on with Brian Gilbert, the director, to create. I found it fascinating to view the "dailies" after each day of shooting and to watch Sally's eyes—they disclosed just what I'd been feeling at the time. I was especially struck by the telling scene in which I told Moody that I wanted to make our life work in Iran—a ploy calculated to buy Mahtob and me the time and space to escape. As Sally put her arms around Alfred Molina, the actor playing Moody in this false reconciliation, the camera zeroed in on her eyes, and you could tell that she was saying and thinking two different things—that her affection was all pretense.

Sally surprised me on my first day on the set. As we walked across the tarmac to allow the crew to set up a new scene, Sally stooped to pick up a piece of litter—a Styrofoam cup, as I recall—and deposit it in the trash. I found it a refreshingly unspoiled gesture for a movie star. Between scenes she would do professional-caliber needlepoint.

From the moment Mahtob and I stepped off the plane, the Uflands paid us nonstop attention. Their limousine took us from the hotel to the set and back every day. They sat with us for lunch and invited us to dinner every night. Harry and Mahtob gabbed nonstop about my daughter's beloved Detroit Pistons, who were headed for the NBA's playoff finals. To Mahtob's delight, Harry kept rooting for Detroit even when they faced off against his hometown Los Angeles Lakers. As we spent time together, my friendship with the producers grew much closer. They were compassionate and protective, and kept in touch with us long after the movie was completed.

About a week into filming the Uflands declared that the escape scene would have to be cut from the script. They'd counted on snow in the Eilat Mountains in the southern part of Israel, but a snowless winter had foiled them. Without snow, the producers reasoned, the scene would lose its dramatic power. Deleting it would be easiest—and most economical. Alan Ladd, Jr., head of MGM-Pathe, had been uncomfortable with a snow scene from the start, for safety reasons.

Brian argued that the escape was essential to the story line and proposed that they shift the scene to Spain, where there was snow—an idea the Uflands rejected as too extravagant and time-consuming. The Atlanta crew was set and ready to film the U.S. scenes; there just wasn't enough time to seek out another location.

Sally was even more upset than Brian—at one point she even threatened to quit. To stave off disaster, Harry worked out a compromise: they would restore the escape, but the scene would stay in Israel—without snow. Sally agreed to stay. Brian hurriedly rewrote the script—my character would now be fighting off heat stroke instead of frostbite—and the show went on.

While we were trapped in Tehran I had made a promise to God—a *nasr*. These vows are common among Iranians. For example: Mehdi, the son of Moody's nephew Reza, was born with deformed feet. He underwent surgery and was required to wear special shoes and braces. His parents made a *nasr* that if Mehdi walked, they would all go to Mashad for a pilgrimage. My *nasr* was that if we escaped, I would take Mahtob to Jerusalem to walk the same paths that Jesus had.

While we attended the shooting, the Uflands offered us a chauffeured car to take us wherever we wanted to go. Mahtob worked on the set nearly every day, but we did take a couple of trips. The first was to Jericho, Masada, and the Dead Sea. Mony Rae, the actress who played Moody's sister in the film, went with us. It was a strange feeling, as if we were traveling with our Iranian relatives. Though we liked Mony Rae very much, she was having a difficult time with us because she was playing such a wicked role against me in the movie. She always felt apologetic, but we developed a warm friendship with her.

Mahtob and I were breathless when we saw where the wall of Jericho had come tumbling down. We entered King Herod's palace on top of Masada and were reminded of the great sacrifices made at that very spot. The Dead Sea was very beautiful, very smelly, and a rare treat. The water is so heavy with dissolved minerals that even I didn't sink when I went for a swim.

Often Mahtob associates a country with an individual child who has been kidnapped to it. When she looked across the River Jordan, she thought of one little boy in particular and lamented, "I wish we could go over there and get him."

Back on the highway we saw tribes of Bedouins living in tents, and camels silhouetted on the mountaintops. It was as if we had stepped back in time. The only people we saw outside the tents were women. According to our driver the women did all the everyday work and waited ceaselessly on the men. In the Bedouin social structure the men had to be rested to fight and protect their families.

It was so incredible to see people still living in these ancient ways. With all the modern conveniences we take for granted, I can't even begin to imagine what life must be like for them.

We also saw reminders of the Seven-Day War along that highway, with rusted trucks and tanks marking the old battle locations. War and its remnants are not ancient history in Israel. The air was charged with the tension of wars past and wars to come. I empathized with parents who raised their children knowing they might be called to fight—perhaps to die—any day. And what of the children, whose futures are so uncertain?

A few days later we went to Jerusalem to complete our *nasr*, with our first stop at the Mount of Olives. Our timing was perfect. It was the Saturday between Good Friday and Easter Sunday, a most thought-provoking time to be there.

Our driver, Uri, was an archaeologist who spoke excellent English, and he pointed out how cities had been built on top of cities in different eras. Mahtob was truly excited by this experience and still retains a special interest in archaeology.

Uri explained to us how his car had been stoned and its windows smashed when he had taken someone else through these same streets recently. Fearful of another attack, he left us at the tomb of Jesus before stopping at a service station for gasoline.

Mahtob and I walked where Jesus taught his disciples, where the Lord's Prayer was given. We saw the tomb and the garden where Jesus' body was laid. Unfortunately, according to our guide, the site of the crucifixion was now a bus station.

There were crowds of visitors despite the ongoing conflict in the area. One section of the Old City was off-limits because of Palestinian demonstrations. We later read reports that three people were killed there the following day.

As we proceeded to the West Bank, we could go only to the edge of Bethlehem because of security risks. As we entered a large shop there, I told Mahtob I'd buy her a gold bracelet. But she chose instead a gorgeous Nativity scene, while I selected a Last Supper carved from olive wood—both future heirlooms.

Back in Jaffa we were invited to a family Passover seder by the film's Israeli script director. Several members of her family spoke English, and they provided English-language *hagadahs*, or Passover prayerbooks, so that we could follow the service. They were extremely kind in explaining everything to us. I welcomed the opportunity to be with them—not only to observe a seder but to get a view of life outside the hotel.

Midway through our stay in Israel, Sheila's mom prepared a birthday party in their hotel suite for Sheila's three-year-old sister, Nicole. Sally and her husband were there, as were their two-year-old son Sam, Sam's nanny, and Mahtob and me. The cake, ordered from room service, was a beautiful surprise when it arrived. It appeared to be a typical chocolate cake, but it turned out to be made from matzo flour, in keeping with Passover.

I particularly enjoyed meeting Alfred Molina. Alfred had questions about Moody and how my husband had related to Mahtob and me. "What would Moody do in this situation? How would he move? What would he say? Around the house in America, what kinds of things would he do with Mahtob? Did he speak to her on an adult or child's level?" Alfred looked nothing like my ex-husband; the actor was taller and slimmer, plus he had a beard and considerably more hair. Alfred took his role seriously. His mood swings were very convincing; he had captured Moody's tone of voice and behavior to an unnerving degree, until I took to joking with him that he must be meeting with Moody privately.

Alfred is a caring, approachable man who mixed well with the others. He preferred to eat at the crew tent rather than in his trailer. Often he successfully tried some of his stand-up comedy routines on those around him, but on the set he took his role seriously. His wife, herself an actress, spent time there as well and helped Alfred tell how they first heard of my story. In 1988, while I was in England promoting the book, they were having lunch at their kitchen table when my interview aired on BBC radio. Alfred told his wife, "That would make a great movie," not imagining that he would one day play the male lead. There was much banter during the film about how convincing Alfred was in acting abusively to my character. His wife jokingly replied, "He gets lots of practice at home." Of course, the rest of us wouldn't let him forget that for the rest of the filming.

With the escape scene "in the can," the next step was to film the pre-Iran American scenes in Atlanta, Georgia. Like most movies, *Not Without My Daughter* was shot out of sequence.

On our way back from Israel Mahtob and I stopped in Paris to visit our French publisher, Bernard Fixot. We'd just passed the 1.5 million mark in sales, and Bernard said, "When you have something great to celebrate, you go to Maxim's."

When my editor, Antoine Audouard, and his wife picked us up at our hotel, they marveled at how Mahtob had grown and at how lovely she looked in her striped cotton dress. At the legendary restaurant my daughter drew more compliments. "Mahtob, your dress is beautiful," said Michelle, our French agent. "Where did you get it?"

Shy in public, Mahtob ordinarily would have answered with a nonresponsive shrug. Not this time. In a matter-of-fact and uncustomarily loud voice she piped up, "K mart." I had purchased the dress off the rack, on the run, at the well-known American discount chain.

As the rave reviews continued, it became apparent that none of our dinner companions shared my amusement. As far as they knew, K mart might have been an elegant children's boutique.

It had been a long trip and I had a lot to catch up on back in Michigan, including a stack of mail taller than I could imagine. We'd been home only a few hours when Bill Hoffer called to report that a friend of one of his co-authors had just had her two children "kidnapped and taken to Iran. Would you give her a call?"

I called Jessie Pars right away, and she told me how her six-year-old son and eight-year-old daughter had been kidnapped the week before. She was desperate; she didn't know to whom she could turn. Arnie and I agreed to fly to Philadelphia two days later to see if there was anything we could do to help.

Jessie and her sister and brother-in-law picked us up at the airport and drove us to her house. When we walked in, her family's Easter baskets were still on the table, with the children's toys around the corner in the living room. Jessie said, "When the children were leaving to go on the visitation with their father, my son Cy waved from the driveway and said, 'Mom, don't forget to invite Bobby to my birthday party.' " She couldn't hold back the tears. "And today is his sixth birthday."

Jessie had recorded her recent phone conversations with her ex-husband. We listened to some tapes, including one with a brief message from her eight-year-old daughter Sarah. In a sobbing voice Sarah said, "Mommy, come and get me. Come and get me!" Tears swelled the eyes of those gathered around that table listening to the tapes. We all knew something had to be done as soon as possible to help these children who were trapped in a village in northern Iran.

We returned home that afternoon, as I had to leave the next day for Atlanta for the rest of the filming of *Not Without My Daughter*. But we kept in touch with Jessie. We encouraged her to maintain a line of communication with her ex-husband and possibly she could convince him to come out of Iran with the children. There just wouldn't be any other way to get the children back.

My friend Mary Ann Morris (my family doctor's wife) went with Mahtob and me to Atlanta. Their daughter Jaime and niece Haley went along to keep Mahtob company. We were later joined by Arnie and Michael Carlisle. I loved being surrounded by people who were so important to me and who could share my excitement during the filming.

Again, I was amazed by the care that the Uflands and Brian had taken to replicate our riverfront home in Alpena, Michigan. The river side of the house was lined with glass overlooking the slope to the river. It looked so similar that many people from Alpena thought the scenes has actually been filmed there (I had hoped filming would take place in Alpena itself, but early May weather there would not have provided the summer effect we needed). I had shipped my Iranian mementos to the set, including Mahtob's cradle and some of her old toys and dolls, which we dressed in Mahtob's own baby clothes.

Mr. and Mrs. Brooks, the house's real owners, told us that

one day a stranger had appeared at their door and said, "Would you let us shoot a movie in your house?" They never hesitated; they were excited from that first moment. After an agreement was signed, the crew moved the family's belongings out and brought in entirely different furniture and accessories. New draperies were made and hung—and then Brian walked in and said, "Take them down—they're not right." A new set was immediately stitched. When the crew was finished, the interior was a near duplicate of the place I'd lived in six years before.

The five days of shooting in Atlanta were extremely difficult. The cast came in jet-lagged and exhausted from the seven-day weeks in Israel—especially Sally, whose two-year-old was still adjusting to the new time zone. Everyone's nerves were on edge.

Finally the shooting approached completion. When the outdoor scenes were finished, a large truck came to pick up the shrubs and flowers that had beautified the approach to the river.

After the inside scenes were shot, everything was loaded and taken away. The wallpaper was changed back to the original and the walls repainted. The crew left as quickly as it had arrived.

As we prepared for the movie's premiere in January 1991, MGM invited Mahtob and me to New York to screen the film in December—my favorite time to visit the city, with its festive spirit of Christmas. This was a welcome opportunity, a chance for us to digest the film privately before sharing our emotions with the world.

The screening took place downstairs from my agents' office at William Morris. Although nervous to see our lives played out on the screen, Mahtob and I felt as comfortable as possible with our support group of Michael, his mate Sally, and his stepdaughter Holly, whom we had met in 1988 in Paris, where Mahtob had adopted her as a friend. Mahtob had specifically asked if Holly could join us. Arnie was also there as part of our support team.

Even though we'd been on the set, this was our first chance to see the film in its entirety. Early on, during the scene where

Moody told me that he would not allow us to leave Iran, I started to cry. I wondered if I'd be able to watch the rest. It was at that point in my life that I'd lost my husband, who'd been my best friend until then, and that Mahtob had lost her father—not to mention contact with our family back in America.

I kept looking at Mahtob, who was holding up incredibly well. I grew concerned that she wasn't showing much emotion and wondered if it was because Alfred Molina didn't really look like her father. Finally she could no longer conceal her feelings. When we reached the scene where Moody told her that I was going to leave Iran and that she would never see me again, Mahtob began crying and trembling. I held her hand, but I didn't want to suppress her feelings. I thought it was important for her to cry if that was how she felt. But as she trembled harder and harder, I wondered if we should leave the theater.

That scene made me relive a day I will never forget. Mahtob had gone into Moody's office in our house in Tehran. She came out with a look of hatred and betrayal on her face. Boldly and bitterly she faced me and exclaimed, "You're going to leave me!" I tried to explain that it wasn't true—that her father was trying to force me to go, and she still had my promise to "never leave Iran without you."

Now, nearly five years later, it became clear that Mahtob still had questions about that day in Iran—questions finally answered by the movie. As the credits started rolling, she looked up at me, glinted a smile through her tears, and said, "Thanks, Mom."

Though I'd never really doubted I had done what was right, it was then confirmed by the one who counted most. If we never sold a ticket to the movie, that moment made it all worthwhile.

The next day we shopped for a dress for Mahtob to wear to the premiere. When she emerged from the dressing room, I realized she was no longer the little girl who had determinedly climbed those mountains to freedom. She was now a beautiful young lady who had used that experience to build character and stamina. She was a young lady I was very proud to call my daughter.

I knew all along where I wanted to have our premiere: in my native rural area of Michigan. I've always been proud of where I'm from. My family is still there, as well as most of my friends. I didn't want a glitzy, glamorous premiere in Los Angeles or New York, where many of the people I most cared about would be unable to attend.

When a local service organization offered to help with the premiere if we could hold it in the area, I gained the confidence to approach MGM. The studio's first reaction was that it wanted the event to be something special, and doubted that a small town could do justice to an event with such major stars as Sally Field and Alfred Molina.

But once the studio's publicity representative met with the service organization, everyone was pleased with the local group's preparations. We were headed toward a premiere that would make everyone proud to be part of the community.

Given the growing turmoil in the Persian Gulf at the time and my association with that part of the world, publicity for the movie took off before I was ready. Suddenly every TV and radio station for miles around wanted to come to my home for an interview.

CNN brought Mariann Saieed, whom I had met at our workshop in November, and whose two children had been kidnapped to Iraq. With the impending war in the Gulf region, the reporters wanted to hear my advice to Mariann. She was so shattered by the disappearance of her children that she had no life here. Although it would not be easy, and there was certainly no guarantee she would ever get out of Iraq, I knew that were I in her place I would have no choice. If Mahtob was over there, I would go to be with her. Amid the excitement of the coming festivities, I could not forget the thousands of left-behind parents out there and the thousands of children who suffer the trauma of international parental child abduction. In the United States alone, eight cases a week—more than four hundred a year—are reported to the State Department.

The publicity was nonstop. Amid all the bustle, on top of

trying to put my house back together after remodeling, I was surprised when my sons said that they really didn't want to attend the premiere. I had taken their participation for granted, and I wanted them to be with Mahtob and me as part of our family. When I asked them about their plans for that evening, they were both abrupt, and I could sense their discomfort. They had not dealt with our family trauma as well as Mahtob had. Rather than openly voicing their feelings they'd avoided the issue—the same way I used to handle emotional pain or conflict. They hadn't read *Not Without My Daughter* and had avoided discussion of our time in Iran.

"Mom, you just don't understand," John said with tears in his eyes. "When you were over there, I would go to bed at night and I couldn't sleep because I didn't know if you were dead or alive." By this time all three of us were crying, and Joe said, "We didn't know if you would ever come back."

I've never doubted that Joe and John suffered more than Mahtob and I did from this ordeal—that *not knowing* is the worst torture of all. While we were in Iran, my most difficult time came when Mahtob and I were separated. The pain of not knowing was worse than Moody's worst beatings.

In the end, Joe and John both attended the premiere.

Friends from Texas, New York, California, and West Virginia joined our family and local friends for the occasion. I finally had an opportunity to share my excitement with the people who had supported us since our return from Iran.

For Mahtob, the highlight of the premiere came when Sheila and her parents arrived from California. Sheila is a beautiful child, such a joy and such an entertainer—on and off the set. The evening before the premiere, several guests joined us at my home for a Persian dinner. Michael proposed a touching, thought-provoking toast to Mahtob, Sheila, and me as the courageous women of this story. After everyone settled down to enjoy dinner, a sudden tap of a fork on a glass drew everyone's attention to Sheila, sitting cross-legged at the *sofray* (Persian tablecloth) on the floor. She made a warm and gracious toast that delighted everyone. I looked at her father as tears streamed down his face.

Mahtob and Sheila developed a friendship that will endure for years to come.

On January 5, 1991, the afternoon of the premiere, hundreds of friends and family members came to my home for a cocktail party. Mahtob's three closest friends since first grade, Angie, Jamie, and Cathie, were a bit jealous at having to share Mahtob with "Entertainment Tonight," there for filming, and all the other guests.

Christy Khan came to the afternoon party with her youngest son Eric, her parents, and some other relatives. I knew that Christy had found *Not Without My Daughter* too upsetting to read all the way through (she initially had obtained the book before her sons were kidnapped, but her husband had promptly thrown it away). Despite the excitement of the flashing cameras and busy TV crews, I couldn't help but notice Christy holding Eric in her arms. My heart ached for Johnathan and Adam, still in Pakistan. Christy couldn't bear to stay to watch the film. The mere sight of the promotional poster—in which Sally Field, a picture of resolute motherhood, carries the young Mahtob to freedom against the backdrop of a Turkish cityscape—almost drove her from the room.

"Oh, that tore me up," Christy would recall. "Sally Field's face depicted everything I felt. It made me remember holding the kids when they were being torn out of my arms. That whole year I was in Pakistan, that is all I strained for—to run away with them and just put it all behind me."

Sharing Christy's pain renewed my hope that the movie might shine some light on this issue and help prevent future abductions.

It was a difficult day for me. A thousand people had come to the opening and received the film with enthusiasm. But the one person who would have been so proud, who was responsible for all of this, was Dad. He had taught me determination, and the conviction that "where there's a will, there's a way." Though I missed him terribly that day, somehow I knew he was there in spirit.

Early the next morning I left for California, where I would

begin the publicity tour. I called home and asked Mahtob, "Did your friends like the movie?" Her reply was "They loved the limo ride." Mahtob's friends knew her by a different name, and Sheila was playing the role of a girl five years younger; they apparently didn't link my daughter to the character on the screen.

Three days after the premiere, Sally and I shared a flight to Chicago, where we were to do the Oprah Winfrey show. She treated me like a long-lost friend, chattering nonstop from takeoff to landing, giving me a generous helping of movieland gossip. Sally was once in a plane crash; conversation helped her cope with her fear of flying.

Oprah, by the way, was wonderful to me, warm and sincere. She came back to the green room and told me that she'd seen the movie *Not Without My Daughter* the night before. Despite the fact that she had followed my story since the first Barbara Walters interview and knew I'd be appearing on her show the next day, she'd had a hard time sitting through the film. She'd kept fretting that Mahtob and I might not make it out of Iran. Oprah sincerely *loved* the movie, and her energy for that show ran extremely high.

But others weren't so generous toward our film.

I expected criticism of the movie from the start, but I was shocked by Roger Ebert's blistering commentary. Ebert's critique was broadcast on January 5, the same day the film premiered in Michigan and a week before its national release. His statement, which the wire services distributed throughout the country, attacked the movie for having a "racist" tone—precisely what everyone involved with the film had worked so hard to avoid.

In writing our book, Bill Hoffer and I simply aimed to say what happened. We didn't consider how our audience might react, and there were few criticisms that we'd been unfair to Iranians.

For the movie we *were* sensitive to the question of fairness and deliberately toned down the script, even at the cost of losing some of the book's flavor. As I told the producers and director from the outset, "It's very important that people don't leave this film thinking that all Iranians are like Moody's family." To that end we scaled back the number of scenes involving Moody's

242

physical abuse. We also made sure to retain several sympathetic Iranian characters, including Hamid the helpful retailer and Amahl, the extraordinary, selfless man who got us out of the country.

In the movie critics' rush to judgment, none of these efforts seemed to matter. Roger Ebert had set the tone with his preliminary critique, and his charge was echoed in reviews throughout the world (ironically Ebert's full-scale review, as aired on his television show days after his original statement, was no worse than mixed).

There were a few unfortunate mistakes in the film—most notably its treatment of our escape. This should have been the climax, as it was in the book, but it was the weakest scene. Losing the snow was a blow; losing what we had actually experienced during the escape was worse. I had truly felt I was going to *die* in those mountains. At one point, paralyzed by the cold, I gasped to Mosehn, the head smuggler, to take Mahtob and go on without me. That end-of-the-road resignation, that terminal weariness, got mislaid in translation to the screen.

My consolation was the inclusion (over initial objections) of the movie's closing scene in Ankara, Turkey, where Mahtob and I got to the U.S. Embassy by following the sound of a flapping American flag. The producers and director had reasoned, "The audience wants to get you out of Iran; they aren't going to sit through your trip to Ankara." I countered that crossing the Iranian-Turkish border was not our point of security, that we didn't feel safe until we could see a symbol of security, our flag. Many viewers have since told me how moved they had been by that closing scene.

Even with the criticism that the movie was racist, it might have prospered at the box office if not for the worst possible timing. On Friday, January 11, our national opening day, the eastern half of the country was snowed in by a winter storm. In San Diego, meanwhile, a theater received a bomb threat, requiring West Coast audiences to pass through metal detectors. Within a few days Sally's life was threatened, forcing her to hire bodyguards.

Over the next three days—Saturday, Sunday, Monday—the

movie did very well, and it looked like we had a hit. But Tuesday, January 15, was President Bush's deadline for Iraq to withdraw from Kuwait, and the next day the U.S. invaded. For the following week or two, Americans stopped going to movies—they directed their viewing to television, especially Cable News Network.

What they saw was Operation Desert Storm, a drama more topical and urgent than any movie. We had devoted years attempting to depict life in Iran from 1984 to 1986. Now viewers around the globe were given live footage of a war as it occurred. As it turned out, the sun and sand shown in the movie's escape scene were in keeping with the barrage of television footage on the war. People who returned to the theaters were seeking diversion and escape from a most distressing reality. A serious movie—one set in Iran, no less—did not stand much of a chance.

When *Not Without My Daughter* was released in Europe under more favorable circumstances, it met and exceeded box-office expectations. In Germany it was the number-one grossing film for several consecutive weeks. Whatever flaws it may have had, I believe the movie provided an example of international child abduction and helped initiate awareness of the tragedy.

10

Moody Reacts

Not *Without My Daughter* was first published by St. Martin's Press in the United States to solid reviews and excellent initial sales. The response grew from there—in waves. The first non-English wave was in France, where the book sold more copies than any other nonfiction book in the history of the French language, as noted in the 1990 *Guinness Book of Records*. The next major wave was in Sweden, where one of every two and a half homes in the country own the book and well over one-third of the population has read it. The greatest wave of all has been in Germany, where more than 4 million copies have been purchased, and the book topped the best-seller list for more than two years (as a result I was named Woman of the Year in Germany for 1990, an honor I will always treasure).

All told, the book has been translated into approximately twenty languages and has sold about 12 million copies.

What made *Not Without My Daughter* a best-seller on three continents (it made the list in Australia as well as in North America and Europe)? With hindsight, I'd say that the book rode the universality of its subject: the bond between parent and child, and the extremes to which people will go when that bond is threatened. Behind the book's emotional and dramatic appeal lies something else: its concern for the *ordinary*. From the outset, even before I realized I was trapped in Iran, I wanted to show the world how people lived there—how they shopped and cooked their rice, how they washed their dishes and did their laundry, even how they used their bathrooms. No matter what people's status, we all have an everyday home life and a natural interest in the routines of others.

Even though *Not Without My Daughter* is the story of an American woman with the most middle-American roots imaginable, the events described there could—and have—happened to people anywhere. In Western Europe in particular, recent immigrations have led to a quantum jump in bicultural marriages and children of mixed ethnicity. The French and the Algerians, the Germans and the Turks, the Belgians and Moroccans—they live and work side by side these days. They hold very different assumptions about family roles and obligations, differences that may not emerge until after a child is born.

Even as we recognized the story's broad appeal, however, no one anticipated that *Not Without My Daughter* would become a worldwide phenomenon.

As I was a neophyte to the world of writing, so I was a newcomer to public speaking. Before I could conjure up all my anxieties about what I was supposed to know but didn't, I was thrust into a major booking: the Beverly Hills Country Club. As it turned out, however, by reminding myself that I was the only expert on my story, I felt comfortable before an audience from the start.

After the book was released, numerous groups invited me to speak. The idea spread rapidly, and since then my schedule has been filled. While I've spoken to groups large and small, one of my most memorable engagements came when Mahtob and I were chosen to receive the American Freedom Award in Provo, Utah, for the July 4, 1991, festival. Mahtob (the youngest recipient ever) and I shared the international honor with Teddy Kollek, the longtime mayor of Jerusalem, and Nathaniel Howell, the U.S. ambassador to Kuwait who risked his life to stay with his staff after the Iraqi invasion. To make it even more special, I was asked to stand in for former British prime minister Margaret Thatcher, who'd canceled at the last moment, and to deliver the keynote address to more than twenty thousand people at Brigham

Young University Stadium. Despite the size of the audience, I've rarely felt so much in tune with my listeners.

After the formal proceedings were over, Mahtob and I attended a reception at the home of Alan Osmond, whose talented sons—the Four Osmond Boys—dedicated to us a rendition of "Danny Boy." To top off the festivities I was inducted as an aeronaut after I ascended in a hot-air balloon. After we sailed over Provo, my hosts invited me to complete a novel ritual. To become an official aeronaut I would have to sit on my knees with my arms behind my back, lean over, and pick up a glass of "champagne" (in this case substituted by grape juice) with my teeth, then drink it down without spilling a drop. I passed the test with flying colors, and knew my next landing would be a smooth one.

My lecture schedule can be grueling, but I've been encouraged to continue by the question-and-answer periods that follow each presentation. Telling my story of abuse in a foreign land struck a ready chord. Many who had suffered similarly, but in silence, responded when they heard me. They had been waiting so long to tell their own accounts but did not until I came forward.

Many members of my audiences are victims of an abusive relationship that may or may not be bicultural. Early in my lecture career an attractive, well-dressed lady told me, "I'm an American, married to an American, living in America . . . and you wrote my story. I was a prisoner in my own home. You were a woman, a non-Muslim, and an American. After reading your story I realized that if you could overcome those odds, then I could change my life. And I did."

I hadn't considered myself to be a battered woman, perhaps because I never fully fell into the cycle. I was always fighting to get out. After many similar responses, I now have broadened my lecture topics to include battered women and women's rights.

Many have asked me about Ellen Rafaee, whose battering was disclosed in *Not Without My Daughter*. She was an American-born woman—she hailed from a town in central Michigan, in fact—whom I met and befriended in a Koran study class in Tehran. Many have asked me about her.

247

In 1987 my brother Jim had gotten a phone call from Ellen's cousin Florence, who was associated with a women's shelter.

I returned the call to Florence and was told that Ellen, her husband Hormoz, and their two children Jessica and Ali, were in Florida visiting her parents. She related that Hormoz had been brutal to Ellen and the children and that Ellen didn't want to go back to Iran.

I phoned Ellen several times, as I didn't trust her enough to give her my phone number. She was pleased to report to me that she had made it to the fifth-grade level in reading and writing Farsi.

Ellen confirmed what Florence had told me and said, "Betty, I hope you can understand. When I was thinking for myself in Iran I wanted to help you, but the rest of the time I was trying to protect us from Hormoz. He blows up at us two or three times a year, at whoever gets in his way." She said it was usually her own fault that she got beaten, because when Hormoz beats the children "he gets mad at me for interfering. He starts hitting Jessica so severely that I don't call that punishment anymore. It gets really bad." On one occasion, she continued, Hormoz had struck their daughter with a wooden hanger. "It was in three pieces and she was crying, and I saw that hanger and I about flipped out!" Jessica described to her mother how Hormoz had beaten her on the back, and when the hanger broke, he picked up the pieces and resumed until they broke again. "I blew up and screamed, and then he beat me. I think he punctured my eardrum even before I met you," Ellen said.

"That was the worst injury, but he brags about being able to beat us up without leaving any marks. He knows all these holds. About a month before we came to Iran, it happened. He started beating on her [Jessica], I stepped in, and so he beat on me. I had bruises where he held my arm too tight, when he was twisting my arms up around my back. The next morning I couldn't move my neck. My back is still bad."

Ellen said Florence had offered to try to get her a job at a center for battered women. "I said, 'Well, maybe I should be a patient instead of a teacher.' Before that, I hadn't said anything to her. I brought it up to my parents this time because I really wanted some support to stay here. But my dad keeps telling me to stay [in Iran] because Hormoz is a good man, and he thinks that maybe he will change."

In Tehran Hormoz had told Moody, in front of Ellen and me, that he had problems with Ellen after they first came to Iran. She didn't like living there, he said, but he beat her and locked her up. She ultimately converted to Islam and became "a good wife." When I heard this, I knew it was exactly what Moody wanted from me. Moody liked Ellen because she had "adapted."

I said to Ellen, "They don't change because they think it's okay. They don't see anything wrong with what they do."

Ellen was working hard to convince herself that her father might be right. "He [Hormoz] swears up and down that he would never beat me again," she said, "and that if he does it again we could leave Iran and go back to America."

Ellen told me she'd read the serialization of *Not Without My Daughter* in *Ladies Home Journal*. She said that Florence had doubted it was all true, but Ellen "read it word for word and I said, 'There is nothing in there but the truth and I can verify all of it, because I was with her throughout. Some of these dates I remember vividly.' "

She went on to say that she and Hormoz had thought that I was happier and had accepted my life in Iran. She expressed her disappointment that I hadn't confided my intentions to her. I knew, however, that I couldn't trust Ellen—ever since she informed me, months before our actual escape, that it was her "Islamic duty" to report to Moody that I wanted to flee with Mahtob.

Ellen told me how she found out Mahtob and I had left. "I was the first person to be investigated. Within twenty-four hours, detectives came to see me. Moody and his nephew, Mammal, came in to see if you were there. He didn't trust anyone."

She told me that some American women I had met in Iran had been under heavy suspicion for helping me. "Moody sent detectives and they were harassed. An American girl that lived in

Moody's sister's neighborhood was taken to the police station with her husband."

"She didn't know anything!" I said. "None of them did."

"She was under suspicion," Ellen continued. "Moody was sure she was lying and he wanted to search her house, because he thought you were hiding there. She had it rough."

Saddened, I said, "That is why I didn't let anyone know what I was doing—because I didn't want anyone to be guilty."

Ellen's information fit exactly with a call I'd gotten from the U.S. State Department not long after reaching home. "Some Americans are in trouble," the caller said. "Moody thinks you are still in Tehran hiding. You have to call him and let him know you are out of the country to save these people." I couldn't consider talking to Moody at that point, so I had my sister Carolyn make the call. Not wanting to let him know we were in America but wanting to relieve the threat to these innocent Americans, Carolyn told Moody that we were in another country outside Iran. He replied that he knew I had no money or passports, and he was sure that I couldn't have gotten out of Iran.

I told Ellen, "I felt I did what I had to do, and it was Moody who destroyed our lives."

"I agree with you," Ellen said. "I don't think you should feel any guilt." She went on, "Betty, you could have been killed! It happens all the time on that border. I can't believe how brave you are. I could never have done that."

In discussing the escape, I couldn't help telling Ellen how brave Mahtob had been. "We didn't have any food for five days. Only once did she say 'Mommy, I'm hungry.' She never complained though she was so cold, tired, and hungry—not to mention scared. She just wanted to go home. I thought I was going to die. I told her, 'I'm sorry, but this is so hard, I don't think I can make it.' She said, 'I can, I'm tough, I'll do anything to go to America.' And she did. She's so strong."

Revealing her desire for freedom, Ellen said, "Boy, I felt that way *really* when I got off the plane in Germany. We had to go to the American Embassy in Frankfurt and pick up my passport. I felt so free. I felt a bounce in my step."

Ellen and Hormoz had seen Moody in May 1987 and asked about his family, to which he replied, "I don't see any of my family now. I've got a class and I'm in with the doctors, and I'm busy." She said that Moody's sister had recommended a new bride for him, but that he hadn't spoken to her for six months. Since we left, she added, he worked very hard, often around the clock.

Ellen said, "Moody has a big dose of paranoia. He thinks everyone is out to get him. He claimed the CIA plotted against him when he was in America, and he even went so far as to say that you are an agent. He's got delusions, really."

I recalled that Moody had voiced similar suspicions to me while we were in Iran and that I had asked why he felt so important that the CIA would be after him.

Ellen said that Moody expressed much anger and hatred toward me, but that he also would get "all sentimental. He said, 'Well, I think she'll come back for the first day of school.' Then it gets near Christmas, and he said, 'Well, maybe she'll be back for Christmas.' Then it gets near something else and, 'Maybe she'll be back for such and such.' "

"How could he think I'd go back after what he did to us there?" I asked.

"I don't know," Ellen said. "I can't believe it. The only thing I can think of is that he's got a split personality. When he gets angry, he gets out of hand, and when he's not angry, he can't remember the bad things."

I told Ellen that we continued to fear Moody's revenge. "It's been difficult, but we try to live a normal life," I said.

"Moody has never been totally honest with us," Ellen said. "I wouldn't relax any of my security if I were you just because he hasn't told *me* anything. There are lots of things he never told us."

I asked Ellen about her plans. I reminded her that her daughter had always told me that when she grew up, she would run away to live with her grandmother and be a Christian.

"I feel sorry for Jessica too," Ellen said. "I'm thirty years old, and I can decide to give up certain things because maybe I give priority to other things. But she gets whatever I can give her until she's old enough to make a life for herself."

I pressed on: "But you know she's never going to have the privilege of making her own decisions in Iran. You know that if Hormoz decides suddenly that she's going to marry someone, she won't have a choice. Then she'll be there the rest of her life."

Ellen admitted that Jessica was "just begging me to stay here [in Florida]. I really feel so messed up—you don't know. My kids are enjoying the vacation, even my husband is enjoying it more than I am. I am just agonizing, Betty. I fear the unknown. I have all these emotional problems, probably mental problems. I've been there eight years, and it sure has had a lot of effect on me. It's like an inferiority complex. I just don't feel as sure of myself as you are. You seem in control of your life, I don't feel that way."

She went on, "I hate living in Iran, but I don't know if I can give up my husband. I feel too insecure to do that. I'm not a person who can live alone."

I asked if Hormoz might consider staying in the States. "No, he just won't," Ellen said. "I've begged him. In fact, I really pushed for him to come with me this time, praying to God that something would come up and we'd have to stay."

I told Ellen I wouldn't try to convince her either way, but that I wasn't sorry for my decision, and that she could make it too. Five weeks after our initial conversation, I discovered that she was leaving. "I'm on my way to the airport with the children," she told me. "They need to go to school. Hormoz will stay with my parents for a while to earn more dollars to take back. He beats us, but he takes care of us."

Ellen's history is far from unique. When her husband told her she couldn't leave Iran, she thought she had to accept it—a standard reaction. I met other women while I was in Iran whose lives were much worse than mine, but I didn't meet one who was trying to get out. When told it was impossible, they resigned themselves to their fate.

When I look back and try to imagine how my life might have been different, I think of the day Moody told me we would never leave Iran. Had I gracefully accepted his dictate that day, I might never have been beaten. But neither would I be home where I have the freedom to tell my story. We'd still be prisoners.

Moody's behavior had a lingering effect upon my family. They had liked and trusted my ex-husband before our fateful trip. Dad and Moody had enjoyed discussing Iran, where my father had served during World War II. My mother revered Moody for the many wonderful things he had done, not least his fathering of Mahtob.

But as my family suffered while Moody kept Mahtob and me in Iran, their love changed to resentment. My family felt so betrayed and abused that they had bitter feelings to spare, and their hostility turned against all "foreigners."

My dad remained remarkably open-minded to the end of his life. But my mom suffered more than anyone, and she was unable to contain her bitterness. In 1985, more than a year after we'd left for Iran, she traveled to Alpena, to appear in Probate Court as conservator of my estate. It was agony for her, to deal with the worldly possessions of a daughter whom she feared she'd never see again.

While she was there Mom ran into our loyal friends, the Parseghians, an Armenian family of three generations: Nana, the kind and ancient matriarch who was orphaned during the Armenian genocide seven decades earlier; two sisters, Vergine and Anahid (whose husband had been killed in the civil war in Lebanon), and their families. The Parseghians had overcome tremendous obstacles to make a success in their adopted land. Moody had special feelings for them, even though they weren't Muslim.

Like Tariq and Farzana, our Pakistani friends who'd tried to help us escape, the Parseghians wheeled into action as soon as they learned of our plight in Tehran. They barraged Moody with calls and letters, begging him to let me and Mahtob come home. They sent frequent packages of food and gifts. Like Dad, they never gave up on the idea that we would return someday. Meanwhile, they helped pay our accumulated credit card bills and moved our furniture into storage from our rented house. After Mahtob and I got back, they gave me money and urged us to stay with them. There was nothing they would not do for us, and they asked for nothing in return.

Mom's grief and uncertainty not surprisingly led to rancor, and she funneled that rancor against the Parseghians. "It's your fault that Betty's in Iran," she rebuked them. "If she didn't hang around with foreigners, this wouldn't have happened."

Mom's anger remained after Mahtob and I moved in with her and Dad. One day Mahtob innocently asked me, "Mommy, will you cook me some Persian food?" Mom burst into a rage and said, "I thought you would have gotten enough of that crap over there."

Dad didn't share these feelings, and he saw how others in the family upset me. "Don't worry about them," he'd say. "They don't understand."

Mahtob, I'm happy to report, has been unaffected by the prejudice. In the small town where we reside, there are very few foreign nationals. One day, driving down the street, my daughter startled me when she saw a woman wearing a *sari* and said, "Mom, look. There's an Indian. Do you think we can be friends with her so she'll make *puri* [Indian bread] for us?"

Since my return to America life has been challenging, draining, and unpredictable. I learned there was another side to the excitement of travel. I had no time for proper sleep, no days off, no vacations. I was prey to jet lag, insomnia, and nightmares. I had more to do than any one person could handle.

The pressure built early in 1991, as I juggled a heavy lecture schedule with my commitments to promote the movie. In January I also appeared as an expert witness in a divorce trial—a particularly stressful event, as I had to face the Middle Eastern husband in court and fend off his attorney, who did his best to discredit me.

It all came to a head on Saturday, March 16. I flew directly from a two-day lecture series in Dayton, Ohio, to address a convention of CEO's in Washington, D.C. On the plane back to Michigan that evening I was struck by severe pain, radiating from my right shoulder into my rib cage. My breathing was labored, and at first I thought I had pneumonia. As I lay in bed that night, and the throbbing spread up my neck and became still more acute, I feared it might be a coronary.

On Sunday Arnie drove me to Carson City Hospital, where I was admitted into the intensive care unit. After a series of tests and x-rays, I was almost relieved to hear the diagnosis: possible duodenal ulcers and an inflamed gallbladder, with a root cause of exhaustion. I stayed in the hospital for five days, telling no one except Mahtob where I was. For months I'd been longing for a single day when I could take the time to catch my breath and relax, where I wouldn't have to talk to *anyone*. I lay on my back in my private room, taking deep breaths and thinking, "Oh, I'm going to take advantage of every second of this." It wasn't Club Med, but I got a needed break all the same.

My main concern was that Mahtob, then ten years old, might be alarmed to see me so vulnerable. But she rose to the occasion, just as she had after John's accident. She cooked several meals, kept up with the ironing and the laundry. She even prepared for the Persian New Year—*No-ruz*—all by herself. "Now tell me all the things that go on the table for the *haft sin*," she said, pen and paper in hand. "I'll have it ready when you come home." I was pleased to see that *No-ruz* had become part of *her* heritage.

Mahtob pleased me again when she called me in the hospital and spoke several words of Farsi to me, a tie in the special bond between us, though she doesn't feel comfortable speaking it in front of others.

I remained very ill for two weeks after leaving the hospital, and felt every one of my forty-five years. It reminded me of a conversation I'd had with Mahtob not long before. "Mommy," she said, "were you born in the fifties or the sixties?"

I could not help smiling and replied, "Well, would you believe the forties?"

Mahtob looked up at me, her eyes tripled in size. Then she recovered and kissed me and said, with the tolerance of the young, "I love you anyway."

So I kept going. . . .

Questions reflect interest, and there have been many who have asked the same questions about various individuals in *Not Without My Daughter.*

What happened to Amahl, the man who helped you escape?

I have maintained contact with Amahl through a third party. He remains in Iran, true to what he'd repeatedly told me: "I will not leave unless my wife and children can leave."

Fortunately, he has not been linked to our escape. I hope someday to meet him and his family somewhere in the world outside Iran.

And what of Helen Balasanian, the woman at the Swiss Embassy in Iran who advised you of just how bleak your plight was?

Whenever Helen Balasanian left Iran for vacation, she would call to check on us. She loved Mahtob so much that whenever she called me, she always insisted on speaking to my daughter, to confirm for herself that Mahtob was doing okay.

One evening I answered the phone to hear a strange male voice that began, "Don't worry, Helen gave me your number." He went on to say that he was an Iranian-Armenian who was living in California. "I am a widower, and I want to marry Helen," he explained. Helen had told her suitor, "Call Betty Mahmoody for permission."

I was truly honored. Since that time Helen has retired from the Swiss Embassy in Tehran and is now happily married and living in the United States.

And your sons?

Joe and John suffered terribly from our ordeal, which was very much their ordeal. Though still not fully healed, they are fine young men and I'm proud of both of them.

John was fourteen when I went to Iran and probably suffered most, because he was more dependent on me. During my absence he lived with his dad and visited my parents; there were many nights he couldn't sleep out of worry for me and Mahtob. He had to grow up in a hurry and feels cheated out of his prime teen years.

He was very close to my dad. John spent hours talking to my father and even cleaned his colostomy bag. One day Dad said to me with tears in his eyes, "You wouldn't find many kids who would do what he does." John lost his best friend when Grandpa died. His automobile accident and subsequent recovery were also very difficult times.

After Dad's death Mom didn't like to stay alone, so John would drive her to our house in the evening. After he recovered from his accident, he started staying with her more and more, because it was easier for her. She loves to spoil John, and he enjoys spoiling Grandma.

Joe was just eighteen and had just graduated from high school when I went to Iran. At one point after I returned to Michigan he came to live with me, working the second shift at an automotive subassembly plant. I would make an extra meal every evening and put it in the refrigerator. When he came home, I would hear the microwave door close, and then I felt secure. At least my childeren were safe at home.

Unlike John, who always had a girlfriend, Joe would hang out with the guys but never brought a girl home. When he was twenty-three, his behavior changed drastically. Even Mahtob noticed and jokingly said, "Mom, you better be careful. Joe wants something." Suddenly I didn't have to ask him to do things around the house—he was unusually attentive. Then one day I answered the phone, and female voice said, "Is Joe home?" As far as I knew, it was the first young woman who had ever called for Joe. Two years later Joe and Peggy were married. He has matured and settled down, and seems happier than ever.

On September 18, 1991, at 8:10 A.M., Carson City Hospital echoed with the cries of a newborn eight-pound baby boy. Proud Joe was standing at his wife's side. It was the same place that John and Joe had been delivered a generation before. It was where I'd met Moody and lost my dad. Now it was the place I would greet a new life—this time from the lounge waiting area.

Sooner than I expected, I looked up and saw Joe—pale, nervous, looking as if he were about to collapse. He dropped limply into a chair. I was afraid to ask anything until he gasped,

"It's a boy," and added a small smile. We walked around the corner and met Roger Morris, who immediately relieved our concerns by saying "Everything looks great."

Brandon Michael Smith was on the table being thoroughly examined. His color was already turning from purple to normal. His lungs were working just fine. I was proud of my son, who seemed eager to assume his responsibility as a father. Uncle John looked on with similar pride. Aunt Mahtob was in school waiting anxiously for a call.

Children grow up in a hurry. Life goes on.

The most commonly asked question is—*how is Mahtob?* In most respects she is a perfectly sunny twelve-year-old. No longer quite a child, she has grown into a striking young person with thick, wavy auburn hair and large greenish-brown eyes. She loves fishing, Michigan State football, Detroit Pistons basketball, and (to her mother's dismay) television. She plays on the girls' basketball team and is trying her hand at cheerleading. She takes piano lessons, only because I don't give her a choice. She prefers the pre-teen's uniform of sweatshirt and jeans—a far cry from the frilly dresses and matching shoes that Moody insisted on before going to Iran.

Mahtob is poised and mature beyond her years, with a droll sense of humor. Tempered by her experience, she has an un-usually keen interest in world affairs.

One day she came home from school and said, "Mom, I was confused in class today. The teacher was talking about Mu-hammad, and I thought she was talking about Islam. The other kids were talking about boxing. I asked the teacher, and she *was* talking about Islam." I explained to her that her classmates had been thinking of Muhammad Ali; Mahtob had a different frame of reference.

With Mahtob's extensive traveling, she knows her geogra-phy better than most. When she was a baby, Moody and I had started a doll collection from the countries she had visited. Her collection has grown until it threatens to exceed her room's ca-pacity.

258

She has fond memories of the places she's traveled to, but always enjoys coming home. After one long-distance tour Mahtob pressed her hands against her cheeks, relaxed her facial muscles, and said, "Good, I don't have to smile any more."

Her priorities are in order, and she knows what counts in life. As one whose prayers have been answered in the most dire circumstances, she is very religious.

Mahtob has a strong sense of ethics and won't easily be persuaded to do something she thinks is wrong. At school, where she is a brilliant and motivated student, her teachers have only one criticism: she will never so much as bend a rule. I know just what they mean. In England, at the end of our grueling European book tour, Mahtob and I gave an interview with an Australian magazine. After taking some photos inside our hotel they wanted to try a shot outdoors, and we walked to a nearby museum.

"Go over there on the grass," the photographer instructed. I complied and beckoned for Mahtob to follow. She wouldn't budge. I went back and told her to come with me, but she refused—rare behavior, as Mahtob is normally very obedient. "Come on," I said a bit testily, "let's hurry up and get this over with."

She said, "No, the sign says 'Don't walk on the grass.' " Despite the pleas of three frustrated adults, she wouldn't do it. Mahtob's stubbornness reminded me of Moody, whose rigid self-discipline had clearly rubbed off. Until recently, Mahtob would be meticulous about taking her socks off right-side out, just like her father. One day she asked me, "Am I really going to hell if I take them off wrong-side out?" Startled, I said, "Why do you say that?" She said, "Because Daddy told me if I take my clothes off wrong-side out, I'm going to hell." I felt obliged to free her of this superstition, though every time I now do the laundry, I'm not sure I did the right thing.

Most days our home life moves in a steady—and wonderful—routine. We cook together; I help Mahtob with her homework. There are times, however, when our normalcy has been rudely disrupted. As survivors of a war zone, Mahtob and I have had our share of flashbacks. Every thunderstorm, so similar to the concussive sound of Iraqi bombs, is still a frightening event for both of us.

Unfortunately, Mahtob can talk openly about Moody and Iran only with me. She feels no such freedom with my family, being reluctant to trigger their disapproval. If my mom asked her whether she missed Moody (an irrevocable fact, in spite of all of Moody's betrayals), Mahtob would say "No way." She is forced to veil her true feelings in their presence; she is split by their prejudice.

When a Swedish journalist asked her if she'd like to see her daddy, Mahtob answered, "Yes, I'd like to visit him—but in prison, so he can't hurt me." There was no rancor in her remark, no appetite for vengeance. It framed a little girl's longing to have a father, yet stay protected—Mahtob's impossible dream.

It was just eleven days after our movie's premiere (and only five days after the film opened in the theaters) that the Allies began bombing Iraq. As the television lit up with the glare of antiaircraft fire, Mahtob looked to me nervously. "I think we should turn the lights off and get down," she said. For the next two weeks she stayed glued to Cable News Network until 11 o'clock each night, even to the exclusion of her favorite shows.

To many Americans the Gulf War was a high-tech abstraction, a sanitized computer game. Mahtob knew what lay behind the charts and scenarios; she'd seen the gore close-up, from the front lines. She didn't assume that the war wouldn't spread or that we were too far away to be hit. Her father had told us that Iraqi bombs couldn't reach Tehran, but they had. How could I convince her we were safe this time?

Mahtob's memories of Iraqi air raids resurfaced powerfully. She and I reminisced about those horrible times when we could hear the planes and screams and sirens, when we could smell the gunpowder and burning flesh. We felt great empathy for those suffering in this new war.

Mahtob worried especially about the people that we knew in Iran and, most of all, that her father might be hurt. Even as I tried to calm her, I was heartened by her concern for her father. It marked how far she'd come toward resolving the most wrenching issue of her young life.

Mahtob and I were always close, from the moment of her first breath. On the day Moody announced that we could not return to America, my daughter and I grew even closer. For the next eighteen months we were partners, wholly reliant upon one another, and our bond remains warmly intact.

Each day with Mahtob is precious. Although my schedule is busy, I coordinate my travel to take her with me as often as possible. Each night I look forward to tucking her into bed and to reciting our prayer: "Dear God, thank you for letting us be together and free."

Our separations are always difficult—even more so for me, perhaps, than for Mahtob. She has adopted a "big sister," Lori, who stays with her when I'm gone. Once when I called her from Germany and told her I'd be returning the next day, three days earlier than planned, she said, "Why are you coming home early?" I knew then she was doing fine.

Routinely I am asked, "Aren't you afraid that Moody might come back for Mahtob?" I reply that I am always afraid. Mahtob and I left Iran more than 2,000 days ago, and not a single one of those days has passed without unusual precautions—some obvious, others less so.

Mahtob is not permitted the privileges most girls her age would take for granted. She cannot ride her bicycle or even walk down the street alone. She has been trained to always look over her shoulder.

I've reluctantly allowed her to attend weekend camping trips the past two summers, even while I kick myself for it. I think of how silly it is to take such care in our security at home, then leave Mahtob unprotected for a day or two of fun. Now she has taken it a step further: she is asking, for the first time, when she might walk to school on her own. I am not ready for that yet, but I know I cannot protect her forever. "I always have to have somebody watching me," she complains. "I wish I could be like other kids." It is such a minimal, reasonable request. Yet it looms so large since Moody vowed more than once, before we left Iran, to snatch Mahtob back and to kill me.

For all of her impatience, Mahtob recognizes the continual danger. After we watched a "20/20" episode about how a mother rekidnapped her children from their father, who had taken them into some cult society, I asked her what she thought. "If that ever happened to me," Mahtob said with utter seriousness, "I would expect you to come and get me."

Mahtob has become emotionally involved in several abduction cases. In one newspaper interview she said, "I'm proud of my mom because she helps other kids."

As I see my daughter blossom, I think of all that Moody has missed with her and all that he will miss in the years to come. Only I can know the full measure of his loss and the power of Mahtob's faith and love. Like anyone else, I have moments when I doubt myself and my direction. Fortunately, my daughter is always there to support me. On Mother's Day, 1989, as a second-grader, she wrote what remains my most cherished tribute:

Dear Mom,

You're the greatest mom in the whole world! I love you so much Mom that if I could choose from all the mothers in the world, I would choose you. You've done so many great things for me that I can't count them all. Mom, I don't care if you are two or one hundred and two, I still love you. I would not change a thing about you, you're perfect the way you are. I don't know what I would do without you, Mom, you mean so much to me.

I Love You, Mom!!!

Love from Mahtob

Like my dad, Mahtob always *expected* me to prevail. "Mommy," she kept saying in Iran, "find a way to go back to America." She never gave me the choice to quit. When it came time to risk everything, to hazard the stark mountains and smugglers of unknown intentions, Mahtob showed extraordinary courage.

There is another meaning to *Not Without My Daughter*. It

is true, in theory, that I might have escaped from Iran earlier if I'd been willing to leave without Mahtob—a course many others in my situation have painfully chosen.

I am convinced, however, that I would be buried there today if not for her. Mahtob was my inspiration. I remember a day, after a couple of months in Tehran, when I picked up a pencil and tried to write. I was so weak with dysentery and despair that I couldn't form a single letter. That is when it hit me that I was going to die—I really believed it. But if I died, I realized, Mahtob would be stuck in Iran. That was the day I went to Moody and said, "I'll live here and do what you want. I want to make this work." Very soon afterward my sickness passed. That was the day I became a survivor.

I haven't seen Moody since I left Iran . . . yet neither have I escaped his presence, his indelible impression upon my life.

On December 27, 1990, Mahtob was spending part of her Christmas vacation with her grandmother. I was alone in my house. After a busy day of publicity and other preparations for the movie's premiere, I fell asleep as my head touched the pillow . . . and then woke myself screaming. It was *Moody*—standing over my bed, leaning over my body, his hands hovering above my neck, his mouth parted in a thin smile of revenge. . . .

I woke up trembling and afraid, drenched with perspiration, my heart racing. The vision had been so lifelike, more vivid than any dream has a right to be. Was it an omen? I could not put it aside. I was thankful that Moody had yet to follow through on his threats to reenter—to destroy—our lives. I could not help wondering how long our good fortune would continue.

There hadn't been a day since Mahtob and I escaped that I didn't think about Moody and all the harm he could do. When would he come? How would he strike? What weapon would he use against me—and how would he try to tear Mahtob from her stable life here? I envisioned countless scenarios but never imagined that Moody would resurface while my daughter and I were halfway around the globe, or that he would choose to attack not my person but the core of my identity.

On July 17, 1991, Mahtob and I set off for my daughter's

first crossing of the international dateline. To promote the movie *Not Without My Daughter*, we were bound for the other side of the world—for the city of Perth, on the remote west coast of Australia. When we reached our hotel late at night, I was startled to find a message from Mitra and Jalal, two of Moody's distant relatives whom we'd known in Iran and who had since moved to Australia.

I'd last seen the couple a few weeks before our escape, which they themselves had tried to engineer several months before. Jalal had enlisted a worker at a nearby bread shop in a phony marriage scheme. After I "married" the man, Mahtob and I were supposed to leave the country on his passport. It sounded promising, but the Swiss Embassy warned me against trying it. If I'd been caught by Iranian authorities, I could have been executed for bigamy.

Mitra, meanwhile, had escorted me several times to the Swiss Embassy, where I collected any messages from my family, always with the hope that somehow a miracle would be waiting.

Even though Jalal and Mitra were two of the friendliest and most supportive people I'd known in Iran, their family ties to Moody made me pause before I phoned them our first morning in Perth. When I heard Mitra's warm voice, however, my reservations melted. They had settled there eight months before, she told me. Jalal had found work as a research scientist; Mitra was studying computer science. "We will meet you any time, any place," she said. We made a date for eight o'clock that evening.

Throughout that day's round of interviews, my mind wandered back to old memories from Iran. Unlike Moody's family, Mitra's was quite liberal, to the degree that they dared to show banned Western movies—Mahtob and I watched *E.T.* with them—on their VCR. We would gather in their kitchen and share whispered hopes for our escape.

Jalal was a brother of Essie, who was married to Moody's nephew Reza. While his relatives were more religious than Mitra's, they too sympathized with Mahtob and me. While social protocol prevented them from intervening with Moody, they showed their love by inviting us to their home. Mrs. Alemoham-med, Jalal's mother, always cooked my favorite foods, such as fish with tamarind. Mitra and Jalal often led us up to their apartment, where they'd play popular American music that made us homesick.

When Mitra and Jalal arrived at our hotel in Perth that evening, I met them in the lobby, leaving Mahtob in our room. After all these years my caution was a reflex; I felt the need to make sure they were alone. When we saw each other, it was like old times—except that Mitra and I had shed our *chadors*. We embraced; Mitra looked wonderful with makeup and her hair styled. Jalal hugged and kissed me as well. They introduced their daughter, Ida, a poised and lovely little girl whom I'd last seen when she was just over a year old.

On our way to our room, my Australian publicist handed me an envelope. I opened it to find a fax from *Quick* magazine in Germany. Distracted by the excitement of our reunion, I laid it aside to read later.

Mitra was still amazed that we were free: "In Iran we talked about you escaping, but you really did it, and that is something else. It was dangerous!" Another friend of hers, she added, tried to escape from Iran some months later and was shot, most likely by the *pasdar* security forces. His body was so riddled with bullets that his family could not afford to retrieve it (in Iran, families seeking to recover a corpse from the police must pay by the bullet hole).

"Remember when we went to the Caspian Sea?" Jalal said, changing the subject.

"Yes," Mitra said, "I remember when you looked at the sea and said you wished you could swim to Russia."

Jalal said, "And *I* remember on that trip that you said, 'I am going to write a book someday'—and you did it!"

Mitra, who'd suffered much harassment from Jalal's family and had long been eager to leave Iran, read *Not Without My Daughter* while living in Ireland. She said the book had helped save her marriage. She gave it to Jalal, who saw parallels to Moody's relatives in his own behavior and decided to change.

Now they were expecting their second child; they had never been happier.

"I never thought about these things before," Jalal said. "I wasn't even aware. When I read your book, I realized I was guilty." He had copied the book a few pages at a time and sent it to his family in Iran. He was certain that Moody had read it.

Mitra and Jalal confirmed much of what Ellen Rafaee had told me four years earlier—that Moody had turned inward after Mahtob and I left him. He cut social ties with everyone except his sister and brother-in-law and their children. Moody's only life was his work, they said. He spent long hours at Talaghani Hospital. He'd even taken a room there, ridding himself of all our family possessions. I had to wonder about Tobby Bunny.

There was also news about Moody's nephews, most of it bad. Majid had been arrested twice and jailed for manufacturing unlicensed cosmetics. Hossein, the pharmacist from Arak, had also been imprisoned for dealing in illegal drugs. Reza and Mammal had quit their jobs and gone into business with Majid.

Three years before, Mitra and Jalal had visited their families in Iran. Baba Hajji, Moody's brother-in-law and the family patriarch, invited them for lunch and a swim in his pool. As the visit drew to a close, Baba Hajji finally said, "All right, what did Betty say about us in her book?"

The hours with my old friends flew by in reminiscence. As we said our good-byes, they promised to come to my breakfast lecture the next morning and to visit with us until Mahtob and I caught our afternoon flight to Adelaide.

After my long day I could think only of sleep . . . and then I remembered the envelope. I started reading the faxed letter, and stared at the *trouble* that radiated from the page. It said that German television had broadcast an interview with Moody the day before. He had claimed, among other things, that Mahtob and I had not escaped from Iran after all—that he'd never held us against our will, that we'd flown out in comfort to Zurich, that he'd even paid for our plane tickets! *Quick* didn't believe him, but they wanted an exclusive response—and someone to verify my story.

The letter's print swam before my eyes. I was hurt, outraged, flabbergasted. I knew Moody was capable of almost anything. He was the smoothest liar I'd ever known. But I never expected he would try to deny a reality known to millions of readers, not to mention State Department officials in both the United States and Turkey.

Moody's timing, as usual, was disastrous. He had cheated me once again. When I lost my father five months after our escape, I'd missed the support only a spouse can provide. Now I'd have to deal with this public furor as far away from home and friends as a person can be.

There would be no sleep that night, as I would spend the next frantic hours on the phone. I was never more grateful for modern technology. There I was in Australia, forced to respond to an incident in Iran, and I was immediately able to reach New York, Michigan, and Germany, all places where it was still daytime. My first call went to my agent, Michael Carlisle. He told me that Anja, my close friend and editor at Gustav Lübbe Verlag, my German publisher, had been overrun by questions from journalists. She was desperate to talk to me.

I needed to respond quickly, Michael said. I asked him to fax a copy of Moody's translated comments to my home so Arnie could drive over to read them. I trusted Arnie's judgment; he always seemed to have some special insight. Aside from his keen mind and formidable energy, Arnie also knew how to calm me down better than anyone else. "Now, listen," he told me after reading Moody's interview. "Just stop and think. If five men had come to your door with Uzis, I couldn't have done anything to help you. But that's not the case. Michael and I are both lawyers. Moody has acted in a way we can deal with." He promptly began to draft a response.

I finally reached Anja in the middle of the night. "It is terrible!" she exclaimed. She said Moody had done the interview from a palatial-looking house with beautiful furniture and Persian carpets—a home he claimed he'd bought for Mahtob and me before we left. It was a far cry from the one-room hospital apartment that Jalal and Mitra believed he was living in. Moody had gone on to say that he'd never beaten me and that Mahtob and I were always free to come and go.

"Moody has lied—we know he has lied," Anja said. "But you have to respond. And if you don't do it immediately, it will be too late."

I begged Anja to understand that I didn't have access to many documents, including my Turkish bus ticket from Van to Ankara, that I had stored at home. I did have my passport, which had been stamped at the police station in Ankara. I told Anja I would send her a copy, along with my statement through Michael.

Soon the fax lines were humming among three continents. Within minutes a copy of my passport had been transmitted around the world.

Before dawn broke in Perth, Arnie and Michael had finished my statement. I decided to put out a general release rather than an exclusive; I didn't want people to think I'd been paid for my response, as Moody had been. My statement read:

> It is revealing that Dr. Mahmoody has waited five and a half years to refute my story. In attempting to do so, he uses no physical evidence and offers no proof of any inconsistencies in my story.
>
> My life with my husband and our daughter was exactly as I recount it in my book. I stand by my story in every detail.

There was still my breakfast lecture to attend. Though my first instinct was to grab the first flight home, I couldn't disappoint all the people who'd bought tickets. Arnie and Michael advised me to broach the subject openly, to shorten my normal lecture and deliver my statement. Up to this point, when someone asked the standard question—"Have you heard from Moody?"—my answer had been easy: "No, nothing." Now it was different—I'd heard from Moody, although indirectly. I didn't want anyone to think I was hiding anything.

After a few minutes of sleep, I had to try to explain to Mahtob what had happened overnight. My first question to her was "Do you remember going over the mountains?"

"Yes," she said, puzzled by my asking.

"Do you remember Daddy ever hitting us, or not letting us come home?"

By then I had confused her. She said, "Yes, I remember. Why?"

"Daddy did an interview," I told her, and we discussed it from there. Mahtob was visibly shaken and hurt, but she gave me a big hug and said, "I love you, Mom."

I apologized to her for her father's behavior and said, "I love you so much, Mahtob, and I'm so proud of you. How did I ever get so lucky to have such a beautiful daughter?"

During the lecture I felt sick and shaky. The event had sold out, and I stepped to the podium to meet rows of expectant faces. The packed ballroom fell silent in attention. As I began to give my statement about Moody, I broke. My throat tightened, and I simply couldn't speak. I could feel the tears coming. I didn't know what to do. I knew I couldn't stop there—no one would know why I was crying.

I took some deep breaths and a sip of water, and somehow gained the resolve to go on. As I gave my response, I could *feel* my listeners' support and compassion. If this was any indication of the reaction in Germany, I had nothing more to worry about.

Yet what would Mitra and Jalal, out in the audience, think? They must be terribly confused; perhaps they'd conclude I'd been dishonest with them the night before. After the lecture was finished and the long line of well-wishers dispersed, Jalal's first words were "How can he say that? He's lying!"

Back in our room we discussed my next move. Jalal said that he and Mitra could affirm the fact that we'd been held in Iran against our wishes. While they'd never seen Moody beat me, they often had spoken to family members who'd confirmed Moody's abuse. In particular, Mitra recalled a conversation with Mahtob shortly after I'd been beaten and the pain in my daughter's voice when she described the incident. Best of all, Jalal said, they wanted to write and sign a statement to support me—which they did.

The statement read:

We are very close friends of Ms. Betty Mahmoody and have witnessed the hardship Betty and Mahtob have gone through. They
were forced to stay in Iran against their will and were not allowed to
leave Iran freely.

We have been in Moody's family and have had close contact
with the relatives and have witnessed the effort Betty was making to
end her ordeal by escaping from Iran.

Dr. Sayyed Bozorg Mahmoody [Moody] physically and emotionally abused Betty and imprisoned her for eighteen months. . . .

It is really not fair to Betty and Mahtob to be treated in this
inhumane way and then [for Moody] to deny his wrongdoings by
lying.

We hope that he does not cause further hardship for Betty and
Mahtob and embarrassment for himself as we personally know there
are so many others who have witnessed the same.

Jalal seemed particularly embarrassed by Moody's fabrica-
tions. "If you steal, you get your hand cut off," he said. "But if
you lie, you are no longer a Muslim."

In the days that followed Moody's verbal attack, my rage
hardened into resentment. I had always been nice to him—too
nice. I'd been the one who'd encouraged him to renew contact
with his family in the first place. I was the one who'd led Mahtob
to remember her father in a kinder light. Now all that healing
was undone. Moody had ignored Mahtob for five years—and
when he finally broke his silence, it was only to lash out and hurt
her again. I had lost my last shred of respect for Moody, and I
couldn't blame my daughter for feeling the same way.

A couple days after the storm broke, when Mahtob and I
had moved on to Adelaide, a promotional spot for our movie
came on the hotel television. The clip cut between two scenes.
The first showed Moody in Michigan, swearing on the Koran
that he'd never keep us in Iran. The second scene showed him in
Tehran, vowing that I'd never see my home again.

"Mom, look at that!" said Mahtob, fire in her eyes. "I like
this part—when they say we went to Iran and he *lied*. Because
that's what Daddy *did!*" Mahtob and I had lost our last illusions
where Moody was concerned. He'd taken everything from us

but our dread—the dark anticipation as to when he might strike again.

In fact Moody *did* lie to Mahtob and me before our trip to Iran. He lied to us in the name of Islam. While in Iran, I had asked him repeatedly if he'd been planning to keep us there even before we left Michigan. He always denied it, but now his deception was revealed. He acknowledged in the German interview that he had intended to stay in Iran all along and knew I wouldn't willingly go there on that basis. We *were* held hostage. Each time I made contact with the Swiss Embassy, a cable was sent to the State Department. Those cables demonstrated that we were being held hostage, that we'd been beaten and threatened with death.

In response to Moody's statement that he'd put us on a luxury airliner from Tehran to Zurich, I had a cable from the State Department of a letter Moody had given to the embassy. The letter notes that Mahtob and I "disappeared" from his house on January 29, 1986, "and have not returned home ever since. . . . I am extremely anxious and concerned about their physical safety."

Had Mahtob and I not escaped when we had, I believe Moody would have held me captive, and apart from my daughter—indefinitely.

I know that Moody is alive in Iran. I know he is bitter; his death threats still ring in my ears. Based on reports from his relatives, I know he is now actively practicing his Islamic religion. As he pointed out in the German interview, Mahtob is unfortunately—but necessarily—being deprived of her other parent and the other part of her heritage. It is always the children who pay most dearly for their parents' sins—and for the world's indifference.

11

Responding to the Cries

With the flood of contacts that were the result of my U.S. hardback book tour in 1987 came the realization that my case was in no way isolated. But more painful was the fact that so many children were suffering the same fate Mahtob and I had endured—and were doing so alone.

Senator Alan Dixon had taken an early interest in this problem. He and his aide Sara Pang had worked on hundreds of cases. Sara and I began frequent conversations, and as I discussed each new case with the State Department, I soon realized there was another often-common thread.

With no legal solutions available, it seemed helpful for many of these left-behind parents to have someone to talk with who understood—who had been there. Knowing that Mahtob and I were successful in our escape gave hope to many who had been told there was no solution. This was especially important because the misery of so many who had suffered an abduction had been cruelly compounded by family and friends who reminded the left-behind parent with an "I had told you so."

Many of the calls were from troubled parents who were desperate for empathy. I could understand the plight of a parent who, terorrized by the expectation of an imminent abduction, felt there was no one to listen, much less feel the utter desperation and terror. So many of these worried parents were treated as I had been—as hysterical, even paranoid, individuals.

With more and more left-behind parents asking me for help, I began to feel frustrated to have so little to offer. I felt a huge responsibility weighing on my shoulders, and all I could bring to bear was a sympathetic ear and some common-sense suggestions.

I needed help. A brainstorming session was organized where state and federal government officials, judges, lawyers, immigration personnel, and a staff member from a battered women's shelter were to attend a brainstorming session.

In the beginning, one attorney leaned back in his chair, with his arms crossed, and said, "Just how many kids are we talking about, anyway?" I responded, "About ten thousand." Again, in his impatient voice: "You mean we are sitting here wasting our time for ten thousand kids? Do you know how many kids there are in this country?"

My response was, "How many hostages do we have in Lebanon?" What the attorney hadn't considered is that these children are all citizens who have lost the rights of their native country. Because these victims were only children and they were taken by a parent, they weren't given the same attention as "hostages." After two hours of discussion, this attorney's arms were no longer crossed. He, like the others, had become aware of the seriousness of the issue. He was ready to help.

Actually, the response of this group was very typical and was consistent with that of the many other groups and professionals I later contacted. Generally, those to whom the problem was presented all agreed there was a problem, but asked me about, rather than suggested, possible solutions. The only real concensus reached at this conference held at U.S. Senator Carl Levin's office was that whatever dismal chances there were for a solution, they would be less dismal at the state level. This was based on the reality that under our system of government these matters were considered domestic matters, responsibilities of the states, rather than of the federal government.

Later that year, I had the opportunity to address the Friend of the Court Association Conference held in Houghton Lake, Michigan. After I discussed some international abduction cases I'd recently been involved with, a woman stood and said, "We had a client in our county who told me this would happen. I didn't really believe it." Another one rose and said, "We had two in our county." It turned out that several other people in the room had been approached by parents who feared their children would be abducted to a foreign country. They admitted that they hadn't really taken these fears seriously. For the first time these officials realized: *we have a real problem right here in Michigan.*

Much of the next year was devoted to rounds of meetings, hearings, and seminars. It was during this time that I was first accepted to testify as an expert witness in a Florida court custody case.

State Representative Francis ("Bus") Spaniola introduced legislation to address this problem and invited me to testify before the Michigan House of Representatives.

Some relief came on November 29, 1989, when our bill was signed into law—to the best of my knowledge, the first of its kind in the nation. The bill allows for a Michigan resident, married to a foreign national and deemed "at risk," to file a divorce action outside their county of residence; the primary purpose is to lessen the chances a noncustodial parent will be able to track down and abduct or re-abduct their children.

The new law certainly made an immediate difference in my own life. Not wanting to alert Moody to our address, I had been buying time. Every six months I had filed for an extension of my temporary custody order. The judge wasn't happy about the continual extensions, which evaded the issue of providing "notice" to Moody.

With the new legislation in place, I filed a different divorce complaint in a court some distance from my home, requesting custody of Mahtob. The papers were mailed both to our last known address in Tehran and to the office of Moody's brother-in-law, Baba Hajji, but Moody didn't respond. My divorce finally came through on June 19, 1991, the day before Moody's fifty-second birthday.

I was relieved to gain permanent custody of Mahtob but felt somehow dissatisfied. I'd always thought that divorce signified a true ending, and I was eager to get that part of my life behind me.

But I didn't *feel* any different. Emotionally, the door had yet to close; my fear of another abduction of Mahtob continues. I pray that he loves her enough to let her go once and for all, and not to turn her into a ping-pong child. I hoped his silence carried a tacit acknowledgment that Mahtob's life must not be disrupted again.

Arnie and I realized that our work wasn't finished, not even on the state level. The new law was a partial solution, not nearly enough. Clark Harder, Spaniola's successor, agrees and has been working on proposals for legislation. In deciding divorce and custody cases, Michigan courts consider several criteria, ranging from a parent's physical capacity to his or her moral fitness. But they are *not* required to consider the risk of international abduction.

All too often, parental child abductors come before the courts and take advantage of the due process requirements afforded any litigant. Frequently they have used court-ordered visitation to snatch the child beyond the trusting court's reach.

As the limits of state legislation became clear, Arnie and I came to support a more effective, if short-term, deterrent: the enactment of federal criminal sanctions against international parental abductors.

In other contexts, kidnapping is universally condemned as one of the most serious crimes. Kidnapping by strangers is a grave—even capital, offense. Within the United States, parental abductions are prosecuted as felonies by most of the fifty states.

To date, however, Congress has yet to pass legislation against international parental abductors. Hostage taking has been a federal felony since 1983, when it was defined as a form of kidnapping. But when a parent steals a child to another country (a far more common phenomenon), it is treated as a "domestic" matter, beyond—or beneath—the attention of our national government. Because the act is not a federal crime, the State Department has little leverage with the haven nation. Extradition is out of the question. The abducting parent sneaks outside the law's reach.

When I tell my lecture audiences about this glaring gap in

275

federal law, they are shocked and offended. When I discuss this abroad, people are even more amazed, as are a growing number of our representatives in Washington. In 1990 the U.S. Senate overwhelmingly passed a bill to make international parental abduction a federal felony. When I testified before a House Judiciary subcommittee in September with other advocates of the bill, our remarks seemed especially well received. I returned home to Michigan ready to begin celebrating, but the bill got caught up in parliamentary maneuvering, and never passed the House.

In 1991 the Senate passed the legislation again, this time as an amendment to its Comprehensive Crime Control Act. The House followed suit, and then the bill was sent to a joint committee for resolution. The bill did not make it back out of the committee in time to become law. The problem is not opposition to it, but the lack of sufficient force to overcome the inertia of our system of government. If the bill becomes law, much of the credit must go to two senators—Alan Dixon of Illinois and Donald Riegle of Michigan—and their aides, Sara Pang and Chris Korest, who have worked the past five years for this breakthrough.

"To us it's a big issue," explained another aide to Senator Dixon. "But to people not familiar with it, it's not. We've had to work over the years to educate people. Once a senator or congressman hears about these cases from their constituents, they always support us."

After my experience in Washington, I could appreciate the expression "it will take an act of Congress." I felt even more admiration for the Mothers of Algiers, who, without any real political power or financial might behind them, got *two* national governments to act in concert. The mothers weren't a force in commerce or geopolitics. But they got the job done.

I look forward to the day when Congress will look out for those young citizens who can't look out for themselves, particularly when they're trapped in another country.

My search for a solution to the problem of international parental child abduction has taken me to many countries throughout the world. I was visiting Germany in September 1990 when I heard that an organization there harbored ill feelings about *Not Without My Daughter.*

The IAF (Interessengemeinschaft der mit Auslandern verheirateten Frauen e.V., or the Association of Binational Families and Partnerships) was founded by the German wives of Turkish and other immigrants to protect their husbands against a political movement to deport them. Declaring that they had the right to live with their husbands in their own country, these women worked to promote understanding between cultures. Eventually they too were plagued by the problem of international parental child abduction.

When I was interviewed by German journalists, most of them would ask about an article in *Der Spiegel* (an influential German magazine) that quoted the IAF regarding my stance toward Iranians. The IAF wrongly believed I was warning people against marrying outside their own culture. They also charged that I'd painted Iranians unfairly and that my book fed on people's ugly prejudices toward those from other countries.

This reaction disappointed me. From the day I arrived in Tehran, I felt compassion for Iranians and all they had suffered during the Islamic revolution and the Iran-Iraq War. I always understood that my ordeal in Iran was created by one individual—my husband. I never generalized about Iranians, especially after so many of them had befriended me and tried to aid my escape.

While fundamentalist Shiite Muslims fostered and reinforced Moody's behavior, many ordinary people in the country did not support such abuse. In fact, aside from his immediate family, many of the Iranians I knew felt insulted and angered by what Moody did to Mahtob and me. They went to great lengths to try to help us, not wanting us to think that all Iranians were the same. Only I know what they did for us, and I recognize that we owe our lives to these people. Although I've said that our worlds are vastly different, I've never suggested that Iranian culture is bad and Western culture is good. I was sure that the IAF must have misunderstood. Despite my German editor's concern for my safety, I knew I had to meet with this group to clarify the matter.

277

Mindful of the hostages in Lebanon and the threat against novelist Salman Rushdie, I was apprehensive. I might not have been brave enough to follow through had Arnie not been with me. I requested that we meet first in a public place—a restaurant as it turned out. As we talked, the six women representing the IAF seemed to begin to understand that our goals did not threaten theirs. We hadn't gone five minutes before one woman said, "I think we had the wrong impression of you." They realized that I held no grudge toward Iranians and that it had never been my intention to hurt anyone. Likewise, I was convinced that the IAF was an honorable, well-intentioned group.

To my pleasant surprise, I learned that the IAF, in fact, had goals similar to mine. Wanting to learn more about this group, I made another appointment to meet them at their facility in Frankfurt, a large high-rise building with numerous offices and meeting rooms. Their impressive library featured books about cultures and religions from all over the world, including several of the group's own books on interethnic marriages and partnerships. Other rooms were decorated with cultural artifacts from specific countries. For example, one could go to the India Room and be entertained with Indian music, read Indian books, walk on Indian carpets, and even enjoy Indian food.

The IAF has gained recognition before German courts, which often ask the group for a recommendation on custody or visitation in international cases. If a child is at *substantiated* risk of abduction, the visitation takes place in the IAF facility, under supervision. The IAF also offers counseling to couples with marital problems and information to anyone planning to marry someone from another culture.

While I deal with the real world, I also realize that no single notion, no matter how well intentioned, can solve this problem by itself. By definition, international problems can only be solved by international action.

12

One World : For Children

T he Hague Convention is the single best solution to the problem of international parental child abduction!

The increasing problem of abductions in Canada led to the formation of the Hague Convention on the Civil Aspects of International Parental Child Abduction. France and Portugal joined with Canada in 1980 to sign the convention.

In 1988, the year after *Not Without My Daughter* was published, the United States became the tenth nation to ratify the Hague Convention. With continued new interest, the Hague Convention has grown from three signators to twenty-four. Ideally, the members of the United Nations would abide by the principles of the Hague Convention.

I made a trip to the Hague in 1991 and had an opportunity to meet with Adair Dyer, who was the treaty's primary author. He discussed with me the history and mechanics of the convention.

Briefly stated, the Hague Convention provides that any child under the age of sixteen who is "wrongfully removed" to another country shall be promptly returned to the child's "place of habitual residence," or home. In other words, the pact restores the preabduction status quo.

The convention imposes no criminal penalties, nor does it attempt to settle disputed custody claims. Instead it recognizes that the most urgent issue, and absolute wrong, is the abduction itself. According to the Hague Convention, custody battles must be waged lawfully in the child's home country. An abducting parent no longer can flee from the established family home to find favor for his or her claims, or to avoid an open hearing.

Traditional haven "partners," such as Germany and the United States, which once harbored parental kidnappers in both directions, are such no longer. Had the convention been in effect in those countries in 1989, Craig DeMarr would have had a legal alternative to his desperate action.

Ramez Shteih would have had the right to file an application under the Hague Convention, which would have initiated the swift return of his daughters to their New Jersey home while the court decided custody. "We're getting people out of the abduction business and getting them into the courts, where they belong," a U.S. State Department official noted. "We're not saying you can't take your child to another country. We *are* saying you have to deal with custody first. You can't just run away."

American parents are being held to the same standards as those from other signatory nations. A case in point is that of Henry and Michele Tyszka. He was a teacher and a U.S. citizen; she was French. Their two young children had lived in France for relatively long periods—fourteen and nine months, respectively—and had attended French schools. In the summer of 1990 Henry bought round-trip plane tickets for himself and the two children to visit Michigan, and Michele drove them to the airport.

But on September 4, instead of returning as scheduled, Henry filed for divorce. He called his wife to tell her he was keeping the children. Michele responded by filing for divorce in France—and by invoking the Hague Convention in Michigan's circuit court system.

In November, just two months later, the circuit judge concluded that Henry had wrongfully retained the children in the U.S. and that jurisdiction over the custody case belonged to France, the children's habitual residence. He ruled that the children be returned to Michele, who took them back to France.

Custody is being sorted out in the French courts.

In a crisis, the Hague Convention has been used quite creatively. In 1987, when a father attempted to abduct his two daughters from the child's home in Australia to Saudi Arabia, they were intercepted during a layover in Zurich, Switzerland. Australian officials had invoked the Hague Convention through the Swiss central authority; had they waited until the children reached Saudi Arabia, a nonsignatory, the convention would have been useless. The mother and daughters were reunited in Switzerland, and remain together in Australia.

Despite such heartening stories, it is difficult to gauge the Hague Convention's general impact. Like rape statistics, child abduction data is incomplete and misleading. The U.S. State Department can tell us only how many abductions are reported to them by left-behind parents; as public awareness has grown, we can assume that a higher proportion of cases are surfacing. Nonetheless, it appears that the Hague Convention is making an impact. After years of sharp increases, the number of parental abductions among many convention participants appears to be leveling off. In the three years since the United States ratified the pact, 800 cases have been processed by the State Department alone, about half in either direction. Of that total, half the kids involved are now home, whether through court-ordered or voluntary returns.

As with the Franco-Algerian Convention, the signatory countries have acknowledged a crucial principle: the welfare of children is no longer purely a domestic matter, to be dealt with inside the family or at a local level. They are saying that children—the future of all societies—are worthy of treaties at the highest level, that they merit the full force of the state behind them. As Anne-Marie Lizin said, "We have to make children as important as a natural gas contract."

For all the Hague has solved, for all its potential, there remain too many safe havens for parents who kidnap. The convention carries no force outside its signatory nations. It leaves Africa and virtually all of Asia unprotected. Unlike the Franco-Algerian Convention, the Hague Convention has yet to make any headway among Muslim states.

This limitation makes the Franco-Algerian accord seem even more remarkable—a fitting model for future efforts. No one has equaled the accomplishment of the Mothers of Algiers. By bridging two such different cultures, by transcending centuries of conflict and uniting two distrustful governments, they have enabled millions of people to honor a universal principle: that children must come first.

Another case involving France, one that lends even greater credence to the need for the principles espoused by the Hague, began in 1980 in Britain. Zana and Nadia Muhsen were typical British teenagers when their father proposed that they take a holiday in his native Yemen. With visions of unspoiled beaches and camel racing, the girls readily agreed. Zana was fifteen, Nadia a year younger; the trip would be an exotic interlude before they resumed their schooling.

But after landing a thousand miles away from home, the sisters learned that their father had deceived them in the most brutal manner imaginable. In accordance with Yemeni custom, they discovered that he had *sold* them into arranged marriages for £12,000. Their buyers took them to adjacent, remote villages, and the girls stepped into a nightmare seemingly without end.

To be a village bride in Yemen is to be a slave. The word of one's husband—or one's father-in-law—is absolute law. If Zana or Nadia failed to comply with a man's command, they were beaten harshly. The backbreaking, medieval nature of domestic work in Yemen, where villages lack running water, electricity, telephones, or medical care, was an additional torture. To provide water for their families, they were forced to walk up and down a mountain up to twelve times a day with heavy vessels on their heads. They spent uncounted hours grinding corn by hand to make bread.

When Zana and Nadia—children themselves—delivered their babies, they did so in their homes without doctors or medication.

I first learned of the sisters' plight during my European book tour in March 1988, a few days after I'd first met with the Mothers of Algiers. I was horrified by their story; it stirred every maternal instinct within me. At the same time, I empathized with them as a married woman who also had been trapped against her will in another land.

By 1988 the girls' mother had finally located them in Yemen and had received some attention from the British press. The Yemeni authorities came under severe pressure from both media and diplomatic channels. They agreed to release Zana that year, on the condition that she sign divorce papers. Even at this point there was treachery. As the papers were written entirely in Arabic, Zana had no way of knowing that she was also relinquishing custody of her two-year-old son Marcus.

"Hurry and come back for me," Nadia told her sister. Although Nadia had agreed to care for Marcus until her sister's return, the boy was taken from her shortly after Zana left, to parts unknown.

Back in England, Zana found herself cut off from her sister for the next three years, as communication proved impossible. But she could not forget Nadia and the children. She filed suit against her father for kidnapping (the case is still pending) and wrote a book titled *Sold*, which she hoped would generate enough interest to help Nadia, Nadia's children, and Marcus.

I obtained the English galleys of *Sold* from my German editor during my movie tour in Germany in June 1991. While the book wasn't especially well written and had sold only 9,000 copies in Britain, I couldn't put it down. The otherworldly setting, the extremity of the girls' ordeal, the rare quality of Zana's courage—all made for compelling reading.

I reported my impressions to my French publisher, Fixot, which decided to take the lead with this book, as it had with *Not Without My Daughter*. *Sold* was rewritten and published in France as the first volume of a "Betty Mahmoody Series." I was honored to write the introduction to this French edition, which stirred phenomenal interest in both France and Germany. Fixot appealed to all French journalists to convey a message to their public: to write or call the Yemeni embassy and demand Nadia's release. The embassy was deluged with urgent responses. More than a decade after the girls had taken their fateful "holiday," their case was a cause célèbre.

On February 5, 1992, six years to the day after Mahtob and

I had reached Ankara, I met Zana in Fixot's offices. She looked like an Arab woman—black hair, black eyes, olive-tanned skin—but her accent was unmistakably British. The years of grinding corn had taken their toll; one of Zana's wrists was deformed and arthritic, and her fingertips were permanently enlarged.

"Sacrée Soirée," a prominent French television program decided to spotlight the sisters' story, and invited both Zana and me to appear on a show, along with the Yemeni ambassador to France. As 14 million viewers heard, to their collective outrage, the details of Zana's captivity, the ambassador grew increasingly uncomfortable.

"These girls have been held against their will," he finally allowed. "These men did something that has caused a bad impression of all Yemeni people." The ambassador promised the show's host that he and his crew would be permitted to accompany Zana to Yemen and to retrieve Nadia and the sisters' children. The power of the media was never so apparent to me as at that moment.

Five days later Zana and her mother left for Yemen, accompanied by the television crew and Bernard Fixot. Tragically, the Yemeni government reneged on its promise. Nadia, now twenty-six years old, was brought to a meeting with her sister and the other visitors, but without Nadia's children, whom she had to leave behind in the village. In the presence of thirty armed Yemeni soldiers, a visibly frightened Nadia trembled while insisting that she did not want to leave. It was impossible to gauge her true feelings. But Nadia may indeed have sensed that it was too late for her, that it would have been too traumatic for her children to transplant them to such a different culture, regardless of her own desires in life.

Despite the fact that Marcus, Nadia, and her children remain in Yemen today, the episode demonstrates an important point: A primarily French public became conscious, actually outraged, that British subjects had been held as captives in Yemen. What happened not only offended their conscience but drove them to action.

The French reaction to Zana must be put into the context of our rapidly changing world. Over the past few years we have witnessed a series of earth-shaking events. The voice of freedom has been heard and accepted by many once under the dictates of Communism. Arabs and Israelis are meeting face to face for peace talks. The war in the Persian Gulf demonstrated how the world of nations could act in concert to repel aggression.

Taken together, these events suggest the emergence of a *global conscience*—a sharing of both principles and action, a growing unity that has been spurred by revolutionary advances in communication and transportation. With new awareness has come a new vision, one that transcends national borders, one that would protect even the least powerful among us.

A central part of that vision—that all children have innate rights and that they should not be violently uprooted from one culture to another—has inspired and sustained ONE WORLD : FOR CHILDREN, the organization I co-founded with Arnie. Dedicated to intercultural understanding and the protection of children everywhere, the nonprofit group was formally organized in 1990 and received its tax-exempt status the following year.

In our statement of purpose, we noted that "ONE WORLD FOR CHILDREN strives to be a part of a New World Order—a world where reason prevails, where the rights of children are understood and protected."

ONE WORLD : FOR CHILDREN has provided a more systematic way to help the distraught parents who call me every day. It promotes understanding of different cultures, provides counseling by left-behind parents for others whose children have been abducted, and refers these victims to agencies and professionals for further help.

We do *not* propose that people avoid romantic entanglements with those from other countries; every time I look at Mahtob, I'm reminded of the gifts that such relationships can bring. But we *do* advise people to learn as much as they can about their future spouse's culture and family traditions. That kind of enlightenment, with open discussion, can only help a marriage—and the children that marriage produces.

285

The vision of the Hague Convention is one shared by ONE WORLD : FOR CHILDREN. My hope is that membership in the Hague Convention will continue to grow, only at an accelerated pace. Perhaps if nations do not formally become members, they will at least govern in harmony with its principles.

I envision of a world where children's rights are protected and cultural differences are respected; of a world where no child need fear losing either parent and where no parent will ever be left behind.

Three years after Teresa Hobgood warned me about Moody, Mahtob remains safe and by my side. All the same, I never go a day without worrying when Moody might strike. And while I am truly grateful for my life with my daughter, I also share the suffering of so many other parents whose children have been abducted or who fear abduction.

Christy Khan, Ramez Shteih, Craig DeMarr, Mariann Saieed, Marie-Anne Pinel—along with thousands of other left-behind parents whose stories remain untold—have endured unimaginable loneliness and desperation. Yet they have persevered, as I did in Iran, driven by the most powerful force known to humankind.

They have forged on for the love of their children.

Appendix

*I*n a case of international parental child abduction, a left-behind parent can invoke the Hague Convention by filing with the destination country's "central authority," the designated enforcement agency (in the United States, applications may be processed through the State Department's Office of Citizens Consular Services). Once a parent's application is accepted, any custody proceeding on the merits in the destination country ceases. Guided by the central authority, the responsible court may rule only on the question of whether the removal or retention was wrongful. If the court finds that a child had established a "habitual residence" in a nation where the abduction took place, it rules that the child be returned.

The convention is triggered whenever a parental abductor violates a custody order. But it also applies to cases with no existing custody judgment, as when a spouse takes children abroad without the other spouse's consent. To minimize trauma and disruption to the child, fast action is the norm. In the United Kingdom, for example, where the courts are notably fair and efficient, children generally are returned within a month of the parent's application.

There are exceptions, but they are narrowly defined. If the child has lived in the destination country more than one year, the court may rule to keep the child there—but *only* if the abducting parent can prove that the child is "settled" in his or her new environment. The court may also refuse to return a child if there is "a grave risk" of physical or psychological harm.

Listing of Central Authority

This list of independent countries of the world, as of April 1992, was furnished by the National Geographic Society, Washington, D.C.

Countries that as of June 1, 1992 were signatories to the Hague Convention on the Civil Aspects of International Child Abduction are indicated by asterisks. This information was furnished by the U.S. State Department.

Some signatory countries do not have reciprocal agreements with all other members.

In case of abduction, or for more information on your country's status with regard to the Hague, contact your central authority or:

Mr. Adair Dyer, First Secretary
(English, French, or Spanish)

or

Secretariats: Mrs. Françoise Franck (French)
Mrs. Sarah Adam (English)
Mrs. Laura Molenaar (English)

The Hague Conference on Private International Law
Permanent Bureau
6, Scheveningseweg
2517 KT THE HAGUE, Netherlands

Telephone: 31/70-363.33.03
Telex: 33383
Telefax: 31/70-360.48.67

OR:

ONE WORLD : FOR CHILDREN
P.O. Box 124
Corunna, Michigan 48817
Telephone: (517) 725-2392

INDEPENDENT COUNTRIES OF THE WORLD

Afghanistan

Albania

Algeria

Andorra

Angola

Antigua and Barbuda

*Argentina

Armenia

*Australia

*Austria

Azerbaijan

Bahamas, The

Bahrain

Bangladesh

Barbados

Belarus

Belgium

*Belize

Benin

Bhutan

Bolivia

Bophuthatswana

Bosnia and Hercegovina

Botswana

Brazil

Brunei

Bulgaria

Burkina Faso (Upper Volta)

Burundi

Cambodia

Cameroon

*Canada

Cape Verde Islands

Central African Republic

Chad

Chile

China, People's Republic of

Ciskei

Colombia

Comoros

Congo

Costa Rica

Cote d'Ivoire

Croatia

Cuba

Cyprus, Northern

Cyprus

Czechoslovakia

*Denmark

Djibouti

Dominica

Dominican Republic

*Ecuador

Egypt

El Salvador

Equatorial Guinea

Estonia

Ethiopia

Federated States of Micronesia

Fiji

Finland

*France

Gabon

Gambia, The

Georgia

*Germany

Ghana

Greece

Grenada

Guatemala

Guinea

Guinea-Bissau

Guyana

Haiti

Honduras

*Hungary

Iceland

India

Indonesia

Iran

Iraq

*Ireland

*Israel

Italy

Jamaica

Japan

Jordan

Kazakhstan

Kenya

Kiribati

Korea, North

Korea, South

Kuwait

Kyrgyzstan

Laos

Latvia

Lebanon

Lesotho

Liberia

Libya

Liechtenstein

Lithuania

*Luxembourg

Macedonia

Madagascar

Malawi

Malaysia

Maldives

Mali

Malta

Marshall Islands

Mauritania

Mauritius

*Mexico

Moldova

Monaco

Mongolia

Morocco

Mozambique

Myanmar

Namibia

Nauru

Nepal

*Netherlands

*New Zealand

Nicaragua

Niger

Nigeria

*Norway

Oman

Pakistan

Panama

Papua New Guinea

Paraguay

Peru

Philippines

Poland

*Portugal

Qatar

Romania

Russia

Rwanda

San Marino

Sao Tome and Principe

Saudi Arabia

Senegal

Seychelles

Sierra Leone

Singapore

Slovenia

Solomon Islands

Somalia

South Africa

*Spain

Sri Lanka

St. Vincent and the Grenadines

St. Lucia

St. Kitts and Nevis

Sudan

Suriname

Swaziland

*Sweden

*Switzerland

Syria

Tajikistan

Tanzania

Thailand

Togo

Tonga

Transkei

Trinidad and Tobago

Tunisia

Turkey

Turkmenistan

Tuvalu

Uganda

Ukraine

United Arab Emirates

*United Kingdom

*United States

Uruguay

Uzbekistan

Vanuatu

Vatican City

Venda

Venezuela

Vietnam

Western Samoa

Yemen

*Yugoslavia

Zaire

Zambia

Zimbabwe